The Junior Officers' Reading Club

The Junior Officers' Reading Club

Killing Time and Fighting Wars

PATRICK HENNESSEY

ALLEN LANE
an imprint of
PENGUIN BOOKS

ALLEN LANE

Published by the Penguin Group

Penguin Books Ltd, 80 Strand, London WC2R ORL, England

Penguin Group (USA) Inc., 375 Hudson Street, New York, New York 10014, USA

Penguin Group (Canada), 90 Eglinton Avenue East, Suite 700, Toronto, Ontario, Canada M4P 2Y3
(a division of Pearson Penguin Canada Inc.)

Penguin Ireland, 25 St Stephen's Green, Dublin 2, Ireland
(a division of Penguin Books Ltd)

Penguin Group (Australia), 250 Camberwell Road, Camberwell, Victoria 3124, Australia
(a division of Pearson Australia Group Pty Ltd)

Penguin Books India Pvt Ltd, 11 Community Centre, Panchsheel Park, New Delhi – 110 017, India

Penguin Group (NZ), 67 Apollo Drive, Rosedale, North Shore 0632, New Zealand
(a division of Pearson New Zealand Ltd)

Penguin Books (South Africa) (Pty) Ltd, 24 Sturdee Avenue, Rosebank, Johannesburg 2196, South Africa

Penguin Books Ltd, Registered Offices: 80 Strand, London WC2R ORL, England

www.penguin.com

First published 2009

6

Copyright © Patrick Hennessey, 2009

Maps and photographs copyright © Patrick Hennessey, 2009
Extract from *Lessons of the War*, Part IV: 'Unarmed Combat', by Henry Reed,
reproduced by permission of Carcanet Press Ltd
Extract from 'Fair Weather', by Dorothy Parker, from *The Collected Dorothy Parker*,
reproduced by permission of Penguin Books Ltd

The moral right of the author has been asserted

Set in 12/14.75 pt PostScript Monotype Bembo
Typeset by Rowland Phototypesetting Ltd, Bury St Edmunds, Suffolk
Printed in Great Britain by Clays Ltd, St Ives plc

ISBN: 978-1-846-14186-7

www.greenpenguin.co.uk

For the world, which seems
To lie before us like a land of dreams,
So various, so beautiful, so new,
Hath really neither joy, nor love, nor light,
Nor certitude, nor peace, nor help for pain;
And we are here as on a darkling plain
Swept with confused alarms of struggle and flight
Where ignorant armies clash by night.

From 'Dover Beach' by Matthew Arnold

Contents

Author's Note

One of my favourite Army stories was told to me by my first company commander. A team from his anti-tank platoon had been up to some drunken mischief or other, and he was charged with finding the culprits. When interviewed one by one they all came out with an identical and well-rehearsed story in which they had been out together and all returned to camp at exactly 23:57 (some ten minutes after the alleged incident had occurred), a timing they all recalled with such precision because each one of them had 'checked their watches' as they came in through the gates. Having heard the same improbable story five times, he called them back into his office together and asked them all to read him the time off their watches; needless to say, no two men had the same time, and at least two were either half an hour fast or slow.

No two recollections of an event are the same, especially an event as frantic and emotionally charged as a battle or the loss of a friend. As Anthony Swofford puts it in *Jarhead*: 'What follows is neither true nor false but what I know.' The following narrative has been constructed as accurately as possible from e-mails sent to friends, my diaries and orders notebooks. Occasionally I have turned to colleagues for their recollections of certain incidents or to official after-action reviews and reports. Some names have been changed. An element of confusion is inevitable and is, in places, intentional – the only realistic sense of the moment. For the rest, the book is entirely the time as I read it off my own watch.

Dedication

In April of 2001 I wrote a letter to my grandfather, also Patrick Hennessey – a retired Cavalry officer, veteran of the Normandy landings who finished his long military career in the RAF and who embodied much that was good about his generation of soldiers – asking for his advice on joining the Army. I hadn't mentioned the idea to anyone else and I've always been glad I sought his advice first. He provided good counsel and measured support, knowing that my parents would probably be more dubious, but beneath all of that he was delighted and proud. He died in November of 2002, quickly and quietly from a heart attack and a life of tobacco, red wine and cheese, the perfect death for a soldier with a soldier's hatred of doctors and hospitals, and I am always caught between happiness and sadness: happy that he died knowing that I was following in his footsteps, off to Sandhurst after university and about to embark upon the life and profession he had found so fulfilling, sad that he wasn't there, for the parades and the medals and stories that would follow.

Four years later I visited my other grandfather, Professor Emrys Jones, for the last time and brought with me something to show him. It was considered one of the great success stories of the family that my father's father and my mother's father – an awe-inspiring academic, humanist, liberal and the driving intellectual force in the family – got along so well. One had been in the first wave of DD Shermans, the swimming tanks that had rolled on to Sword beach, queasy in the early hours of 6 June 1944. The other had driven ambulances throughout the war, a conscientious objector with quiet and strong conviction. One devoted his life to military service, the other to shaping and improving post-war communities.

They were brought together by their children, my parents, smiling and improbably young in photos in front of Durham Cathedral, outside which they had first met as students – glamorous, my father in his naval uniform and my mother in her wedding gown. What must they have thought, these two men, being presented in turn with a pad-brat naval aviator for a son-in-law – child of military bases in Germany and Cyprus, up at university with a portrait of the Queen on the walls of his room and anxious to get back in the cockpit – and a spirited and beautiful musician and feistily clever university administrator for a daughter-in-law.

Sometime in August 1982 they must have all stood together over the slightly ugly six-pound baby, their first and only grandson, and wondered. Military Grandpa might have pictured another young Hennessey in his regiment, a continuation of a long and unbroken family line of military service to crown and country, and Professor Taid (Welsh for grandfather, which was how we distinguished) might have wondered if that bundle might be a thinker, might follow him into academia and print. Taid did not murmur when I announced that I was going to join the Army. Immersed as I was, or so they thought, in literary study it must have seemed a safe bet that the gowns and mortar boards had won out over fatigues and helmets. I know the decision came as a big surprise and slight disappointment. Taid didn't agree with my thinking but understood and respected the thought process. He couldn't have been more supportive. A few days before he died, I had been presented with my first Operational Tour Medal for service in Iraq. Taid had strenuously objected to the war, but we had stayed in close touch while I had been out, and he had come to see that perhaps some good was being done, and that what else was not being done was not the fault of the young men and women in uniform working hard in difficult conditions. I showed him my medal, and, like Grandpa when I wrote him that first letter, I knew he was proud.

I am happy and sad again because, just as Grandpa had died that bit too early to see me stomping the parade square at Sandhurst, so Taid died a few months too early to see the first article I ever wrote in print, a whimsical piece for the *Literary Review*, which I think would have appealed to him, about the books we take to war and what fraying paperbacks I found on transit-camp bookshelves throughout Iraq. Still writing in his last year, gamely mastering his laptop in his eighties as he ploughed through his twelfth book, Taid would have been my constant guide in writing this, and my sadness is he didn't live to see a book with his grandson's name on the spine to be placed in distinguished company on the bookshelf at home with all of his own.

They were towering, inspirational men: a fine soldier and an outstanding scholar. I am neither, but dedicate this book to them to show how I tried to live up to them both.

It's one thing being able to read a map (although beyond an alarming number of my contemporaries) but it's quite another being able to draw one. A young officer spends a surprising amount of time drawing maps: with his fingers and rocks in the sand, with sticks and ribbons in the mud, with arty chalk on farm walls and heartbreaking permi-pen on lad's mags and, when all else fails, in biro on the back of the biggest guardsman in the platoon. The following rough approximations of Sandhurst, Iraq and Afghanistan are not the most accurate I've ever drawn, but they may be the most honest.

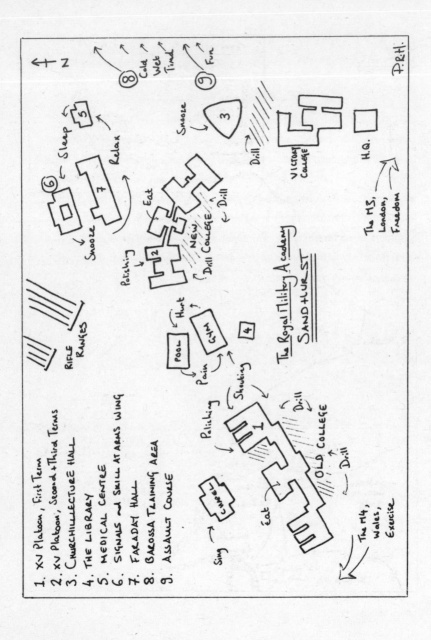

The Royal Military Academy
SANDHURST

1. XV Platoon, First Term
2. XV Platoon, Second & Third Terms
3. Churchilllecture Hall
4. The Library
5. Medical Centre
6. Signals & Skill at Arms Wing
7. Faraday Hall
8. Barossa Training Area
9. Assault Course

N

8 — Cold
Wet
Tired

9 — Fun

5 — Sleep

6 — Snooze

7 — Relax

2 — Polishing

New Drill College — Eat / Drill

3 — Snooze / Drill

Victory College

H.Q.

The M3, London, Freedom

Pool — Pain

Gym — Hurt

4 — Shooting

1 — Polishing / Shooting / Drill

Church — Sing

Old College — Eat / Drill

The M4, Wales, Exercise

Rifle Ranges

P.R.H.

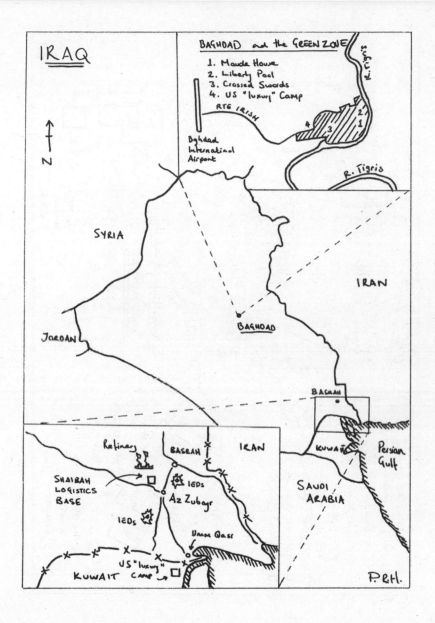

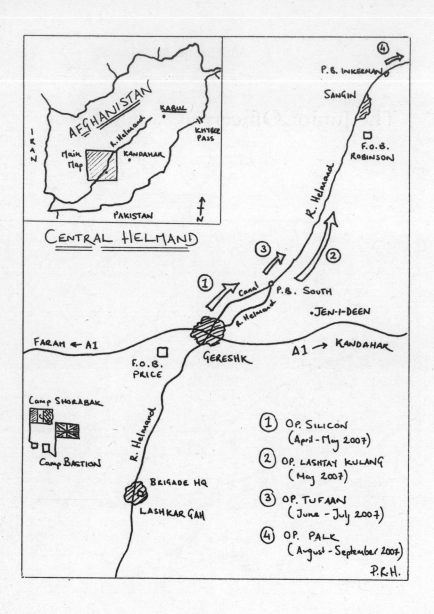

CENTRAL HELMAND

AFGHANISTAN

KABUL

R. Helmand

KHYBER PASS

IRAN

Main Map

KANDAHAR

PAKISTAN

N

P.B. INKERMAN

SANGIN

F.O.B. ROBINSON

R. Helmand

④

③

②

①

Canal

P.B. SOUTH

R. Helmand

•JEN-I-DEEN

FARAH ← A1

A1 → KANDAHAR

F.O.B. PRICE

GERESHK

Camp SHORABAK

R. Helmand

Camp BASTION

BRIGADE HQ

LASHKAR GAH

① OP. SILICON
(April - May 2007)

② OP. LASHTAY KULANG
(May 2007)

③ OP. TUFAAN
(June - July 2007)

④ OP. PALK
(August - September 2007)

P.R.H.

The Junior Officers' Reading Club

Prologue

On the Dam

And suddenly we're on the dam.

Four wizened Pashtu Gandalfs sit impassively sipping *chai**
around a dining table in the middle of a rose garden, and my
first thirsty thought is not the obvious *WHAT are we going to
do?* nor the reasonable *WHY are these four improbably old white-
bearded guys sitting taking tea in the middle of a fire fight?* but
*HOW is there a dining table in a rose garden in the middle of the
dam?* It's an interesting point of speculation, but one cut short
by another burst of fire, and to the cracking above and the
thudding as bits of crumbling masonry and rose petals drift
down into the broiling water beneath our feet is suddenly and
worryingly added the melodic pinging of bullets bouncing off
the sluice-gates and rusty turbines below.

Qiam, wisely, is already across the now perilous structure and
gesticulating wildly for us to follow, but something holds me
back, and I just have to have a sip of the *chai*, I hope out of respect
for the Pashtunwali codes of hospitality, but maybe it's just
the thirst. My mind is a whirlwind of half-remembered training
nonsense, and I catch myself trying to work out who the senior
man at the table is, because he's always furthest from the door,
only there isn't a door, and he's usually a *mullah* or at least *haji*,†

---

* Tea.
† *Mullah*: a preacher. *Haji*: one who has been on a pilgrimage to Mecca,
a term of respect.

and so maybe I should apologize for having my boots on, even though we're not strictly indoors.

God this is difficult.

I've lost track of time in the ambush and am trying to work out if it's still *sob bahir* or now *char bahir** when another burst rattles out, and the wall behind me becomes a cartoon of bullet holes everywhere but where my head seems – inexplicably – still to be. I've been an eternity on this extraordinary fucking dam (which wasn't even an objective, only a landmark), even though it's only been a matter of seconds, when I'm grateful to the elderly *sahib* who, taking stock of the situation and possibly sensing my general confusion, calmly finishes his tea, produces an AK47 from under the table and, smilingly, gestures me across the dam as he stands up and sprays a wild and deafening burst of covering fire in all directions.

It was surely never meant to be like this.

It was never meant to be like this in the orders group as we patiently explained how it would go to the childlike Afghans. Moving the little blocks of wood which were US up the little ribbons which were TRACKS and over the coloured powder which was CANAL into the little tins which were the VILLAGE where we would spend the quiet little night 'SECURING' the line of departure.

It was never meant to be like this in training on the Plain, where the enemy were always in BMPs, and I could never remember whether they were the scary armoured personnel carriers or maybe those were the BTRs, and none of it mattered because the worst course of action was always the Russians reinforcing with the seriously scary T80 tanks, which you always sensed were just behind the woodland in the direction of Hampshire, and hopefully they don't have an

---

* *Sob bahir*: good morning/day. *Char bahir*: good afternoon/evening.

AGS-17, whatever one of those is, but either way the right plan was always left-flanking with bags of smoke and avoid the machine-gun post.

It was never meant to be like this as with deep euphoria we rolled the entire *kandak*★ out of the gates of Shorabak and drove them bold as brass down the main road, the only road, with i-Pod blaring from the WMIKs and all the excited chatter on the radios of Gereshk and the crazy market and the stares of the locals and our firepower and the fact that we're leading the operation and the fact that we haven't got lost and the fact that we're nearly at the objective and the fact that there suddenly was the dam.

And then it was chaos.

I noticed Will on the other side of the canal, and everything was going so much to plan that the first rattle was almost offensively incongruous, and the temptation was to ignore it because if we didn't really hear it then maybe it didn't really happen. Then, rudely and undeniably, RPGs boom in from the front and the flank, and the ground and the hedgerows are alive with the sudden intensity of fire that's now bouncing like popcorn off the vehicles, and before we've even registered where it's coming from the Afghans are in the ditches to the side of the track pouring back fire and answering boom with boom. And the frozen pallor of our faces might be fear or adrenalin or just the excitement and realization that the three-year, ten-year, twenty-year expectation of various military careers is finally being fulfilled but it only lasts that split second it takes for me to snatch for the radio and whoop with delight 'AMBER 63, CONTACT, WAIT OUT,' and I've said it.

★ *Kandak*: an Afghan National Army battalion, consisting of about 500 men.

3

I've said it.

I've said it first and I beam across at LSgt Rowe, who understands, and up at LCpl Price, who's ecstatically letting rip with the GPMG, and then we're bounding gleefully from the vehicles and firing, actually firing real bullets, at the invisible and unperturbed enemy. Actually firing our weapons in glorious and chaotic anger. Actually firing.

I knew, deep down, it was always going to be like this.

I

The Junior Officers' Reading Club

We had founded the Junior Officers' Reading Club in the heat of the Southern Iraqi desert. Marlow and me, the smart-alec Oxford boys, with surfer dude Harrison and the attached Coldstreamers. Basking in boxers on improvised sun-loungers, we snatched quick half-hour escapes from the oppressive heat and boredom routine – caught our breath among the books, wallowing after patrols and riding the adrenalin come-down. Convened behind the junior officers tent, the 'Crows' Nest', flaunting non-regulation underwear in a gesture of defiance to the quartermasters, we might have thought we were the Army's Bright Young Things, but we weren't the first and we won't be the last.

The club was a product of a newly busy Army, a post-9/11 Army of graduates and wise-arse Thatcherite kids up to their elbows in the Middle East who would do more and see more in five years than our fathers and uncles had packed into twenty-two on manoeuvres in Germany and rioting in Ulster. 'Too Cool for School' was what we'd been called by the smarmy gunner colonel on a course down in Warminster, congratulating through gritted teeth the boys who'd picked up gallantry awards while he'd been flying his desk, too old now to win the spurs he never got the chance to getting drunk on the Rhine.

But in a way he was right: what did we know just because we'd had a few scraps in the desert? The bitter, loggy major sat next to him had probably been to the Gulf back in '91, when we were still learning to read; probably been patronized himself when he was a crow by returning Falklands vets who in turn had been instructed by grizzly old-timers sporting proud racks of World War Two medals, chests weighed down by North-west Europe and Northern Desert Stars, which told of something greater than we could comprehend, the stuff of history imagined in black and white when no one was anyone without an MC. Our grandfathers were heroes, whatever that meant, and they had taught the legends who charged up Tumbledown and who had returned to teach us.

We who didn't believe them.

We who had scoffed as we crawled up and down Welsh hills and pretended to scream as we stabbed sandbags on the bayonet assault course. We tried to resurrect the club at the start of our Afghan tour, lounging on canvas chairs on the gravel behind the tin huts of Camp Shorabak. Same sort of base, same sort of desert, just a few thousand miles the other side of Iran. By the end of the first month it was obvious that there would be no club. Each of us, wherever we were and if we could at all, would be reading alone. We went into battle in bandanas and shades with Penguin Classics in our webbing, sketch pads in our daysacks and i-Pods on the radio, thinking we knew better than what had gone before.

In the end we did and, of course, we didn't.

★★★

Out in Helmand we were going to prove ourselves.

This was our moment, our X-Factor-winning, one perfect fucking moment; we finally had a war. From university through a year of training at the Royal Military Academy at Sandhurst, from Sandhurst to the Balkans, from the Balkans to Iraq, and now from Iraq to Afghanistan, it felt as though our whole military lives had been building up to the challenge that Afghanistan presented.

The only problem was we were bored.

We landed in Kandahar with high hopes. The whole battalion, 600 men, mustard keen to get stuck into the unfamiliar and exciting task of working alongside the Afghan National Army (ANA) for seven months. A task which promised as much action and fulfilment as the last few years had failed to deliver. Of course, there was nothing exciting about arriving in an airfield in the middle of the night, but the taste of Mountain Dew the next morning was the taste of expeditionary warfare.

But those first March days of 2007, sat on the boardwalk, acclimatizing outside the Korean takeaway, watching the many multinational uniforms amble towards the 'shops' for souvenir carpets, we had to pinch ourselves to remember this was a war zone. The indeterminate South African accents of the military contractors mixed with the sub-continental sing-song of the shit-jobs men jumping in and out of the ancient jingly wagons which rolled haphazardly past millions and millions of dollars' worth of hardware while the Canadians played hockey on the improvised pitch, and I was bored. As bored as I'd been when I decided to join the Army, as bored as I'd been on public duties, guarding royal palaces while friends were guarding convoys in Iraq, as bored as I'd been once we got to Iraq and found ourselves fighting the Senior Major more than Saddam. Stone-throwing, chain-smoking, soldier-purging bored.

Waiting for the onward staging to Camp Bastion, it was pretty easy to forget that Kandahar was already in the middle of nowhere. An iso-container city where big swaggering joint headquarters with lots of flags sat side by side with puny National Support Element tents and the luxury of the semi-permanent pods of the KBR guys, who were the real power in places like this. All right, the Taliban weren't in the wire, but surely Kandahar was at least dangerous enough not to have

7

LSgt Dragon sums up the mood of the early stages of the deployment –
Kandahar, March 2007.

a bunch of Canadians playing roller-hockey in the middle of
its airfield.

Bored of the coffee shop at one end of the complex, we
hopped on an ancient creaky bus, drove past the local market,
where no doubt the Taliban info-gathering went on each
Saturday as the RAF Regiment juicers bartered for fake
DVDs, and hit another café 500 metres down the road. A
sign by the bin, overflowing with empty *venti* coffee cups,
announced that here six years ago the Taliban had fought
their last stand. A worrying thought occurred: surely we
weren't late again?

From Kandahar we decanted into Hercules transport aircraft for the jerky flight down to Camp Bastion, the tented
sprawl in the middle of the 'Desert of Death' that was the
main British base in Helmand. There we conducted our

reception staging and onward integration package under an oppressive and drizzling cloud. The mandatory and in equal measures dull and hilarious set of introductory briefs and exercises completed by all British soldiers entering an operational theatre was as vague as ever. All anyone wanted to know was: were we going to be shooting people? and: would we get in trouble if we did? The answers, to everyone's relief, were 'yes' and 'no'.

★★★

After days which seemed like weeks we arrived at Camp Shorabak, the ANA sister camp next door to Bastion. This would be our home base for the next seven months. The photos 'the Box' – the broad-shouldered commander of the Inkerman Company – had taken on his recce had shown a horizon that symbolized everything Op Herrick (the umbrella name given to ongoing UK operations in Afghanistan) was going to be that previous tours hadn't been. The view shuffling at night to the loos down in Iraq had been depressingly eloquent – the burning fires of the Shaibah refinery and silhouetted pipelines told you all you needed to know about that war. The Hindu Kush, on the other hand, was the symbol of the great adventure, the danger and hardship that we hadn't endured last year. But a bubble of brown and grey cloud blocked out the sky the week we arrived, and we couldn't bloody see it.

To add insult to injury, it even rained. At least in Iraq it had never rained.

The Marines we were taking over from didn't care. They were going home and had lost too many guys too close to the end of their gritty, six-month winter tour. Patience sapped by working with the Afghans we still hadn't met, they shamelessly crammed into the gym to work on their going-home bodies, laughing when we asked them questions about what it was like 'out there'.

We were trying to get to grips with the theory of our task. A normal infantry battalion, the basic building block of any army, works in threes. The basic fighting unit in the British Army is an eight-man 'section' (sub-divided into two four-man 'fire teams'). There are three sections in a platoon – each platoon headed up by a young whippersnapper lieutenant or second-lieutenant and a wiser, grizzlier platoon sergeant – and three platoons in a company – each company led by a more experienced major and an even wiser and grizzlier company sergeant major. These three 'rifle companies' are the basic elements of a battalion, supported by a fourth company of specialized platoons (support company) and a large headquarters company which provides the logistic and planning support in the rear echelons. A tried and tested system forming up a happy family of nearly 700 fighting men, a system which we knew and trusted and which worked.

A system which, for the purposes of our job in Afghanistan, had been thrown out of the window. We were to be an Operational Mentoring and Liaison Team (an OMLT), the set-up of which was simple, but bore no relation to anything we'd ever done before.

Gone was the familiar comfort of the formations and tactics they'd spoon-fed us at Sandhurst. Suddenly we found ourselves in much smaller companies of about thirty, the platoons reduced to mere six-man teams loaded with experience: captains and colour sergeants you would normally expect to find in more senior roles and the junior men all corporals and lance-sergeants who hadn't been the junior men for a few years. In these teams we were to attach ourselves to an ANA formation and mentor them as we both trained and fought together. Each six-man platoon would be responsible for an ANA company of 100, each company of thirty responsible, therefore, for a whole *kandak* – an ANA battalion of 600 men – with our own battalion commander no longer commanding his companies but sat on the shoulder of the Afghan brigadier, advising him on how best to deploy his brigade of thousands. We would use our experience and expertise and superior training and resources to form each Afghan battalion into a credible fighting force. The potential for fun was incredible, the potential for fuck-up immense.

So we should have been glad of the enforced lull at the start, should have been grateful for the time to get our heads around what everyone soon referred to as *omelette*. But, as weeks passed and the training continued and the cloud stayed down, what we were dreaming of was getting out there and having a fight.

★★★

The invite to my going-away party had promised 'The Great Game, Round III – Beards, Bombs and Burkhas', but we were getting bollocked for not shaving before early-morning PT, and as for bombs, we fucking wished. It was only a matter of time before the creeping bullshit would start; before those with nothing better to do would start to patrol the huts, complaining that the mosquito nets weren't in straight enough lines or that we should be carrying our weapons in the showers. The sergeants, infuriatingly tidy and unfailingly up at 0530, would crash around the hut and have us pining for the little eight-man tents we'd resented back in Iraq. Like clockwork they would order 'lights-out' at 2200, and the hut would become a profound dull tunnel lit by the blueish glow of laptops being watched on camp cots. Padding back from the showers, I'd pick my way past rows of fluorescent faces, featureless and blurred through the mosi-nets, each man absorbed in the snug little world of the nylon domes, somehow finding a privacy in the headphones and pretending to sleep through the telltale rhythmic rustling of the cot next door.

The frustration grew when the Inkerman Company, lucky bastards, were crashed out in the middle of the night on a real-deal, this-is-not-a-drill, load-up-the-wagons tasking. As it turned out, they spent the next week bored and cold and with no sight of the enemy, but what was worrying was how selfishly and childishly jealous we all were. With nothing remotely gung-ho to boast of, we couldn't even be bothered to write home and moodily sat out at nights on the Hesco fence, watching the thunderstorms. Towering clouds hurling magnificent bolts of lightning silhouetting the mountains to the north drifted over our heads as we sulked and, in the finest tradition of bored soldiers, sat around throwing stones at each other.

The days ticked by. The heat and dust grew more oppressive, and the reports from elsewhere in Helmand grew more exciting, and our own boredom intensified with each passing day we didn't get out 'on the ground'. Occasionally we would catch the whisper of something, the sniff of an American op going in to the north. But we were scheduled to spend the next two months training our *kandak* in camp. The idea of spending months trying to force Sandhurst on the ANA was unthinkable. Other companies started getting sent on real patrols and getting into real fights. Marlow was down on the Garmsir front line, and the daily SITREPs – situation reports sent back from the boys on the ground – were tantalizingly full of heavy engagements. The ANA soldiers, who had watched with amusement as we played our incomprehensible touch sevens on the helipad, started to get bolshy, trying to

Life in Camp Shorabak. My fellow platoon commanders 2Lt Folarin Kuku (top) and 2Lt Will Harries (bottom) deal with the boredom in time-honoured fashion – playing with guns.

play football right through our games. We were already telling our new comrades to piss off in their own country – as someone shouted from the wing: how the fuck was it 'their' helipad when their army had no helicopters?

They barely *had* an army.

★★★

205 Brigade of the 3rd (Hero) Corps of the Afghan National Army, though they didn't know it and though certainly not enough of us knew it, were the solution to Afghanistan. We were trotting out the right phrases – 'An Afghan solution to an Afghan problem' – but we didn't believe them. Back with the Operational Training and Advisory Group (OPTAG) on pre-deployment exercises in Norfolk, we had asked one of the instructors what special preparation we should undertake to be an OMLT, and he had made a gag about eggs. It wasn't OPTAG's fault, not that the training they delivered wasn't a waste of time. The problem was all in the name; 'mentoring' and 'liaison' sounded like holding hands and building bridges. If we'd wanted to build bridges we'd have joined the Engineers; we were combat soldiers, teeth arm, and our culture demanded more. If they'd called the task OBFET (Operational Blow the Fuck out of Everything Team), then every battlegroup in the Army would have been creaming for it, but the Afghans might have objected.

Afghanistan was only going to work if the ANA could eventually do it for themselves. The Paras, first out when the war began, had been thrust into a fight they couldn't win on their own and forgot about the ANA in the midst of keeping the Taliban from their throats. The only story anyone heard about the ANA during the whole of the first British deployment into what the papers soon exclusively referred to as 'the lawless Helmand Province' was the one about how they ran away when Tim Illingworth of the Light Infantry won his Conspicuous Gallantry Cross. The Marines had come in six months later with a whole lot more people and, in theory, a whole lot more sense. They dedicated almost a whole Commando, the OMLT Battlegroup, to the task of bringing on the ANA, but they hadn't found it sexy enough and had sulked, taking it out on the ANA, alternately over-working and ignoring them.

So of course, if we're honest, the Grenadiers hadn't wanted the task either, and we'd sucked it up when we were told we were going to be 12 Brigade's OMLT. After all, we were going in with 1st Battalion The Royal Anglians, who had been the lead infantry battalion in 12 Mechanized Brigade since forever and even had previous Afghan experience, although we all knew by then that the Kabul peacekeeping tours of pre-2006 had nothing to do with the war in Helmand. The Grenadiers were tired from their tour of Iraq and an unknown quantity down in Aldershot; the Anglians had trained hard for the task of proving that, if the Paras and the Marines could do it, so could the line infantry.

We knew they'd get the *important* jobs over us; we'd only just got back from a no-notice deployment out to Iraq so we could finally wear the yellow medal that everyone else in the Army already had. Bumming around Shaibah Logistics Base, feeding detainees and cramming down lobster in the American D-Facs in Baghdad was no adequate preparation for what – even by autumn 2006 and presumably to the justified annoyance of those Falkland veterans marking the twenty-fifth anniversary of what was hardly a picnic – everyone was calling 'the most intense fighting the British Army has experienced since Korea'. A square-bashing Guards battalion was never going to be on the 'main effort' – our reputation was as unreconstructed traditionalists, stuck in the obsolete mentality of the Victorian era that was our heyday, so obsessed with pageantry and protocol that we were lesser soldiers for it. Grenadiers certainly weren't going to be favoured by an 'airborne' brigade commander – a Paratrooper who'd missed out on commanding his own troops and would have to settle for 'hats'.* The Paras had forgotten who'd had the imagination to set them up in the first place; their reputation was as unreconstructed hooligans, stuck in the obsolete mentality of the Second World War which was their heyday and so obsessed with being 'ally' and killing everyone that they were the lesser soldiers for it. We could play with the Afghans and teach them how to use their rifles for the time when the real soldiers had blown up all the Talibaddies and could hand a peaceful if not prosperous province over with smiles and handshakes and flag-ceremonies. Just like the British Army were supposed to be doing in Southern Iraq.

Problem was, down in Southern Iraq the Rifles and the Irish Guards were getting hammered. The Americans were pouring everything into a surge which nearly bled them dry, but was starting to work, while we were handing over the bases, doing dodgy deals with the militia and then stepping back as Basrah descended to anarchy. And this in a region we'd walked around years earlier wearing berets and smiles and gloating about how good we were at hearts and minds. But even then, Helmand was something else, and no one down there really knew it.

Except the Afghans.

They couldn't shape their berets. They didn't get up early and they stopped everything for meals, for prayer, for a snooze. They had no discipline. They smoked strong hashish

* The apparently derogatory term used by the Parachute Regiment for the rest of the Army.

and mild opium. They couldn't map-read. They had no tanks, no planes, no order to the chaos of their stores. Their weapons weren't accounted for. Their barracks weren't health and safety compliant. They wore what they wanted, when they wanted and walked around holding hands. They lacked everything that British Army training believed in and taught – and fuck me if most of them hadn't killed more Russians than we had ever seen.

I loved them.

I liked that they had more balls than I ever did to just stand up and say 'why' or 'no' or 'I don't care if there is a war on and a massive IED threat, I like watermelon so I'm going to steal a car I can't drive and run a Taliban checkpoint in order to go to the market.'

I couldn't train them at all.

The video-funnies – spoof Marlboro adverts with all-American cowboys covered in scratches herding cats – didn't do it justice. We would wander over to the Afghan side of camp mid-morning, the sergeants already gritting their teeth in fury because they'd been up since half-five and couldn't understand anyone who hadn't, hoping for the best. The best would usually be half of the soldiers we expected, lounging around on mattresses, sharing *chai*. Well, we reckoned half of the soldiers, but since we had no idea how many there were supposed to be, how did we know how many were half? And since there was no commander, or headquarters, or any sort of structure, how could we find out? I spent my first week with *toolay se, kandaki awal* – 3 Company, 1st Battalion ANA – trying to find out who commanded it.

★★★

Miserable March turned to April, and without warning the temperature soared, and the peaks of the Kush were suddenly hidden in haze, not cloud. The remaining ANA were supposed to have come back from their leave, though still only half our Afghans were in camp. The combination of the rising temperature, the continued lack of action and our utter failure to make any progress in their training was starting to take its toll. The frustration was starting to show in shorter tempers, and the old-school lot were itching to form the whole *kandak* into three ranks and thrash them round Shorabak like Sandhurst cadets.

Instead we took those we could find out on the range and gulped hard and reassessed our desire to fight alongside them as they missed target after target with rusty and broken AK47s. As the gap between what we were realizing we would need to do in Helmand and what it was obvious we could never teach the ANA to do widened, so things descended into farce.

I guess it was inevitable that I would get told off for conducting the body-bag lesson from inside it.

Every so often something would stop us in our tracks and almost force a reassessment of our new allies. The blasé way in which the young and impressive sergeant mentioned that he was hoping to go back north with us because he had earned his reputation up there years before, capturing a number of Taliban during the civil war and, unable to take them all prisoner on his own, throwing them one by one down a well and tossing a grenade in after them. Even Mahjid – quiet, considered, intelligent Mahjid, with whom, standing in for all the other officers in his company, I daily talked over *chai* and too-sugary boiled sweets and liked more and more – mentioned how he too hoped we made it to Sangin so that he could avenge himself on the man who had shot him in the leg last year, pulling up his trousers to modestly reveal barely half a thigh distinguishable beneath monstrous scarring.

It forced us to remember that we were the tourists here. We were action-starved soldiers who had flown in for our seven months of glory. The Afghans were in no rush – they lived it all year every year. The mandate for OMLT was to be completely integrated with the ANA: if they went out for a fight, we went with them. Brilliant in principle, except that at every rotation of Op Herrick a fresh bunch of British soldiers arrived hungry for some action and started a frenzy of planning and grand ideas, involving the tired Afghans who had just accompanied the previous lot.

Lieutenant Mahjid was weary, a good officer who looked twice his thirty years and who'd never go far because, for all his balls and brains, he had no patronage. He was only supposed to be second-in-command, but there was no company commander and no platoon commanders either; come to think of it, there was no company sergeant major, so it was pretty much his show. His soldiers were from all over the country but mainly, thankfully, far away from Helmand, where Pashtun tribal loyalties undermined what little military command structure there was. His best fighters were northerners, battle-hardened Tajiks and Uzbeks with ruthless eyes and Hazaras with their Mongol fighting blood, guys who had stood alongside Massoud, the Lion of the Panjshir, who had fought for the only team ever to defeat the mighty Red Army and then been the last rearguard against the insanity of the Taliban. Problem was, they all lived many hundreds of miles away in a country with no roads and they needed to go home once a year. They needed to keep making children.

We had forgotten, if we ever knew, that this 'training' we were delivering wasn't important, was, in fact, insignificant compared to bringing up a family.

And what the hell did we know? It took me three long

days of haggling and translating and drawing pictures and taking digital photographs just to get what I thought was a nominal roll of the hundred or so soldiers I was supposed to be working with. We had the audacity to be cross because thirty of them were still absent, trying to maintain their families on the other side of the country. We had the nerve to be pissed that thirty of those who were in camp refused to turn up to our training sessions, or that twenty of those who

1st Kandak, *3/205 'Hero' Corps, Afghan National Army, the ragtag bunch who'd done it all before – Camp Shorabak, April 2007.*

did left their shirts untucked. Christ, we must have looked stupid as we trudged back across the sweltering helipad dejected to lunch after another failed attempt to teach vehicle checkpoint drills or safe weapon handling. It was the ones we labelled troublemakers early who turned out to be the best soldiers, lazily pretending they didn't know how to handle a weapon when later it turned out they knew better than most and were just taking the piss because why would they bother to handle their weapons 'safely' when all they used them for was firing at Taliban, not manning gates in Surrey with empty magazines. We grumbled in the cookhouse afterwards over Black Forest gateaux about how the hell were we supposed to go to war with a ragtag bunch like that, forgetting for one crucial moment that most of that ragtag bunch had done this before.

2.iv.04 – 'An introduction to Terrence'
and we're OUT, we're finally out on patrol and after weeks of thinking too precisely on th'event, Afghanistan finally starts.

we'd come in excitingly enough as the Herc' had thrown an aggressive corkscrew landing and the first-timers jumped just perceptibly as chaff briefly lit up the cabin in a red phos' glow and we slammed the runway like some cheap African airliner when the storage cabins overhead all fall open except there is no storage, just us sweating in helmets and body armour so we all leg it off the back and into the middle of the desert.

later – much fucking around later – and we're tearing down Highway 1 in the middle of a sandstorm and the world is a blur of dust and green through the LUCIE night vision sights and though we've successfully wedged the i-Pod speakers into the dashboard of the WMIK, the combination of wind and static cackle on the radio is drowning out even Metallica's 'For Whom The Bell Tolls' which – after extensive debate – has pipped Too Many DJs Prodigy vs. Enya 'Smack My Bitch Up (Orinoco Flow)' as the soundtrack of choice for our first foray 'OUT' and even if we could have heard it, the shattering cannon smack of the .50 cal booming through the night would have drowned it out and anyway I'm concentrating too hard on the ridiculous exhilaration of firing 6 rounds a second of 7.62 1-bit ammo – crack and tracer crack and tracer – out into the cloudy dark to care, until i wonder idly over the radio if maybe we actually shouldn't go easy on the fireworks given that there might be some nomadic herdsman or the odd mud hut getting ripped to pieces 500m to the north by our self-indulgent over-response to the remote possibility of 'Terrence' in the vicinity.

and when we've calmed down a bit and the last of the strangely beautiful red firefly tracer has burned out like a shooting star thousands of metres away I peer hopefully into the dark, reassuring myself that the rounds have tipped out in some harmless sandbank or – optimistically – shaken up some passing Taliban night move, but keep my fingers crossed that we haven't exploded the camel of some innocent clueless herder whose temporary stop to shelter from the storm just turned nasty in a cacophony of over-excited ISAF troops.

in a way it's a blessing to have far too much to consider as we rip down towards the mouth of the Sangin valley with essential cigarettes and Haribo and batteries and bullets and football scores for the poor suckers further forward who should have been going home by now but have just had their tour extended by 4 weeks in what the Nam-heads call 'the A Shau valley' after the notorious ground of Hill 936 a.k.a. *Hamburger Hill*. I haven't time to dwell on the absurdity of blasting out live munitions while driving down the Afghan equivalent of the M25 because within seconds we've got to slow down because fuck fuck FUCK the Afghan fucking police are firing at us.

not that we can blame them.

with characteristic *sang-froid* the British Tommy has come to know and respect his enemy in Afghanistan as 'Terry'. (*a la* Vietnam as in Viet Cong = VC = Victor Charles = Charlie, so Taliban = Terrence = Terry). Unfortunately Terry is a kind of funny name conjuring up images of Terry Thomas in tennis whites twirling his moustache and saying 'good show' in a silly voice – difficult to take seriously. Whether the Taliban who snuck into the police checkpoint we've just passed the night before were wearing tennis whites or had moustaches history doesn't relate but what is as certain as the nightmares of the boys who went there to take over the shift the next morning is that snuck in they did in the middle of the night and decapitated the policemen on sentry duty leaving the headless torsos still sitting round the table where they had been smoking for the oncoming guard to discover.

which should have been pretty incongruous in the foothills of the breathtaking mountains which rise like jagged walls from nowhere as the desert stops and the Kush starts. in the lush valley of the Helmand River the poppies are head height and in full bloom where fields of bright turquoise give way to a ludicrous pink, blossoms swaying in a delightful mockery of our desert combats and the dark green US Marine Corps hand-me-downs of the Afghan National Army or local drug lord militia (which is pretty much usually the same guys depending on which side of bed they got out of that morning and whether they pick up the rifle we gave them and come along and fight with us or pick up their own AKs – all Westside pimped-up with flashy stickers and painted magazines and in one inspired case a brass door knob for a cocking handle – and shoot at us instead).

should have been incongruous, but wasn't. isn't.

out here, it seems, anything goes.

back in the camp in the rear with the gear (which sadly isn't the Baghdad swimming pool or the Kuwaiti Ice-Cream parlour or a Saigon-style Baby-san massage hut so this war really needs to sort out its perks) exhausted, filthy, hungry soldiers drop their kit on their beds and head straight past the kitchen to queue for a desperate fix of Facebook. Before bedtime in the stinking hut with 30 blokes under mosquito nets, the Light Dragoons are in the middle of inventing a brilliant new game. You sellotape a peanut M&M above the double 20 of the dartboard, aim for it and laugh with each chip of coloured shell (the milk chocolate melts in your mouth and not in your hand) that falls to the floor as your opponent is obliged to lick it off the dusty concrete, that is unless the mice get there first. This is our entertainment and I shrug as Kuks or Will or one of the other guys I live so completely on top of that even after only three weeks our senses of humour have morphed into one grotesque entity misquoting constant Coogan-Gervaise-Morris-Atkinson-Ferrell-and every war film you ever saw, walks past and winks and in bad Afrikaans intones our favourite borrowed line from *Blood Diamond*.

'TIA bru'. TIA.'

This Is Afghanistan.

Of course, as soon as we started having fun, it all got serious.

As if the weather had known what was coming and every-thing was getting a bit biblical, a plague of flies descended on the camp and crawled in food and eyes and ears until, fool-ishly, we wished anything would clear them away. Then midday turned to chocolate dusk as the sandstorms rolled in, and we spent the next half-hour running around camp like kids in a snowstorm, shocking each other with the static. Of course, the storm brought the giant cricket locusts, which were uglier but less annoying than the flies, but nothing topped the first round of DnV,* which I only avoided by taking lunch of greasy rice and lamb with the Afghans until I saw them prepping the raw meat in the dirt next to their shitters.

Not that any of this bothered anyone when the news of the first casualties came in. The UN aid workers blown up in Kabul by suicide bombers as we'd arrived were too distant and we were too fresh. But when only three weeks in six Canadians a few miles north got killed by a mine like the one which had bounced Dave Groom's Humvee 2 foot up in a puff of smoke we realized how lucky he'd been to walk away and more importantly how lucky we'd all have to be too.

But it only properly hits home when we're stood on the tarmac at Bastion, watching the silent and birdlike then deaf-ening and grey hulking flypast of the Hercules taking Private Chris Gray's body home. Private Gray had been shot by the Taliban during a clearance patrol up in Now Zad. It didn't matter that we'd never met him, didn't know his platoon, weren't even part of his regiment. It mattered that he was nineteen years old, someone's son, someone's brother and someone who'd been shot in a fire fight doing the job we were all there to do. Grief was etched harder on the faces of

* Diarrhoea and vomiting.

the Royal Anglians at that first repatriation ceremony, but we were all thinking hard. Private Gray was any one of us, and we all knew he was the first but not the last. How many more solemn hours would be spent stood by this runway? Who would be next in a box?

We should have taken the moment to question our desire to get out on the sort of deliberate ops the Anglians were conducting. Was there starker evidence of the lunacy of our desires than the familiar geometric blocks of crimson and blue draping the coffin being carried by the six guys with the worst job going? I caught myself thinking about our dog-tags, about how we always laugh at the idea that there are two in case the one round your neck comes off when your head gets blown off, about how every twat in a provincial nightclub at home seems to be wearing them as fashion accessories. Glancing up and down the lines of sombre faces, I do a quick count of how many of my guys are nineteen; Gdsm Lloyd, certainly, LCpl Price, probably, Mizon?

It wasn't until we were bouncing back down the road to Shorabak, quiet except for the odd purge in the back of the trucks about why the British Army is borrowing bone-jarringly uncomfortable wagons from the Afghans, that I was overcome by a surge of revulsion at the hypocrisy of the thing, the crap being peddled by the padres that somehow make it all right for a nineteen-year-old to die if he's going to heaven. That surely can't have been the same heaven the suicide bombers who blew up the UN workers were off to. After the Old Testament trials of the week I'm done with the religious bullshit dimension of what is going on.

Done with uncomfortably referencing *A Bridge Too Far* in the padre's canvas token 'church', droning 'Abide With Me' because we have to 'show support', even though we're only there for the sweeties. Done with the ANA lunatics who drool over the cleavage-flashing, butt-wobbling Tehran diva on Iranian NMP (state-approved MTV, rock and jihad for the McBurkha generation) even while Ahmedinijad parades our pathetic sailors in a hijab. Done with the hypocrite soldiers who demand *halal* rations, but prefer the American non-*halal* MREs because they've got M&Ms. Done with the yanks who bless their hummers as they roll out of camp with the callsign 'WidowMaker' spray-painted on the backs to fight an enemy which shouts 'God is Great' as he runs obligingly into our torrents of .50 cal cannon fire.

And just when I think I can get no lower I find that Fergus, bitter because he's heading home early, has left a sticker he got from a copy of *NME* hidden in my helmet. It says: 'I'm Going to Glasto and You're Not'.

Which is true.

★★★

The contrast between the sparse desert camp where we watched our comrades being flown out in boxes and the international REMF★-fest up in Kabul airport couldn't have been more pronounced. We'd been sent up to escort a new batch of ANA recruits down to Helmand. A Mickey-Mouse task, the hardest part of which would be convincing some of the more sceptical ANA to get on a flying machine at all, but were grateful for any chance to get out of camp routine and now stood in disbelief outside the bar where it was multinational karaoke night, and the Kiwis were sipping cold beers while a couple of French Paras murdered 'Brown-eyed Girl' on a makeshift stage in the corner.

The next morning at the best breakfast we'll have all tour, we count dozens of different styles of uniform in the

★ Rear Echelon Mother Fucker.

cookhouse, and they all stare at our dusty, unpressed combats and the weapons we're carrying because we've nowhere else to put them like we're vulgar gatecrashers. A rainbow of flags, the ISAF partners, flutters outside to signify who's feasting at the coalition trough for US dollars and spurious international prestige; but we're stuck in the airport for two days because most of our 'partners' refuse to fly down to Helmand because *it's too dangerous.* Kabul was *too dangerous* once. Hemmed in by the snow-capped mountains, the *Muj'* used to hide in and pop rockets at the fat Illyushin transport aircraft flying terrified Russian conscripts in and out. If you were lucky, so they said, you'd get blown up on your way in, not your way out. The foothills are still dotted with the rusting hulks of burned-out Soviet T72s as if to remind anyone coming what happens when you take on Afghanistan. Difference is now it's F15s and giant C17s rolling in and out and the troops – thousands of troops doing we have no idea what up here – stroll from the beauty and massage parlour to the Thai takeaway and then maybe back for a spot more karaoke in what was once the most dangerous airport in the world.

On the way back down south to the desert we stop at Kandahar. A riot breaks out among the young ANA recruits we're escorting because now, too late to slip a ten-dollar bill to the posting clerk back up in HQ in Kabul, they've found out where they've been sent. Some argue furiously with bored-looking officials, and I think some do a runner, take their chances with the fence and the long run to the hills rather than join the 205 'Hero' Corps. Perhaps they know something we don't. The wind has changed direction and they're burning the shitters so the whole base is hung with a cloying, sickly-sweet, gag-inducing stench, but the radio messages from base are why we really want to get back down to Helmand.

Nervous ANA recruits waiting to fly out of Kabul International, once the most dangerous airport in the world – April 2007.

Op Silicon was on. Not some poxy, over-excited resupply patrol, not some hand-holding training task. Our first proper mission, a real-life op.

Op Silicon

Op Silicon was to be the first push up the Lower Sangin Valley from Gereshk towards Sangin itself. Terry's country and no two ways about it. The security of Gereshk was at best dubious while Sangin was under siege. Months back the Marines got a few kilometres up the towpath before bugging out under heavy contact and mine-strike-triggered ambushes and were lucky to tell the tale, judging from the lesson the French SF and the Estonian recce guys learned the year before, sliced up and decapitated by the Taliban in the same valley, the stuff of nineteenth-century nightmares. Op Silicon was going to be 12 Brigade's first major operation, thousands of coalition and Afghan troops, and, joy of joys, 1/3/205, our own lovely half-AWOL *kandak* of mad ANA was going to be on it. The planning maps were like pictures from history books, Battlegroup boundaries and symbols we had only ever played with before. Assets in support which beggar belief and even our own company area of operations – square miles of real estate to play in; to CLEAR and DEFEAT in capital letters.*

That afternoon, we marched the company into the briefing room for an impromptu, psych-ourselves-up movie night. An evening of roaring with homoerotic bloodlust at *300,* the boys bellowing every time the characters screamed 'Sparta!' and cheering each stylized gory death. Standing at the back, I couldn't help feel that the narrator's voice, the voice which knew deep down that the Spartans were all nutters, was posing an interesting question. *Why? Why are you delirious with excitement for the first time on this tour?*

I knew why, of course, but didn't want to admit it. I knew it was because the summer had started and the baddies were coming down from the mountains and the brigade had decided to start flexing its muscle and because Silicon was ON and because the orders had been full of wet-dream mission verbs like DESTROY and HOLD. I knew it was

---

* Doctrinal mission verbs were an amazing concept – words which when in formal orders (and capital letters) didn't mean what every English-speaking person might think they mean. To HOLD actually meant 'to exert pressure to prevent movement or redisposition of enemy forces'. My favourite was COVER, which was nonsensically defined in our Tactical Aide Memoires as 'to protect by offence, defence, or threat of either or both'.

because what was going to come next was going to answer all the old questions and pose all the new, unasked ones.

Because you're going to kill or be killed.

Was this the stark truth? Was the frightening reality that the tension of the last few weeks had evaporated because we were finally getting what we wanted? Because, if so, what we wanted was actually the one thing that I should have thought years ago before all this started that I would never want. The one thing that no sane and civilized human should ever want.

Standing at the back of the room, I remembered how scared I had been watching *We Were Soldiers* on a coach journey back to Sandhurst, still nervous in the first term and suddenly questioning the whole thing with the horror unfolding around Mel Gibson. It was a bad film, and Gibson was a bad actor, but it got one thing right that the slick porno-violence of *300* forgot: soldiers fought and it hurt and they died. And sat in the back of the coach, surrounded by sleeping cadets, fresh off an exercise of simulated violence, I had wanted nothing to do with that.

So how, I was wondering in Afghanistan, did I get here? Somewhere, something got lost. Not all at once, but small increment by small increment while we'd been at Sandhurst; a bit in the gas chamber, a bit on the bayonet range, a bit on the final live-fire exercise, when I finally let go and went for it, screaming down the individual lane just to shut up CSgt Coates. Somewhere, something shifted, and, even if we laughed it off, we were taking it more seriously and we were enjoying taking it more seriously.

Enjoying not being the banker in the room when we got out on leave weekends, standing on the fringes of solicitors and estate agents at parties joking that we were the guys who 'travel the world, meet exciting new people and kill them'.

We suddenly enjoyed being the guys in the room with something to say, flirting with the old girls with a new angle. Engaging Raya in genuine conversation like the kind we had all been too cool to have for three whole years at university, explaining what I'd been doing away for the last fortnight on exercise learning counter-insurgency and actually getting the sense that someone was interested. I hadn't even left the factory that was Sandhurst at that stage, but couldn't escape the buzz of holding those big eyes in a way no one was ever going to by describing his week at law school.

Four years previously I had known, more than anything else in the world, that I didn't want to die. Four years previously as Boylan, my cynical but unerringly perceptive friend, had teased me from the idle comfort of university that Iraq would be the new Vietnam, a quagmire that we'd still be in if and when I ever found myself wearing a uniform, I hadn't believed him. Even standing there in the ops room in Shorabak with the map boards, dotted with the gritty incidents of 365 days of unprecedented violence, I could see that the Spartans were nutters, that the big winner was the guy who got sent home. I still knew I didn't want to die. But I didn't want to go home either.

II

A Call to Arms

Officer recruitment shot up after 11 September 2001. At least some of the students walking into milk-round jobs paying higher starting salaries than their parents earned were moved by the apocalyptic spectacle and signed up for Sandhurst.

My recruitment began in the polish and glamour of the mess at St James's Palace, where the Grenadiers were on guard and where Fielding (whose fault the whole thing was since we'd become friends and he'd wondered over a few bottles if I'd never thought of the Armed Forces) had invited me to dinner. Still enjoying the remnants of his gap-year commission in bastard-smart uniform surrounded by silver and pretension, he was transformed from a roguish ginger student into something more substantial. I was eighteen years old, and the promised £1,000 bursary the Army paid yearly to undergraduates would make a welcome dent in the Brideshead-imitation overdrafts I'd racked up playing credit card roulette in Pizza Express, but it wasn't the lifestyle or the money that drew me in, it was boredom with everything else.

Potential entrants to Sandhurst were sent on the Regular Commissions Board (RCB), the week-long test of 'leadership potential' which I pitched up for at Westbury on the same day that American and Coalition troops launched Operation Enduring Freedom and invaded Afghanistan. You couldn't make a connection between the glamorous hunt for Bin Laden stories in the papers I'd been reading in the train on the way down and the quiet anonymity of the red-brick town on the edge of Salisbury Plain. At Westbury we had to climb walls, jump through imaginary windows and negotiate barrels

33

with planks. It was like *The Crystal Maze* without Richard O'Brien's charisma, and I thought I must have failed because I said MILAN was a city in Italy (*idiot*: it was a wire-guided anti-tank missile).

I still don't know what goes on at Westbury. By the time I had finished Sandhurst I could fly over walls, and the MILAN had been replaced by the Javelin, which is much harder to confuse with European cities and which I have fired in anger, which is almost certainly more than any of the directing staff on my RCB had ever done. The unlucky ones were deemed to lack some elusive quality which couldn't be taught at Sandhurst, and to this day I'm not sure what that is. I've served with a number of men who struggled so severely to learn fundamental lessons that even to pass them out of Sandhurst was highly questionable and to select them over other, far better, men who never even got there is only to see how early in the process the Army can get things strangely wrong. I should have noted that, along with the portentous drab coveralls and scratchy blankets which were omens of things to come, but I needed to get back to a house party to try and kiss Parker, the beautiful new fresher, and had run out of underwear, so my mind was on other things.

I passed RCB and was pencilled to start Sandhurst after I finished my degree. It was fun to shock the parents and impress the girls and tease the future lawyers with having signed up for something a bit different, pretending you were off to hunt for Osama after finals. None of it was serious until Boylan and I sat up all night watching the next invasion of Iraq on CNN; bang after bang after bang and inferno visions of Baghdad silhouetting an unheard-of Rageh Omar. This was the green night-vision war-porn we'd been too young to enjoy in '91. Back then I'd been confused by the notion that my father was somehow involved, didn't know why the grown-ups found it funny that my younger sister thought he was away 'playing Gulf', nor why my mother did the ironing late into the night listening to Verdi's *Requiem* on full blast while scuds rained down on Kuwait.

Suddenly it was a bit serious, because how could young guys who had been brought up on 'Nam films in Mr Riddick's history lessons not find it exciting that *The Day Today* piss-takes had been right all along? Even as we got bored of the increasingly smug and increasingly familiar blue-body-armoured, schemaged reporters we couldn't help but chuckle – 'As I swirled the last dregs of toothpaste from my mouth, a soldier's head flew past the window shouting the word "Victory".'

The only fight I'd ever been in had been a pathetically staged affair with Nick George in the Fives Courts when we were fourteen. I'd only won by default because I'd accidentally hit his new braces. When we got bored of the coverage of real fighting we stuck on a DVD of *Fight Club*, which was somehow more realistic, more relevant. We were sat there, pampered, comfortable students, and there was Edward Norton all respectability and IKEA furniture with a smile on his face we couldn't quite recognize, actually alive for the first time because he could taste the blood in his mouth and was getting the shit kicked out of him.

Perhaps that's what the Bullingdon boys were actually up to each time they trashed a restaurant. There was something vital in the wanton destruction, and rather than join the tedious student union protests I was inspired to cycle down to an abandoned warehouse in the rain just to see if I had it in me to put my fist through a window. It hurt, but there was an inexplicable elation in doing something, anything, to show to yourself that you weren't just another overprivileged, over-educated, under-sexed student.

I received my joining instructions for Sandhurst in the midst of the haze of early summer 2003. Exams had finished, and fun was in full swing, but the papers spoke ominously of discipline and physical training and hardship and contained photos of muddy and cold people. I was warm and comfortable and had almost forgotten where my bursary money had actually been coming from.

There were many times when, with more or less justified melodrama, I endured 'the worst moment of my life' during my year at Sandhurst. With breathtaking prescience and wisdom the commanding officer at my first ever potential officer interview had advised me as a clueless student not to bother with Officer Training Corps at university. 'At least,' he observed, 'when you sit out in a field at Sandhurst getting pissed on and miserable, it will have novelty value.'

Sandhurst isn't meant to be easy. My joining papers spoke of the modestly entitled 'finest command and leadership course in the world'. Filled with pictures of lots of cheerful-looking types in uniform, the brochure depicts a kind of CentreParcs with more guns and less cycling. Some of the cadets look smart in dress uniform, others warry in combat face paint, a group stand in jacket and tie laughing in a bar.

Not one of the groups was wearing an all-in-one olive pyjama suit.

The brochure had mentioned that 'the first few weeks are intensive' but stressed that those weeks were working towards the mission of the Academy: 'through military training and education to develop the qualities of leadership, character and intellect demanded of an Army officer'. Unfortunately what I began to discover is that LEADERSHIP, CHARACTER and INTELLECT are best developed by MARCHING, IRONING and SHOUTING.

★★★

Explaining Sandhurst to people who weren't there became easier once Harry rocked up, and with the blanket press coverage our little habits and customs and bits of jargon fell into the wider lexicon. Prince or no prince, I quickly realized that the Sandhurst year was really like a condensed version of your entire schooldays.

The junior term, based in and therefore also known as Old College, was the early years – 270 students, school-leavers and change-seeking City types formed up the first commissioning course of 2004 (CC041) and were straight back to prep school. The mornings you cried because you didn't want to leave home, the lessons you learned seemed for their own sake and just to spite you, and all you dreamed of was the long holidays and maybe the joy of being ill for a day. We were bullied by all and sundry and firmly at the bottom of the food chain. Our yellow lanyards pathetic like ourselves, we trudged through juniors like fearful fourth-formers from incomprehensible Latin to some sadistic games afternoon, stood out on the wing soaking wet with hands thrust down tiny shorts praying that the ball didn't come slapping in on our thighs.

In Old College, sorted into three companies of ninety (ominously named after atrocious, life-guzzling battles: Gaza, Marne and our own muddy Ypres) and further into three platoons of thirty, we endured a crash-course introduction to the military. Discipline would be harsh, sleep deprivation routine and life generally miserable, but in fourteen weeks the Academy would turn us from stinking civvie students into soldiers.

Intermediate term was the two years of GCSEs. Hectic

37

and busy cramming in more than was necessary or than we wanted but at least with a vague sense of purpose and the growing maturity to recognize that, while we might not like what we were doing, it had a point. The years we would realize that some masters were actually human, and that the system could be played, and that cooler boys than you got away with skipping maths and hiding in the music school practice rooms with the obligatory Tangos and Cool Original Doritos and maybe a bacon and chicken Tesco sandwich. The years that the more enlightened teachers began to treat us like grown-ups and we responded in kind, and when the papers were marked and the counting was done, we realized that some of us might actually be good at some stuff.

In that second term, now boasting blue lanyards and living in New College, we would spend more time in the field on exercise, not just being pushed but actually learning tactics and skills. We would spend more time in the classroom on theory and start to practise the leadership for which we were presumably all there. We would have a little more freedom but be far too tired to enjoy it.

Eventually we'd make it to the senior term, the sixth form. We were elevated, the tops of the pile, with the new junior intake getting a very public thrashing and the intermediates running around like the blue-arsed flies we'd been just weeks before and we ourselves strolling around, no longer required to march everywhere in a platoon, wiser and more confident and with an end firmly in sight. We'd have chosen what area of the Army we were joining, our future regiments would have accepted us, and with our red lanyards and our eyes on the real world we'd suddenly understand why people seemed to have enjoyed Sandhurst.

The practice was somewhat different from the theory.

it is the most crushing moment in a young man's life when he wakes one morning and quite rationally says to himself: 'i'm at Sandhurst.'

last Sunday night was about the worst i have ever spent. I made a note in my diary on the way here, simply says 'bugger'.

today was I was given time off for good behaviour because I managed to stamp in the right place at the right time with particular excellence and decided to send you all the first of what I hope will be a series of e-mails chronicling my year at what I have been many times assured in the last two weeks that it is my PRIVILEGE to be attending, the finest leader-ship course in the world.

not that we've done much leadershiping as such. Ours is a day to day struggle for survival, the priority being not to do anything which might upset the malign despot who rules our waking (and sleeping) hours who is known as THE COLOUR SERGEANT. Daily the misdemeanours which incur his wrath change so we can never be sure when we might be pleasing him or not. Three days ago during my morning room inspection the bristles of my toothbrush were facing left – an offence which resulted in the throwing of said toothbrush, along with everything else on the shelf above the sink, out of the window. Yesterday I took great care in facing them to the right – an offence which resulted in everything being thrown out into the corridor.

occasionally, and almost always without warning, we will have done something right. When our shoes are nice, our mobile phones are unlocked early (they are kept with unnecessary precaution in a locked box in the Colour Sergeant's office) and the guilty pleasure of an extra hour's texting is indescribable. The crap here is so extreme and unrelenting that the pauses in it seem like paradise which is one, albeit slightly backward, way of getting kicks.

it goes in waves.

the famed gallows humour of the British Army is clearly forged in basic training when there's nothing to do other than laugh (or cry – which more than a couple do). Sometimes the banter is strong and the complete strangers you have been thrown in with seem like the best and oldest friends. Across the corridor my 'oppo' (opposite number, basically a buddy – another massive challenge here is effectively having to learn another language) hates ironing but excels at the precision bed-making which is required of us. I have no problem with the ironing so I do his trousers in the morning while he makes the bed, an absurd parody of a married couple which reduced us both to hysterics every morning until we were found out and punished for our unwarranted display of initiative and cooperation.

i haven't quite decided yet whether to be Captain Blackadder or Lt the Hon. George, most of the time at the moment I'm just Baldrick.

A typical day during those first five weeks went like this.

Up at 0430, having slept on the top of my bed because I am so bad at making 'bed-blocks' that I don't want to ruin the hospital corners I did the night before and frantically try and iron down the rumpled creases of my own sheets while they're still on the bed. Our rooms are freakishly nothing. A bare desk, a bookshelf with only a bible on it. A noticeboard with the misleading plan of the prescribed layout of a room. Cupboard doors are open to display everything hanging in correct order from left to right. Drawers are pulled out each one an inch further than the other in descending order to reveal the perfect formations of underwear (socks correctly bundled into a 'smile' and not a 'frown') and random military equipment. A quick shower to wake us up and a thorough shave – then as much time again drying out the sink in which a residual drop of water counts as dirt. By 0525 we are all seated in coveralls in the main corridor of our platoon lines awaiting the arrival of Colour Sergeant White. On the first morning we made the mistake of being there at 0525 when we had been told to be there at 0525, which is to say we were five minutes late because 0525 means we should have been there at 0520. Press-ups first thing in the morning prove an effective way of teaching this lesson in timekeeping, and at ensuring no one has been tempted not to fill to the brim their litre water bottles which, having been inspected, we drain in a painful, gag-inducing struggle, demonstrating we have finished like toddlers or rugby idiots by holding the empty bottles over our heads until we are waved off to dress and stampede towards breakfast to minimize the fifteen minutes' allotted eating time which will be spent in the 270-man queue.

We learn little tricks. To remove our shirts before brushing our teeth after breakfast to avoid tiny white flecks of toothpaste. To cover all the surfaces in our rooms with cloths to be whisked off last thing before an inspection, revealing a perfectly dust-free environment. To change boots having come back from breakfast in case the boots you wore on the way there got scuffed and have to be freshly polished. Most mornings are room-inspection mornings, so we stand at ease outside our doors until the appearance of the CSgt, at which point we brace up and then spring to attention and state our names as he enters our rooms. The longer the silence the more the tension builds as you hear him pacing around, picking things up, pulling open drawers. An established tactic, damage limitation, was to leave something obviously wrong – a speck of water on the mirror, a ruffle in the counterpane, the sash window not left open at the regulation height – which will immediately be noted and can then be rectified, satisfying the true purpose of the inspections, which is to find fault no matter what. The alternatives were worse, either Kafkaesque retreat into bamboozling complexity (forget left and right, my toothbrush bristles weren't pointing north) or the discovery of something really serious.

On the occasion of a stone having become lodged in the tread of my 'breakfast boots', which I hadn't noticed as I had changed into my 'inspection boots', I was almost too awed to be scared by the perfect pitch of the CSgt's screaming rage, the very capillaries in his eyeballs popping apoplectic red as he spat sheer Glaswegian terror, wielding the offending boot like a cudgel so close to my face that he was either a practised genius of intimidation or lucky not to break my nose. During such bollockings there was nowhere to hide, not even in the face of the man standing impassively opposite you, trying under normal circumstances to hint with a twitch of the eyes or inflection of the head how the inspection might be progressing while you strain every muscle in your neck not to turn around and check yourself.

Only one cadet took it all in his stride. Donaldson was so at ease with the whole thing he used to play the fool and entertain us by seeing how far he could pad up and down the corridors while the CSgt was tossing drawers out of windows and screaming at someone round the corner. We were amazed by how unfazed he was by it all. Donaldson had been a field marshal or something in the Officer Training Corps at university and knew all the tricks. Earlier than any of us he realized it was one big game and he played it as well as anyone. But the rules of the game were stacked against us, and when you thought it couldn't get any worse, there was always drill.

Drill was when we put on our most uncomfortable clothes and our heaviest and shiniest boots and marched up and down the square. It's not actually something one can actually be very good at – good, yes, but to be very good would be to stand out, which would be bad. Being bad, however, was pretty easy, and with drill lessons lasting anything up to two hours we had plenty of time to practise.

It never ceased to amaze me how people were incapable of doing the very simple things they were asked to do on the drill square. Sandhurst crams into five weeks for its officers what soldiers endure in basic training for fourteen: a course so hard and fast that our ears were full of *left, right, left, right* (which became, appropriately, a hoarse approximation of *love, hate, love, hate* in CSgt White's throaty Glaswegian), *left turn, right turn, about turn, saluting on the march – salute to the left . . . SALUTE!* (in your heads *up, two, three, four, five, down, swing . . .*) and so on it went until the blissful release of *HALT!*

And people were shit at it. People who must have known MILAN was not a city because they had passed RCB, these people couldn't tell left from right, couldn't count to four, couldn't even stop at the right time in the right place.

On good days the hysterical, colourful insults and withering mockery were impressive. In our relief that we weren't going to get thrashed, we would have gladly laughed at the more tried and tested lines ('Mr shagging X, don't tell me you don't know left from fucking right, you're fucking mental, you're supposed to have been to fucking university, you're supposed to have a brain the size of a planet, what a shame it's only shagging PLUTO!'), but the colour sergeants prided themselves on élan and would often put on a bravura performance. Notable for its surrealism was the ten-minute bollocking of one particularly inept cadet in 14 Platoon whose CSgt (an equally ferocious Scot known as the 'Badger' for his Argyll and Sutherland Highlanders sporran, a badger which we no doubt believed he had killed with his teeth as a boy) performed an elaborate pantomime in which he phoned the cadet's mother to sympathize with her for having a son who had been born with an acorn instead of a normal human head. Running with the theme, he offered to use a bayonet to carve eyes and ears into it so he could see where he was going and hear the words of command, or as an alternative, to put 'acorn-heed' out of his misery, to get a blowtorch and roast his head off there and then on the square.

What was really terrifying was a 'warm-up'. The warp-speed over-reaction to a mistake that involved the whole platoon trotting across the square in a vain and comic attempt to keep up with an impossible time being called out. Fifteen *change steps!* in a row and then a hard *about-turn!* with another run in the opposite direction. By far the most powerful tool for punishment was the *mark-time!*, a drill move which seems to have been designed only for the purpose of punishment as entire formations march on the spot, straining to keep the knees up, thighs parallel to the ground, chins up and eyes straight forward. With the steam rising from our heavy wool blues uniforms, the heat from our aching bodies evaporating the sweat in the cold January air, we would stand there in a painful frenzy of activity, nostrils flaring for breath, mouths correctly clamped shut, eloquently going nowhere.

I hated marking time. I hated whichever idiot had caused

44

us to be marking time. I hated CSgt White for making us mark time. I hated myself for having undertaken this nonsense course which had thirty young men marching on the spot. I hated how demeaning it was, I hated how brainless it was and I hated how symbolic it was, going nowhere.

Just when we thought life could get no worse, we deployed on our first field exercise, and the 'hundred ackere wood' was ruined for me for ever.

★★★

Exercise Self-reliance (universally known by the cadets as Exercise Self-abuse) was five hellish days of dribbling through three hours of sleep a night in a muddy trench. By the third day I think I had shell-shock, and we weren't even being fired upon. There is something uniquely minging about being so caked in dirt that four baths later you still feel filthy, being able to feel the squelch of inches of mud beneath your sleeping bag and the stabbing pain of cold-numbed hands grappling on the floor to try and pack up all your kit in the pitch black at four in the morning for a forced march through the rain to breakfast.

The exercise had promised glorious release from the oppressive routine of our training. Supposedly (laughably) we would get more sleep. We would be out running around the green fields with guns, playing soldiers, which was surely why we were all here. (Why are we all here?) Those who had gone before had painted an appealing picture of a happy week of no ironing, no room inspections, no woman, no cry.

It wasn't until the mild drizzle which had come down all morning turned to rain on Monday afternoon that I began to worry. The 0300 wake-up was insufficient variation from our routine to ruffle us. D-day was to be an instruction day, our introduction to living 'in the field' a challenge, surviving against the elements, using nature as an ally not an enemy. I was going to be Ray Mears. Even the colour sergeants had smiles on their faces, cracking jokes in our introduction to the twenty-four-hour ration pack (when we commission we will get special officer-type rations with Ferrero Rocher and a copy of the *Telegraph*, tee hee hee).

For more than a split second, for a couple of hours, it was going to be fine. Then we started crawling.

And crawling and crawling and crawling. And maybe a bit of 'fire and manoeuvre', where you dash a few yards forward, throw yourself to the ground, fire off an imaginary shot, get back up to your feet and start again from the beginning. On and on and on. Across fields, down tracks, up knee-ripping elbow-bashing lung-bursting hills every time wetter and colder and more and more knackered.

And then we set up our platoon harbour, the area of wood in which we would spend the night, put up ponchos and cook up our boil-in-the-bag meals and roll out our sleeping bags and finally rest. Or more accurately the area of wood in which we would dig shell-scrapes, coffin holes filling with mud and rain as quickly as we could dig them around the painstakingly scraped triangular track plan imposing military straight lines on our little copse. If we had thought room inspections were bad we hadn't a fucking clue. At least wardrobes and shelves incline themselves to order; trees have to have it imposed.

Impossibly complicated stag-rotas contrived to ensure the minimum of sleep; any lapse from the disciplined order brought collective punishment. Shivering miserably on the stag position until somewhere someone is caught.

And then it's more screaming and shouting and bloodcurdling threats and everyone up in the dark hauling stiff

46

frozen bodies out of damp sleeping bags and crawling, crawling, crawling round the track plan.

With only twenty-four hours to go the upside to neither having the time nor the inclination to eat all the meals in the provided rations was demonstrated when I dropped the bag of hash-browns and beans (the worst of the universally vomit-inducing breakfasts) into my lap, where it promptly started steaming off my soaked trousers. Friendships were forged like lightning in that adversity. Donaldson everyone's saviour, helping clean weapons, carrying extra kit. With nothing but the guy next to you to share your misery, we became intimately close to guys we'd never met. My basher-buddy Bowmont and I had been engaged in a miserable discussion which had moved depressingly from what we were doing one month before (he – beach in Brazil, I – lounging in Paris) to what would induce us to come out from under our poncho (apparently not even Elle McPherson offering a blozzer 20 metres away) but now, cracked by the fatigue and the absurdity of it all, we just broke down in hysterics and boiled up more and more of the leftover meals, rubbing them all over our trousers to dry them out, stuffing them into our pockets for the warmth and finally, if only briefly, finding something to laugh about.

On a navigation patrol we came to a clearing in the woods, and Winnie-the-Pooh's playground was laid out below us. Acres of gentle rolling woods so impossibly peaceful and redolent of childhood innocence that we couldn't equate them with our muddy platoon harbours and the nightmare camping trip in which we were trapped.

I suppose what is clever is that, when we finally got back, pale and broken imitations of what we had been four days previously, the halls and corridors which we had loathed for the last two weeks suddenly felt like nirvana.

Clearing up after Exercise Self-reliance, pale and broken in our fetching coveralls – January 2004.

***

I overcame the trauma of my first week in the field – a week which, had I been one of the admirable Afghans, I would have scoffed at and, at the first hint of rain, wandered off the training area to find the nearest village – not only by writing self-pitying e-mails but by driving my little red car in circles round the Academy car park. It was another of those lovely Sandhurst customs, customs we would have found quaint were we not being throttled by them, which rounded off the relative luxury of a Sunday.

Sundays would begin with a church parade which had very little to do with religion and far more to do with putting on uncomfortable clothes, shouting loudly to military hymns and falling asleep somewhere no one could really see you or could shout at you if they did. Gambling men played the numbers

48

and weighed up the brevity of the Catholic service against the anonymity of the larger Anglican congregation. Floppies – overseas cadets so called because they could never shape their berets correctly – were excused to sit in their rooms and order up deliveries from the Edgware Road to be smuggled in by the servants they all had staying down the road at Pennyhill Park Hotel.

My only experience of Sandhurst, before arriving clueless with naive enthusiasm, big hair and ironing board on the first Sunday of 2004, had been my grandfather's funeral, and I drew unexpected strength from the proximity of the chapel to our daily comings and goings. The names carved on every spare inch of wall and pillar and pew may have suggested to more thoughtful souls the futility, not the glory, of war and I was pretty sure that whatever God was being sung to had better things to do than check we were standing to attention during the national anthem, but I liked the idea that Grandpa was keeping an eye on things, and Sundays were good days because of this.

They were also good because in the afternoons those of us who had brought our cars were permitted to go and run the engines for an hour to stop the batteries dying. The sight of a slow, grateful traffic jam trundling round the grounds would have been farcical if it hadn't meant so much. In the seats in which we had driven so many miles we recalled our outside selves as if everything we were missing was channelled through the steering wheel.

★★★

The mantra at Sandhurst, particularly in the first term, was 'progressive training'. The assumption, on which I had depended, was that everyone would be treated as complete military virgins. This was most true of physical training we conducted. By the end of our year we'd all be tabbing bored as hell over long, combat marches barely noticing bergens the size of small children digging in our backs, dreaming of Friday. The physical endurance events could only get progressively harder, building up to competitions like the dreaded 'log-run' slowly otherwise the course would end up breaking more than the roughly one in twenty cadets it did.

Most of the PT stuff was psychological anyway. Red-faced little instructors in tight vests and immaculate white Hi-Tecs screaming falsetto because someone had forgotten to remove their watch before starting a run, or had been caught walking in the gymnasium where only running was allowed, no standing still, only jogging on the spot. My platoon were lucky, our dedicated instructor a giant of a man and transferee from the Infantry who towered above his chippy colleagues and had nothing to prove to himself or us. Nonetheless there were the odd undeniably painful sessions; half-drowning trying to do sit-ups on the side of the pool, while your partner completed a length, willing him to finish so you could swap over and enjoy the release of the swim, but knowing you'd have to thrash yourself anyway so he wasn't stuck on the side for too long like you were now. Long shuttle runs up and down the steep hills in the training area, someone too fit or too stupid risking a smart-alec comment from the back, and then it was everyone back to the gym for an agonizing ten-minute introduction to 'stress positions'.

And then, six weeks in, there was Exercise Long Reach.

14.ii.04 – 'Climb every mountain'

on return to boot camp, life improves. After 5 weeks I am considered to have completed the 'basic training' that everyone in the army must complete and now embark on specific 'officer training' with some of the perks that entails – our 0630 lie-ins had been keenly anticipated, the hard part of this 44 week extravaganza had been done, bring on the war studies lectures.

or so I thought.

it seems that our blissful first leave weekend was a ruse designed to lull us into a false sense of security, that just when we thought we were getting the hang of things, something of an obstacle was placed in our way.

more specifically fifteen extremely high mountainous obstacles to be raced over in a non-stop, 36 hour, 80 km marathon. Shit.

i have just returned from the Black Mountains having heaved my sorry arse, along with 6 other wrecks all faintly resembling the human beings they had been two days previously, further over hill and dale than I would ever have thought possible. Exercise LONG REACH, we were briefed, is one of the most difficult endurance tests the army does. Period.

as it happened I could deal with the constant weight and aching shoulders, the dull pain in the feet that sharpened with every stage until by the end every blister was a dagger, I could even deal with the draining fatigue and strange hallucinations, looming farm buildings twisting like funfair rides, idle tractors becoming menacing elephants – what was by far the most exhausting thing was having to haul the other bastards along with us.

should any of you ever find yourself in a similar situation – a simpering weed crying over his blisters and refusing to go on, a grossly overweight clown of a man having to be pushed up each slope, a shell-shocked looking thirty year old or young kid who have withdrawn into themselves with the remainder of you losing energy fast with all the others' kit you're carrying and share of the work you're doing just to keep your team together – let me give you an excellent tip. Once every six hours, 400mg of Ibuprofen, 2 x Proplus and 2 x Dextrose.

i dread to think what state our livers are in but we damn well got up those mountains.

only to find at the top some infuriating get-the-red-barrel-across-the-river-without-touching-the-green-stick *krypton factor* bollocks. Your mind becomes so degraded that by the time you're hitting the last few checkpoints all rational thought has flown out of the window – got to change the tyre on the Land Rover, don't bother with a jack we'll just hold the thing up even though half of us are too weak to even carry our kit much further. Had it not all been so painful there might have been an excitement in the breathless anticipation of the track junction or phone box that you hope more than anything else you've ever hoped for in your life is 200m round the corner of the wood because if it's not then you've got lost and are going to have to do even more walking. Pathetically, laughably, reduced to keeping up the spirits by singing 'Bat Out of Hell' to yourself in the vague knowledge that it's ten minutes long and so singing it six times will pass an hour which is really measured in three or four if you're lucky slow, hard kilometres. As it was it mostly just hurt.

but would you fucking believe it, we all finished. Long Reach is what they call here a 'benchmark' exercise and though I hate to admit it, having finished you do feel like you could take anything anyone could now throw at you.

hilariously, hundreds of cadets are now back in Sandhurst hobbling up and down from the medical centre, ridiculous in trainers with combats and sick-notes for blisters and ankles and everything else imaginable. In the lines a pile of bloodied socks (what sicko chose white as the colour for an inner sock) sits at the end of the corridor waiting to be thrown out and, we hope, ceremoniously burned. The problem is that you can't really remember pain and so that now the trepidation of stepping off up that first huge climb to checkpoint x-ray – the light of the Welsh pub in the village below getting depressingly smaller with every step – has been forgotten in the euphoria of completion and the anticipation of our next leave weekend, we probably think we all enjoyed that.

we didn't really.

It's funny how history writes itself. Having lost my journal I can't recall much of the rest of the first term, nothing to tie it down in my memory; it is a vague blur of annoying discomfort and camaraderie in the midst of the strangeness. We might have suddenly been allowed to lie-in till 0630 and we might have been allowed our mobile phones in our rooms, but we still had midnight curfews and were being worked sufficiently hard that we didn't want to escape that much anyway.

Petty bullshit was still the watchword. A moment of realization came when our section failed a pre-deployment inspection because, instead of taping five ten-pence coins to the back of our notebooks, we had all taped five fifty-pence coins. Instead of being congratulated for recognizing that the packing list was ten years out of date, and you couldn't have found a phone box which would have taken ten pence if you'd been a general, we were thrashed up and down the hill to Barossa for our impertinence in ignoring the strict instructions.

We had an epiphany on that run. The platoon commander was, as ever, running on the shoulder of the guy at the back, screaming obscenities in his ear as if the opinion of a deeply mediocre Engineer captain was somehow going to bother the cadet from Dubai who just tried to close his eyes and picture the Brabus Mercedes waiting for him at home. CSgt White was keeping his head up at the front, growling low encouragement and keeping watch over the rest of the platoon as we started to really feel the unexpected climb, and I looked across at the boys and felt a surge of warmth, a previously unknown kinship with these men, these strangers; the aristocratic Charlies, Bowmont and Church, tall and languid even in the run and even in the ranks cousins, side by side. I could feel Oscar beside me starting to giggle. Oscar of the gargantuan lungs, the fittest man I'd ever met and the bastard had the surname next to mine which meant I was partnered with him and his gazelle legs for every fucking event. Donaldson the other side, rolling his eyes as he caught mine, and they must have been feeling it too, because the snicker started to spread, and the Charlies were joining in and then lazy, handsome, only-joined-the-Army-for-a-bet Jonty behind and even little C-T, the pantomime dame of the platoon, feeling it more than anyone on his little legs, spluttering with suppressed laughter even through the burning lungs.

It was all just a game.

We muttered 'Leadership, Character and Intellect' under our breath as we scored our own little victories; diverting the energy and effort we should have been putting in on the drill square and in the classroom by planning and executing the perfect covert operation – streaking the long Old College corridor. The beauty of Op Naked Parade was that, though they'd have kicked us out if they'd caught us, stood perfectly to attention, chests thrust out – look large, be massive – like the Academy Sergeant Major himself, they'd have had to admire the attention to detail in the planning, the precision of the O-group and the level of control in the execution of the op; it was what we were being taught every day.

For actual military instruction, we watched videos.

Sandhurst relies on scenes from war movies for roughly 57 per cent of the course teaching material, and there was barely a lecture we attended that didn't make use of one of the stock Sandhurst war films for an element of instruction. For this reason there is almost no one in the Army with less than five years' service who has not seen all of *Band of Brothers* (Damien Lewis is, basically, the 'perfect' officer; our own platoon commander had got confused and thought he was supposed to emulate David Schwimmer's odious character), most of *Gladiator* (Maximus' exemplary employment of both fire support (catapults) and surprise in the battle with the Goths) and *Saving Private Ryan* (Tom Hanks probably a bit too thoughtful, but the fight up the beach sufficiently horrific to make up for it), not to mention significant sections of *Full Metal Jacket* (the opening half-hour), *A Bridge Too Far* (General Horrocks' definitive 'summary of execution' paragraph) and, for reasons which escape me, *Heat*.

In the evenings we would put on our convict pyjama coveralls and sit together in the corridor, polishing our boots on our knees. If we'd been good that day maybe some doughnuts would appear from the NAAFI and, on someone's laptop, the CSgt would play his own favourites: *Tumbledown* obviously (but none of the scenes of Colin Firth fopping it up in Chelsea, from which we might have drawn officer comfort) and Mel Gibson's porno-violent *We Were Soldiers*. I assumed my own favourites – *Apocalypse Now*, *Black Hawk Down*, *Platoon*, *The Life and Death of Colonel Blimp* – contained some hitherto unseen subversive elements and were on the Sandhurst junior term blacklist. We didn't even dare consider a little *Zoolander* for light relief.

***

By the end of the first term, even when some transgression or other so petty I can't even remember it brought the dreaded 'return to weeks one to five' that had been the threatened punishment ever since we had been allowed our duvets and half-hour extra in bed, it had the pre-planned air of going through the motions. All the platoons in the intake had been 'put back' for more or less minor infringements, the volume and pitch of the colour sergeants' screams had been steadily increasing as weeks eleven and twelve of the fourteen-week-long term passed, and the Old College staff realized they wouldn't have us as their playthings for much longer. The final exercise of term was round the corner, and the final intensification of the bullshit had been another of the things we had all been warned about before arriving, the final over-reaction of protective parents about to lose their kids to college and the power of veto in their lives.

We polished random brass plaques and resumed evening shining parades under the CSgt's watchful glare and some-times, for a treat, the more terrifying scrutiny of his ten-year-old son, who would walk up and down the corridor brandishing a small broom handle while his father eulogized about the Jocks tabbing across the Falklands, and we all just sat there, giggling and bulling and bulling and bulling and sometimes, for the sheer post–modern irony of the thing, watching the *Brass Eye* episode with the experimental borstal which had us all wondering what came first, the Sandhurst system or Chris Morris' pastiche of it, and had the CSgt wondering where he could get hold of a giant brass moustache to hide behind the notice board or whether forcing us to bury our beds would be a health and safety violation.

And when we had been good we were allowed to sit in the canoe – because it was all just a game.

Far from Milk Wood

Unfortunately Exercise Crychens Challenge was not just a game.

Crychens Challenge was our first proper test exercise. Fully tactical, we would be deploying with a 'realistic' scenario and enemy forces to live and fight four bitter days of conventional warfare. Beyond lay the prospect of four glorious weeks of leave and escape from Old College for ever, if only we could survive.

We were going to Brecon.

Even clueless Old College cadets understood the symbolism of Brecon. We had been given a passing introduction to inhospitable Wales on Long Reach, but that had been the Black Mountains, with the faint whiff of a national park that they carried, distant memories of Duke of Edinburgh's expeditions and regular glimpses of a red fleece which reminded you that misguided people did this sort of thing for fun.

Sennybridge was not about the fun. It was about the Infantry. It was about the pitch-black woodblocks and the freezing streams that weren't obstacles to be crossed but covered approaches to be crawled along. It was about the cattle grid on the track up from the main road which always signalled an ascent into freezing fog and about the cloud and sense of despair that always seemed to linger over Dixie's Corner. Even to those of us who wanted to join the Infantry, the dread promise of Brecon had been enough to make the ridiculous recruiting videos of the otherwise untouchable rear-echelon corps and services – the lingering zoom-out shots of the four-tonners making their way across the desert before an enormous blood-red sunset to the power ballad strains of Maria McKee's 'Show Me Heaven' – seem quite appealing.

Sandhurst had an air of grandeur about it, a certain elegance and even, beyond the shouting and marching, a certain gentility to its stables and polo pitches and black-and-white photographs of back in the day when cadets sporting preposterous moustaches practised bicycle drill. Brecon was raw and non-commissioned, and we were definitely in someone else's back garden. After fourteen weeks of basic training recruits pass out and become soldiers. When we qualified as platoon commanders, we would be instructing guardsmen, troopers, riflemen or privates, who had done only twenty-odd weeks of training. Out in Iraq and Afghanistan kids who had done four months of training and just turned eighteen were on patrol with loaded weapons. The first five weeks of Sandhurst had been breaking us in, a short, sharp military inoculation. The first term was the groundwork, everything beyond it was extra. Crychens Challenge was about making sure we could, at the very least, soldier.

We couldn't soldier.

Once your feet froze in your sleeping bag, you couldn't sleep let alone soldier. With crumbling fingers and Neutrogena at a premium (hard-working hand cream for hard-working hands) we stumbled in and out of impenetrable woodblocks as we tried to get to grips with the agonizing slog of advancing to contact – patrolling towards the likely enemy positions until engaged, defeating him, regrouping and then doing it all again – that was the bread and butter of the Infantry. Mile after mile, each rotation more stupid than the last, what sort of idiot plan was it anyway – to just walk at the enemy until he shot you? Effective enemy fire, we were instructed, was when the incoming rounds start landing at your feet; keep going till then. As if! After each attack we'd get a welcome five-minute break for a debrief. Sat perched on our sodden day sacks, sulkily eyeing-up the grinning Gurkhas who were playing enemy and who didn't mind because they'd be in warm beds in Sennybridge Camp that night, we'd be told what we'd done wrong and how much worse it would all have been if it had been for real. Worse?

We couldn't soldier.

Day one had been wet, but not cold. The cold came sometime on day two, which was probably why everything froze, but at least it kept us awake with shivering on the long stags, not even bothering to look through the night sights, bulky CWS which had already been outdated in 1982, when the troops had gratefully swapped them for the superior ones they captured from the Argentinians.

At night it was a toss-up on the lesser of two evils. Staying behind in the harbour, freezing and blind on the stag positions, actually watching the frost form on your trousers, feeling the water sliding in to the shell-scrapes and trying not to anticipate the grimness of stuffing the mud-soaked sleeping bags back into our mud-caked bergens the next morning. Or, for a laugh, out on a recce patrol. Even less sleep than if we'd stayed behind, but the highlight of the exercise when the platoon commander, coming along to critique, had fallen straight into one of the chest-deep holes of freezing water that pockmarked the foul training area. A break in the cloud and a sliver of moonlight revealed the section trying to hold back grins for the deliberate split second too long it took anyone to offer to help him out. The double bonus was the patrol being cut short because the poor bastard was so cold.

We shouldn't have been amused, but you had to find what humour you could. The CSgt was best, his stream-of-consciousness rants by now the stuff of legend among thirty of us who had as clear a case of Stockholm Syndrome as ever you're likely to see. Hanging on every word of this man whom we had feared and hated in equal measure but now worshipped and envied, his professionalism, his experience, his implied hardness and the fact that he would come grinning into work after a leave weekend with impressive bar-brawl scars, growling at us that we'd better not piss him off that day because he loved his wife and if we annoyed him he'd have to beat her because he wasn't allowed to beat us. He was an awesome soldier, and the more we learned about soldiering and the more we found it nigh impossible, the more we revered him and the more we laughed nervously when he snarled down the suggestion that landmines were unethical things that we shouldn't bother learning about because we'd signed the Ottawa Convention banning them.

And with a nod of satisfaction and half a smile he'd turn away to his steaming flask of whatever delicious brew he'd picked up before coming out to our pathetic harbour that morning, leaving us just enough aware he was joking to be laughing, but just enough unnerved by his grin to think that perhaps the Scots Guards Close Observation Platoon *had* assassinated the Princess of Wales in a stand against her position on landmines.

And then, at around GR 852, 346, we got to the Company Assembly Area for what would be the final night, except it wasn't a harbour, it was a farm.

It was about four in the afternoon, and it was a farm, and the weather had finally broken, and spring was here, and we had the roof of a warm barn over our heads and were sat in straw, peeling off damp socks and just wriggling our toes.

Next came the norgies – giant thermos flasks for food – full of I don't know what but it was hot and tasted good with lots of Worcester sauce and the white sliced bread that came with fresh apples for pudding and I went outside and sat on the step for a smoke.

And I was happy.

At four in the afternoon on a Thursday I was pissed wet through, shattered and filthy and having fun and for the first time, and, although I knew I couldn't soldier, I suddenly remembered why I wanted to.

The First Long Summer

On practically my first meeting with my platoon commander in Old College he had called me a *cunt*. On my first meeting with my new platoon commander he called me a *goobah* and smiled. We didn't even know what a goobah was, but in a thick Aussie accent this seemed like the sort of progress we had hoped for and, although we pined for CSgt White like we pined for nanny, CSgt Coates promised to be a decent, if eccentric, *au pair*.

The whole point and promise of New College was that, *au pairs* not nannies. Terms two and three at Sandhurst were not about the mindless crap, they were about learning and improving as warriors and leaders of men.

I guess that's why we spent the first weekend back polishing the skirting boards.

Straight out on exercise within days of having returned and without having caught our breath set the tone for the middle term, which was a busy thrashing. I lay on my back in the stag position, neglecting my arcs but staring enviously up at the planes coming and going low overhead out of Heathrow, flashes on the wing-tips so bright you felt you could climb the tall conifers and touch them, full of comfy, warm, pleased-to-be-coming-home, pleased-to-be-going-on-holiday smug bastards.

Out on the training area, as we tried to inject some aggression into our final attack, the new CSgt called a halt to the pathetic affair and, as we braced ourselves for the inevitable assault, he launched instead into a passionate and thoughtful discussion on the horror of war and the terrible reality of killing another man. The terrible reality that in our world people are still called upon to perform this act and the terrible responsibility that lies on our shoulders, having volunteered to oversee it and make sure it is not abused.

If we thought this was new and exciting, I could scarcely believe the events of the following Sunday, when I had been caught without my name-tag (no one had told me I needed one, nor provided me with one) and had been prepared for the worst.

CSGT: (*Stern and incredulous crescendo*) Mr Hennessey, you forgot your name-tag?
MYSELF: (*With heartfelt remorse*) Yes, Colour Sergeant.
CSGT: (*Pause, suddenly* piano) Mr Hennessey, there's a war on at the moment.
MYSELF: (*Confused*) Yes, Colour Sergeant.

CSGT: (*Resuming his attempts at Coldplay*) Then let's have some fucking perspective. Now, piss off!

For a wonderful week we thought we had broken clean. In the new *digger* lingo of chain-smoking Captain Hindmarsh the 'field' became the 'bush', which seemed a much cooler place to be crawling around. For a wonderful week we thought that now we were allowed to sign out in the evenings and not be required to be back in until the first parade next morning things would be different.

But then we had our introduction to rifle drill.

Rifle drill was just drill, but with a rifle. With anything as remotely exciting as the rifle ranges firmly behind us we spent the evening hours we'd imagined escaping to London polishing and brushing and ironing and buffing and first thing Saturday morning trooped out on to the square for four solid hours of marching, just this time with a 4kg rifle to be held, swung, switched from arm to arm and, apparently, slapped – hard.

Four kilograms is not particularly heavy but, under the unseasonably harsh sun and the even harsher scrutiny of the prowling colour sergeants and snarling company sergeant majors and even the immaculate, terrifying form of the legendarily ferocious College Sergeant Major, we spent the first weekend of the term in which we'd been promised 'grown-up' lessons and 'real' military training in a dull ache. Striking, seizing and grasping inanimate metal and plastic: *STRIKE! SEIZE! GRASP!*

As I tried to detect a flicker of irony in CSgt Coates' features as he explained to us that, if our hands weren't bleeding, *we weren't fucking doing it properly*, it wasn't the painful pointlessness of the *present arms!* which really hurt, it was the sense

63

that we'd been duped, lulled into a false sense of expectation that the bullshit was somehow over and the real work was about to begin. As the CSgt had already said himself, there was a war on at the moment, and you couldn't help but wonder how much *strike, seize* and *grasp* they were doing down in Basrah.

★★★

Then again, down in Basrah they weren't fighting the Russians either.

In Sierra Leone in 2000, in the early phases in Afghanistan, throughout the whole of our time in the Balkans and certainly down in Iraq, I'm pretty sure that we weren't fighting the Russians. Russian influence, yes, Russian rifles, yes, hosts of Russian weapon systems and even the odd legacy Soviet vehicle here and there, but the Motorized Rifle Brigade, which was forever threatening us at Sandhurst, no. I had no problem with the theory behind preparing us for any eventuality: the British Army has a fine tradition of being so distracted by what it is currently up to it stubbornly refuses to look round the corner, let alone into the future. We've known this since long before Liddell Hart tore up the corridors of Whitehall in the thirties desperately trying to get people to listen to him about tanks while the crusty generals bickered about their horses. My problem was not with the theory of considering all eventualities; my problem was with basing everything we did on those eventualities while different realities were staring us in the face.

I'd grown up on Northern Ireland and Bosnia, and even to a kid at school, the first Gulf War had been an anomaly, the last hurrah of the Cold Warriors who finally got a chance to use all their armour and artillery without the hassle of a decent opposition. Whichever genius it was who put a portrait of General Sir Anthony Hogmanay Melchett somewhere on the top floor of main building had really known what he was doing, and I couldn't help but recall him as I tried and failed again to focus on the troop of T80 tanks which were apparently threatening us from somewhere north of Camberley. Two hundred and seventy of us were going to commission from Sandhurst in seven months' time, and within a year we would be in Afghanistan, Iraq, Bosnia and Northern Ireland and not one of us would see a T80, let alone three unfriendly ones. When it came to theory it seemed that, as the great man said himself, 'When all else fails a blind refusal to look facts in the face will see us through.'

'A war' vs. 'the war' is an ongoing debate: how do we balance allocation of resources for what is currently happening with what might happen in the future? The Navy is still hungover from celebrating securing the most expensive ships the British will have ever built, and never mind that we can't afford to man them or run them and have no planes to go on them because they'll be built in key constituencies, so that's all fine. The RAF have justified their very existence with the delivery of fighter jets that were becoming obsolete when the pilots were losing their baby teeth, planes which they tried to save money on by not buying the option for air to ground support, then spent more money on developing a balancing weight to go in the void than the gun would have cost in the first place and only then realizing that they needed the gun all along so having to order at yet greater expense what they were originally offered. All on the basis that we fight 'a war' not 'the war'.

Even at Sandhurst, as we started our academic studies – lessons in Leadership and Management (Slim Studies), War Studies (movie-night) and Defence and International Affairs (Defence Against the Dark Arts) – we could see that as much energy was being devoted to protecting little empires by the guys at the top as it was actually fighting our battles, that defence procurement was a Dickensian mess, the MOD a lumbering hippo of a department whose money was evaporating paying for kit and equipment out of Urgent Operational Requirement (UOR) budgets at such a rate you had to ask why the stuff hadn't been bought in the first place. We loved the idea of the Royal Navy cruising around in two kick-arse aircraft-carriers as much as the next men, but even at Sandhurst we could see that there wasn't any money around and that, if it was being spent on Eurofighter to fight hypothetical Russians and ships to fight hypothetical battles in the South China Sea, then it certainly wasn't being spent on body armour and decent vehicles for the fights involving real people stuck out in the desert.

No wonder Mike Jackson looked so tired: something had to give and it was the bags under his eyes. He was probably knackered from being the only one in the room looking at what was actually going on while the Navy and RAF looked forward and backward and the politicians looked at the floor and nobody seemed to have noticed that we were deployed all over the place, fighting not 'the war' but 'the wars' and for the time being none of them being taught at the Royal Military Academy.

★★★

I still haven't decided whether the Sandhurst course is astoundingly brilliant or robustly fortunate. The things that matter, we seemed to learn without actually being taught them. The things we were taught, largely useless. The intermediate term was about digging holes and being gassed. We learned that in the event of a nuclear strike the correct procedure is to lie flat on the ground with your head towards the blast and hands covering your balls and wait for the *second* wave before standing up and dusting the radioactive material off yourselves with a nearby tree. We went on huge marches in Noddy suits and banged rifles till our arms were fit to drop off, and none of it have we done since.

But we have fought the three-block war.

A US general, Charles C. Krulak, had coined the term 'three-block war' in *Marines* magazine in July 1999, addressing an only slightly hypothetical situation faced by young Corporal Hernandez, who would have his place in history as the first 'strategic corporal'. The idea was brilliantly simple: In the post-Cold War era – a future that was not 'the "Son of Desert Storm" but the stepchild of Somalia and Chechnya' – soldiers would face 'the entire spectrum of tactical challenges in the span of a few hours and within the space of three contiguous city blocks'. We would have learned this up at Far-away Hall if the Defence Against the Dark Arts teachers hadn't been such sympathetic good academic eggs and allowed us all to sleep unmolested in their classes. As it was we learned it anyway, enviously watching Josh Hartnett in *Black Hawk Down*. Krulak drew on the experiences of the 'grey zone' operations that had erupted in the wake of the Cold War and saw a new future for soldiering. We'd have probably drawn the same conclusions at Sandhurst if the British had fought in 'Nam but instead we'd managed to pick an improbable fight down in the Falklands so were still digging and clearing trenches.

Sandhurst justified the lack of mission-specific training it delivered; it was a generic leadership academy. Specific instruction – flying for chopper pilots, building bridges for Engineers and counter-insurgency for the Infantry – would come later. It never did. I remembered those assurances a year later when I was sent on the fourteen-week platoon commanders battle course in Brecon, waiting for the up-to-date, fresh-from-theatre-with-sand-still-in-their-boots instructions on new tactics while we spent two weeks cutting plastic triangles and planning ranges and only one morning discussing what we called, with unwitting genius, Operations Other Than War (OOTW). No one was denying for a second that at the spiky end of OOTW the skills required to fight would be the same as in conventional warfare – shooting a guy in the head was shooting a guy in the head no matter what the legal terms of the deployment of troops. The problem was, while we maintained the false distinction between conventional and non-conventional and privileged the teaching of the former, the British Army was doing itself a disservice.

Even our own thinking generals had caught up with the Americans, Rupert Smith in *Utility of Force* realizing that, although we couldn't second-guess who the enemy would be and where and how we would fight them, the one thing we could be sure of is that *all* future war would be war among the people, war that still required at one end of its spectrum, yes, the guts and determination and aggression to stick a bayonet in another man, but was crying out at its other end for the intelligence and moderation and subtlety of approach that Krulak invested in his fictional Cpl Hernandez and that the Americans were sparing no expense in teaching their young grunts.

Once I finally got round to thinking about why I was doing what I was doing, bristling with comfortable guilt and righteous indignation at the contrasting bungles unhappily (but brilliantly) chronicled in the likes of Romeo Dallaire's *Shake Hands with the Devil* and Michael Rose's *Fighting for Peace*, I realized that these were the battles I wanted to fight. These were the battles that a Sandhurst of 85 per cent graduates (compared to a Sandhurst of 85 per cent non-graduates only twenty years earlier) should be fighting. And we were still being given Sidney Jary to read in our first term.

Jary's *18 Platoon* was a punchy, simple little book on his experience as a platoon commander in World War Two. Jary's leadership was clearly inspirational; it always amused me that he fell firmly into the category of iconoclasts who excelled *despite* their training not because of it. Rather like sending people into Basrah with a copy of *Stalingrad*, it prepared us for the worst, but I couldn't help thinking there was more relevant stuff out there. We knew we weren't going to be Jary and we didn't want to be. We joined the Army to fight the three-block war.

And if there's any value at all to the experience of the Reading Club, it's that, for all the frustrations and silliness, in three years we did.

We rocked up at Sandhurst to train for the theoretical 'a war' when there were two very real and increasingly bloody 'the wars' our Northern Ireland experience was no longer equipping us to deal with. In 2004 we joined the most over-deployed British Army in years and couldn't understand why Sandhurst wasn't hammering that home. Those of us who formed up the Reading Club were on the verge of three years, three operational tours, each one a step up the spectrum towards what we all trained for and watched the movies of but only ever vaguely hoped we'd do. In the meantime, we were sent out digging.

★★★

We deployed on Exercise First Encounter – the week of digging and sleep-deprivation which was supposed to mark the nadir of our Sandhurst year – with a pre-mixed special brew of super-strength Javan coffee and Pro-Plus which

would see us through the nights of digging, digging and more
digging. And probably, secretly, we'd been looking forward

*Digging and sleep deprivation through the long nights on Exercise First
Encounter – Norfolk, June 2004.*

to it because there was nothing the platoons liked better than
getting thrashed and comparing horror stories afterwards:
whose colour sergeant was the most ferocious, who had
crawled the most punishment miles and slept the fewest
hours. Screw the Sovereign's Banner – the official, year-long
competition to see which platoon across the whole academy
was the best! What mattered was the post-exercise punditry
and one-upmanship and who had lost and broken the most
men.

But when we actually lost Donaldson for real – not lost
like the non-hackers who bolted when they first got shouted
at and went to join the police, not lost like the unlucky ones
whose ankles and knees and backs hadn't been quite up to it
and were languishing in the remedial platoon – but lost, dead,

like never coming back, having come off the motorbike he'd bought himself as a reward for finishing the first term, it put all the whingeing, all the point-scoring, the whole fucking thing into horrible, unfair, grief-stricken perspective.

Sleepless exercise nights, blistered hands and bullshit we'd signed up for, not funeral drill and delivering eulogies and losing friends. My platoon – XV Platoon – didn't win the Sovereign's Banner, wouldn't go on to win the drill competition or the log-race, but we couldn't have given a shit because we put more effort into our drill at James's funeral, put more care into polishing boots to impress his mum and then hold up our heads and come back to Sandhurst to be better soldiers, as James had always been, than any of the other platoons could have imagined.

★★★

Summer at Sandhurst was particularly strange. Half of our friends were still at university, finishing their finals and hitting all the end-of-term parties that only a year ago we'd have been at ourselves, bouncing around in fancy dress and buggering the consequences.

Straight from some party or other we deployed on a week-long urban operations exercise. Ex Dragons Challenge was a terrifying Stalingrad meets Basrah with lots and lots and lots of shooting. It was also the first exercise where they really hammered us with casualties as part of the scenario.

At first being a casualty seemed great. In the middle of an exhausting attack to be suddenly tapped on the shoulder and told to lie down – fantastic. Maybe an overzealous DS would encourage some screaming, nominate a lower-limb injury just to make sure that you couldn't be hobbled back to the aid post by one man but had to endure the gritty poncho-stretcher drag in which you feel worse than all for the four guys straining to carry you across the ground on a glorified bin bag.

But the urban warfare instructors just loved to emphasize how basically, as soon as war comes to town, *everybody dies*. Anyone suspected of enjoying the stalling momentum of each attack as point man after point man was killed off moving from room to room was subjected to lots of shouting and, after we're all sat down in front of some footage of the US Marines ripping through Fallujah, we had as little appetite for FIBUA (Fighting in Built-up Areas) as we did for trenches.

I survived the week by my own ineptitude, not quite throwing myself quickly enough up the ladders, which we were somewhat alarmed to learn still represent our most sophisticated urban assault kit and which we were taught to throw up against bedroom windows like naughty window cleaners with grenades instead of squeegees. On the final attack only ten blokes of the twenty-eight in our platoon were left 'alive', which was apparently standard figures for that sort of game.

Urban warfare had been brutal up to a point, but I don't think we lost control of ourselves. For that unnerving experience we had to wait until we got back and were thrown, with the frenetic pace and intensity of intermediate term, deliberately not letting us draw breath, into bayonet training.

25.vi.04 – 'The horror, the horror'
bayonet training is unchanged since pretty much WW1, it should be one of those things which is obsolete but quite alarmingly it's not. the rumour fuelling all the excitement and extra spice to our current stabbing tuition that the Argylls (a lunatic Jock regiment if the staff we've so far come across

are anything to go by) fixed bayonets and fought through the position last month outside Basrah – gritty.

i approached the lesson with my usual cynicism, play the game, say the right things and laugh at the absurdity of it all inside your head . . . the more violent the activity, however, the more difficult it is and the instructors are well aware of this. We were beasted and beasted until we hated the world and the only way to stop the pain was to give in completely to all the screaming and aggression which goes with charging around the assault course sticking sandbag effigies. Everybody has to give in and then we're just running around screaming at each other like animals, picturing the faces of everyone we ever hated and going mad with horrible big fuck-off knives.

back in the halcyon days before 'health and safety' was invented they used to run the cadets up and down the hills on Barossa after an unscheduled four-am wake up and have us mill at the top, beating each other until the testosterone was charging and then pack the sandbags full of knock-off offal from the local butchers. For dubious realism the Colour Sergeants spray fake blood from water pistols as we go round but you can tell they miss the old times.

the bayonet is a nasty weapon and yet it gives the army a hard-on. Logically i would prefer to use a bullet, in fact, fuck it i'd prefer to be twenty miles away pressing a button and pounding artillery on whoever was trying to kill me, but there's something iconic about this weapon, something personal about it at the top of the hierarchy which everyone understands is all about how close you get to the enemy and so we can't help but get into it. Then we watched the videos of ourselves on the debrief and I felt a scared judder down my spine – the mad-man charging around screaming obscenities till he has no voice left, exhausted from plunging the end of his rifle into sandbag after sandbag is surely not me, surely?

Bayonet training wasn't even the worst of it. Chaotically busy as we were that summer, it's the second term which makes or breaks the cadets as exercise after exercise is crammed into the programme and no let-up for the training in between; we were still dutifully plugging away on our essays. At the time I was reading Norman Dixon's *On the Psychology of Military Incompetence* but, having at first enjoyed it, I was now finding it all too close to home.

If all the current strategic discussions, not to mention what was actually going on in hotspots around the world, begged questions of the very conventional, Cold War framework of our course, Dixon's study questioned the very nature of military training itself. Dixon argued that man is not naturally aggressive, that if we observe the animal kingdom at large there are any number of mechanisms within inter-species conflict to ensure that the participants don't actually kill each other. Armies are required, therefore, to instil in their soldiers an unnatural level of aggression, and we'd certainly understood that as we lay exhausted on our beds after the bayonet assault course. The problem Dixon identified was the requirement for this artificially heightened aggression to then be contained. This is why the military requires large amounts of bullshit. And boy did we get back into the bullshit.

On our guard duties, one of us would sit behind a desk all night at the entrance to the College, which was never used, and preside over The Occurrence Book, into which everything had to be written in CAPITALS in black ink and on to a ruler; certain things had to be double-underlined in red, and what was best of all was that one of the most senior men in the Academy actually checked the thing each morning, ripping cadets in half for inky smudges on the pristine pages let alone an actual mistake.

As we prepared for the drill competition we were busily polishing the actual soles of our boots, being instructed by the colour sergeant which brand of shower gel was best for cleaning the smooth sylvet cloths we used for the hallowed task of bulling our boots in the hope of one day attaining toe-caps so magnificently shiny that – what? The inspecting officer would see his very soul reflected in them?

It was a relief, albeit a painful one, to switch to preparation for the log-race. We didn't know where running around the Academy grounds with a tree on a rope came into the preparation of the cream of future Commonwealth leaders to meet the demands of the volatile international climate, but at least we weren't cleaning shit.

★★★

Our feelings towards CSgt Coates by this time were so mixed that Batty invented the tactical hand-gesture for him, the yo-yo. Coates should have loved us. His eccentricity was a watchword throughout the Academy, his thinking defiantly unconventional, the horrible Infanteer who had come top on his platoon sergeants battle course, who liked to let the rumours linger that he had escaped from Dartmoor prison to join the Army but who sat in his office strumming Coldplay on his guitar. Rumour had it that he had once overtaken the Academy sergeant major, himself no slouch on a bike, screaming down the M3 at well over 100 mph *standing on his saddle*. I could never work out whether it amused him or infuriated him that we religiously polished to *The OC* on a

Sunday evening, working away the Marissa/Summer fantasies in concentric circles which made the drill boots glisten with an extra shine of sexual frustration. He shouldn't have minded as long as we did what was asked of us.

And mostly we did. By that stage those of us who weren't incompetent were making up the ground, and some of the stuff we were starting to do had barely been covered by those who had arrived six months before thinking they knew it all. Sandhurst was still Hogwarts with guns, but we weren't in the first book any more. In fact, XV Platoon was beginning to find itself, to show a character which both explained and belied the fact that in the Sovereign's Banner competition, a buzz which had been only mildly distracting in the junior term but which was starting to bite annoyingly, we were placed firmly last.

Over the three terms and based on points allocations for certain key events – the log-race, the drill competition, military skills test scores, etc. – the Sovereign's Banner competition 'rewarded' the best platoon of the nine at Sandhurst with a multi-coloured lanyard for their last few weeks. The honour was purely theoretical, while everyone else spent the run-in to commissioning relaxing, the winners were frantically rehearsing the extra drill they would have to perform in the final parade.

But XV Platoon had taken Dixon to heart. Loved his idea that good generals differed from bad only in the degree to which they resisted the psychopathy of the very organization they served. Prematurely, arrogantly but not without a sense of fun, we cast ourselves as the Fullers and Liddell Harts and Slims raging against an Academy of Elphinstones and Haigs. And we weren't competitive. In fact, as we took more pride in being 'good in the field' we got less competitive. To foster the required sort of spirit, the pride in your turnout and drill to be a Sovereign's platoon front runner, you needed to care about the trivia. We didn't. We dealt with the extra weight and hassle of combat body armour when it was introduced because we knew it was not something we were going to turn down if we ever did have to assault an East German town (though we prayed that we never would have to assault an East German town and, in our smart-alec moments, wondered aloud if the Army might not be better served if it conducted less of its urban training on mock-ups of East German towns – there's only so much realism injected by taking the cross off the top of a church and replacing it with a crescent moon). Our problem was that, when we didn't care, we didn't play.

Perhaps that's why we got rough treatment when it came to dreaded NBC – Nuclear, Biological and Chemical training.

★★★

We weren't allowed to call it the 'gas chamber', of course, but we weren't concerned about the sensitivities by the time we arrived panting and sweating buckets in the charcoal suits that we had been thrashed around the Academy for half an hour in, scarcely believing that the rumours were true and that the sweat actually does begin to accumulate in your rubber-clad boots.

NBC should have been the nightmare because, well, it was a nightmare. We'd already been fairly darked out by some pretty horrific footage of the town of Hallabjah after Saddam Hussein somewhat unsportingly decided to test his new nerve agent on it. War, we were learning, was nasty enough without having to contend with nerve agents that killed you in nine seconds: three seconds, dizziness; four seconds, cramp in all muscles; five to six seconds, involuntary shitting and vomiting; eight to nine seconds, collapse, seizure, death. We thought the worst of it might have been the extra hassle of more kit to carry and clean and lose, or at the very least the exhausting games of midsummer NBC-suit rugby, but nothing compared to 'the confidence test' when they made us take the masks off and get a taste of it just to see what we were missing out on.

CS gas is a whole world of pain.

I can only really describe it as drowning in Tabasco. As soon as you remove your mask, eyes firmly screwed shut and having taken a big enough breath to hope that you get through your *NameRankNumber* without taking another, it begins to burn the skin, around the eyes and the lips, as you're garbling out as fast as you can *25181380 OfficerCadetHennessey*, except that the sadistic bastard colour sergeant had other ideas and, still barring the way to the door and sweet lungfuls of leafy Surrey air, threw in his curveball: 'Name two of your top ten hits.'

And I'm stumped.

Stood there, blind and immobile, feeling the burning, creeping in at my neck and nostrils and a simultaneous fire as my lungs start to scream for air that I can't inhale, I hadn't a fucking clue what he was talking about until Chad leaned forward behind me and muffled 'Travis' through his respirator and I remembered that for some inexplicable reason the CSgt thinks I look like the lead singer of Travis, and, even though I can't think of anything other than the pain at my chest, I remember Fran Healy looking stupid in a kilt and blurt out 'Why Does It Always Rain on Me?', which seemed pretty apt at that juncture, and if I could have opened my eyes I'm pretty sure I'd have seen the colour sergeant laughing behind his mask, but I couldn't hold it any longer and exhaled, gasping for breath . . .

Even though at that exact moment he stood aside and

bundled me out of the door, my gag reflex was triggered, and it felt like pepper avalanching down my throat, and with the choking came more inhaling, which only exacerbated the whole cycle until all my skin and throat and lungs are on fire, and there was no air, only sting.

Emerging coughing and spluttering from the gas chamber – Sandhurst, July 2004.

The temptation is to curl into an agonized ball on the grass, but it must be resisted as the only way to calm things down is to walk around like a vomiting idiot with your arms out, allowing the air to get to you. The small consolation is looking wonderfully stupid on someone's digital camera, foaming at the mouth and trying to pull 'blue steel' through the tears as you exit the chamber.

In retrospect I should have gone for 'le tigra': it's softer, more of a catalogue look.

But we emerged from the chamber, coughing and spluttering into more than clear air; through loss and digging and essays about what we should have been learning but weren't while we attacked houses with ladders and sharpened boots and polished bayonets and smacked rifles through a sea of bullshit, suddenly, finally,

over

were   the

we   crest

of

the

hill.

★★★

With fond memories of the expeditions which had passed into Sandhurst legend – the Middle Eastern cadet whose group had done a sailing trip on his father's fully crewed yacht, the group who had been on a 'cycling' expedition and had taken only handlebars, posing for photos cut torso high, the exped that had been planned and submitted on physical relief maps only, a challenging trek through California which, if someone had bothered to check the grid references with a more conventional map, they would have realized was actually a bunch of guys walking up and down the streets of LA – we set off dutifully at the end of term for our own adventure training expedition. A hastily planned 'challenging trek' through the High Tatra Mountains which we had no desire whatsoever to complete.

But we did all want to go to Prague.

And of course we had forgotten to mention to the instructors at Sandhurst that the mountain range was equipped with a newly installed cable-car system, so of course we didn't bother to mention that instead of climb the vicious beasts we just took the leisurely chairlifts and enjoyed posing for photos at the top. And of course we were too drunk to remember whether or not Hancox had actually been sick out of the window of the sleeper after we found that all they served in the buffet car was vodka, gherkins and dodgy sausages. Out of Sandhurst and out of green kit and let loose without a pause after three months of digging exercises and house-to-house exercises and NBC exercises and bayonets and grenades and of course we were too drunk.

And after day one of the planned five, when we realized that all the photos looked the same, of course we got bored, so it may or may not have been an integrity issue, but why not just head back to Prague and find the absinthe bar with the piano on the ceiling and the American ballerinas. Of course we did.

I'd like to think we enjoyed the senior term because, a mere eight months into our training, we began to learn things that were relevant. With a sleight of hand that couldn't but shock us, the CSgt dismissed everything we had learned for the last two terms and began our training in counter-insurgency and peace support operations with, in his own words, 'what the Army actually does'. Finally our lessons were not backed up by what had been done in the Falklands, but by what our instructors had done themselves in Ulster and Bosnia and some of them recently Iraq. Finally the enemy was not the Russian Shock Army but the real guy in the balaclava and the schemagh, and the game wasn't to hold the tanks up for at least twenty minutes till we all die but we'll have bought enough time for Washington to nuke Moscow, it was winning hearts and minds and working out how the hell we were going to get the PWRR out of CIMIC House.★

We deployed on Exercise Broadsword for ten days of rioting in Hampshire and marvelled at the satisfaction of whacking people with batons, suddenly understanding police brutality and sympathizing entirely. Broadsword was a revelation. The exercise didn't involve hours of running around and living in little triangles in the woods but was written by the academic department at Sandhurst and based on real incidents. As one of the exercise supervisors said, it was all the worst bits of thirty years in Ireland, ten years in the Balkans and the last two years in the Middle East played out over ten days in one village – and you thought you had a bad day at the office.

Shooting at Gurkhas behind sandbags had been one thing; dealing with actresses playing women claiming to have been raped, starving people looting aid drop-offs, religious leaders with bombs in their mosques, suicide bombers, mafia bosses, dodgy rebel generals, not to mention press conferences and daily newspaper reports about how bad/good you are almost made us yearn for the bad old times. After relentless days we were exhausted and felt nothing but admiration for the guys out in Iraq. The odds might have been worse back in the day, but at least you wouldn't get misquoted or indicted taking a trench.

★★★

★ From 5 to 28 August 2004, Y Company of the Princess of Wales's Royal Regiment fought a frantic defence of CIMIC House, the former Governor of Maysan province's residence in the southern Iraqi town of Al-Amarah, repulsing over eighty attacks by the Mahdi army in scenes which, according to many, recalled the defence of Rorke's Drift during the Zulu War.

The most important thing about being in the senior term is that you knew where you were going. All through the junior and intermediate terms you were a hopeful nobody, visiting various regiments with high hopes, on best behaviour and nervously wondering how your report card compared to the other guys who also wanted to join. The regimental selection process was like Sandhurst's version of applying to university, and competition for certain places was fierce.

The Combat Arms, the so-called 'teeth arms', were top of most people's lists. The Cavalry and Infantry regiments who'd be punching and scrapping through enemy positions were surely what the Army was all about. The Army Air Corps were in the club but they didn't really count because, well, you could either fly a chopper or you couldn't. Equally popular were the Combat Support Arms: the Gunners of the Royal Artillery and the Sappers of the Royal Engineers, the scaly-backs* of the Royal Signals and the sneaky Intelligence Corps, specialist and pretty important jobs and big organizations who would take thirty to forty cadets from each intake compared to the one or two the smaller Cavalry and Infantry regiments would take. In the rear, literally and figuratively, were the Combat Service Support Arms, the logisticians and educators and administrators and mechanics who we all knew deep down were a far more valuable commodity on the battlefield than the grunts we wanted to be but weren't exactly who we'd dreamed of being when playing soldiers in the back garden when we were seven.

The first two weeks of senior term were a whirl of final board interviews, some nightmare sweaty-palm jobs with six guys sat in the corridor interviewing for three places, others

* So called because of the acid burns they used to get carrying the old radio batteries in their packs.

mere formalities and shaking hands with the regimental lieu-tenant colonels we'd met many times before as potential officers and well-looked-after sponsorees.*

The whole thing should have been done long before, but Sandhurst itself was resistant, worried that once we knew where we were headed and started flitting off to London to be measured-up for our smart new uniforms we would lose motivation. The Academy preferred to keep the uncertainty and threat of a dreaded 'bottom-third' report hanging over its cadets for as long as possible. The whole thing was a bit of a joke because in many cases the regiments already knew who they wanted and had subtly communicated it to the grateful cadets. The recruiting officers knew that being good at Sand-hurst and being good in the 'real' Army weren't necessarily the same thing. It was far more important to make a good impres-sion on visits to the regiment you wished to join, to bond with the other young officers who'd become your family and for whom the opinions of the idiot captain that had taken a dislike to you in the first term would have little impact.

The problem was that the whole process was built on the myth that you could turn up at Sandhurst without a clue what the difference between the Household Cavalry and

* There was a rather nice 'third way', which was to have the man in charge of the whole Army in your regiment. The story which did the rounds during our interviews was that four guys had interviewed for three places in the Parachute Regiment. General Mike Jackson, himself a former Para and then Chief of the General Staff, had conducted the interviews and been extremely impressed with all four candidates and had asked his aide-de-camp how many places they were offering. On being told three he had nodded and said, 'We'll take all four.' The ADC, thinking he had misheard, repeated that there were only three places available, to which the general had smiled: 'It's my Army, we'll take all four.' The general had obviously known what he was doing, the alleged 'fourth man' that year going on to win a Conspicuous Gallantry Cross in Helmand in 2006.

the Royal Military Police was. A Cavalry regiment with an exciting role on the battlefield, formation reconnaissance in mini Scimitar tanks, might have three places a year, which meant one place per intake of maybe 270 cadets. Guys who really wanted to join the Light Dragoons would have been on visits before even getting to Sandhurst, maybe even before fully deciding to join the Army. If you were the guy who'd never heard of the Light Dragoons, let alone knew what they did or that they'd been formed by an amalgamation of the 13th/18th Hussars (Queen Mary's Own) and the 15th/19th King's Royal Hussars in 1992 and your great-great-uncle had been in the Charge of the Light Brigade with Brigadier fferignton-Camembert-Smythe (pronounced 'Fanshawe'), well, you *might* get a place above all those who did, but you'd have to be fucking good.

So those who were fucking good, those who had done their homework and chosen wisely and the small handful who were following Grandpa enjoyed finally being able to shape regimental berets in the mirror with the door locked and whooped joyfully on 'uniform-fitting' trips down to London while the unfortunates waited hopefully as the Academy staff called in favours to try and get them squeezed into the Adjutant General's Corps so at least they'd have a uniform to wear at the commissioning ball.

The Grenadier Guards offered three places on CC041, one to me, one to Mark and one to Fergus. My contemporaries were the super-fit, super-fast son of a general from the platoon on the verge of winning the Sovereign's Banner competition and a suave, trumpet-playing lady-killer with a laid-back style we loved (and his instructors hated). Those in the know on Army courses extolled the virtues of being 'the grey man' – finishing a race in the middle of the pack to avoid expectation at the top and pressure at the bottom – so I reckoned I was perfectly placed for when we would finally all arrive at our new battalion.

★★★

Not that there wasn't still hard work to be done, not least on Exercise Bayonet Point, our introduction to live firing. Scenario realism might make way for safety as the coastal ranges down on the tip of the Pembrokeshire coast were patrolled by safety staff in high-vis vests, but there was something a little different from field firing, a metallic taste in the mouth from the live rounds and the adrenalin buzz that the overhead fire gun was spitting real 7.62 just above, that the grenades in our pockets were primed.

Live Fire Tactical Training (LFTT) is something the British Army does better than anyone else. No nation is so thorough in its planning and safety regulations, nor able as a result to exercise so realistically and so dangerously. While the Americans with all their billions of dollars and real estate and resources develop paintball games and crawl underneath machine-guns, our LFTT is the envy of the world.

The hard work came in short, sharp bursts, and, when it did, those bursts were exhausting. Sitting behind the bun-line waiting to go down the individual lane, 800 metres of loose gorse, patrol forward, targets up, down to the prone, leopard crawling into a fire position and then returning live fire till the targets down and on again and again until your legs feel like empty shells.

Called forward, I didn't look left or right as I made my way to the start-line, blocked out the banter from whoever it was coming, panting back up the range with words of warning and encouragement, and stared the horizon down. Determined that even the first slide down into the mud would be immediate, that from the start there would be no crawling pain in knees and elbows, that my hands were unfeeling solids against the hot magazine changes and cold metal of the rifle, I crossed the line and, as the first target popped up, went mad.

I may have even screamed a little nearing the exhausting end at the final impudent targets, popping up long after I'd spent all my ammo and was lobbing smoke grenades I was supposed to have saved for later. I don't really remember. If I did it wasn't the theatrical yelling of the bayonet range, the bloodthirsty curdling they wanted to hear, it was something more personal from somewhere deeper down and bollocks to anyone who was listening. I don't really remember the range but I will never forget the expression on the CSgt's face, an expression which, more than all the kind words and good reports and prizes and post-mortem assurances, meant that I did learn something that year.

'Fuck me, Mr Hennessey!'

And nothing. No usual sarky comment, no allusion to how unsuitable I was to be joining *his* Infantry or *his* Household Division (even if it was the Grenadiers so he was minded to let me pass out just to undermine them, as he liked to say), nothing at all.

Fighting the system was all very well, but the only way to succeed was to give in.

***

And once we had, it was easy.

We fooled around, enjoying the elevated sixth-former status of being last-term cadets. Laughing at the guys in the junior term being thrashed from pillar to post as if it hadn't been us just months before and devised elaborate games to see who could get furthest away from Sandhurst and back in one night, living by the motto 'when in doubt, go civvie'.

Dashing down the M3 for a midweek bender and bluffing

your way hungover through the pistol range the next morning was our own little protest at the tendency of the Academy to try and drive a false wedge between the 'civilian' and 'military' worlds – an outmoded affection for muscular Christianity it had still to fully shake off. Our commandant had written the updated *Values and Standards* of the British Army, his Academy had a strong moral feel to it, but once we were no longer scared by the whole system, we began to question it and wonder at the creeping social conditioning.

Earnest student campaigners probably wouldn't have believed it, but Sandhurst was gloriously, effortlessly diverse. From the former rankers who had all the real military knowledge (and to whom we clung like glue) to the ever-fewer chinless Cavalry types, from Celtic exiles pining for real hills and space to the London boys for whom 30 miles down the M3 was too far, it didn't take much to realize that the diversity of the intake was something to be celebrated, not ground down by the sinister homogenizing process which turned everybody over the course of a year into prematurely middle-aged turds affecting crimson trousers. We teased each other within our own platoons (sniggering like cruel schoolchildren on the back of the bus at the guy who'd never been to London before and who we convinced the Natural History Museum was the Houses of Parliament) but furiously rejected the implication that there was, or should be, an officer 'type'. More importantly, once we'd given-in on the ranges and abandoned ourselves to the colour sergeants, we didn't wonder but knew in our hearts, our exercise-loving, combat-arm-wannabe hearts, that the fitness of the man next to you was more important than his tie and whether he swore or not during the run.

★★★

And through star-gazing nights on final exercise in Cyprus, each day ticked off in a glorious countdown to Endex which would see us just two weeks short of the long-anticipated commissioning ball piss-up and all our Christmasses come at once, it was having given in that kept us going. Having given in that had us smearing on thick layers of cam-cream, the waxy combat make-up that had previously been an annoyance, had us roaring like wide-eyed madmen up the steep rock slopes in the driving rain because every sodden minute and aching step further was one closer to the end.

Even when I became briefly and amusingly *hors de combat* – eyes infected from long hours practising beach landings, squinting in the bright sun and of course not allowed to wear sunglasses because only Americans wore sunglasses and they look *scruffy* – the proffered get-out of sitting the last few days in the medical tent seemed an affront. It was an offer we'd have jumped on at any point over the last year, cried for in those freezing muddy days on our first ever exercise, but I didn't dream of taking it. I damn well finished the exercise, stumbling with an eye patch through the long night march to the final attack; more warry and more scruffy than if I'd been allowed shades anyway (which amused and upset the Academy and College sergeant majors in equal measure when they realized that, instead of an American, I looked like *a fucking pirate!*).

We posed for photos after a champagne breakfast among the ruins of the training village, the sun obligingly breaking through after the thunderstorms of the night before, and all of us, eye-patched, ankle-bandaged, exercise-fatigued, grinning inanely because we'd finished final exercise, and the rest was formalities. Final exercise was the final hurdle, but in reality we'd cleared it months earlier, the moment we'd given in and started thinking about what came next.

Because what came next was for real. What came next was not marching around the square, playing hide-and-seek with the colour sergeants and make believe in Surrey woods. What came next was joining your regiment, what you actually signed up for the Army to do. What came next was our new homes, battalions and units spread across Great Britain, Northern Ireland, Germany, Cyprus and Borneo. What came next was maybe even straight out on operations. After the proud. smiling parents and speeches of the final parade, the solemn slow march up the Old College steps and with 'Auld Lang Syne' still in our ears, what came next was the terrifying prospect of responsibility.

What came next was command.

III

On the First Block

There are those who believe in progressive training, starting everyone off at a low level and slowly building them up, and there are those who believe in throwing people in at the deep end, literally. Gurkha swimming lessons, so we'd been told, involved chucking poor Jonny in at the deep end and fishing him out just before he sinks, letting him grab his breath and then chucking him in again, until he learns to stay afloat. Stood in the knee-deep snow on the tarmac at Pristina airport, waiting for an onward flight into Bosnia and scarcely believing that with lingering hangovers from our commissioning ball we were in an operational theatre, we felt for the hapless drowning Gurkhas.

Second-Lieutenants Fergus Lyttleton, Mark Bowen and myself commissioned on 10 December 2004 into 1st Battalion Grenadier Guards and were sent straight to join our new family, in the Balkans. The Grenadiers were midway through the six-month winter tour as the UK Light Infantry Battalion supporting the NATO/EU mission, Op Occulus/Althea. It was cold and tedious, and Bosnia and even Kosovo had long calmed down – the tense stand-offs with Russian-backed Serbia and the KLA a distant memory of four years before and the heroic patience of the original Bosnian peacekeepers of the previous decade already the stuff of modern history. Not that the Grenadiers minded – they were just ecstatic to be out of London and earning a medal for their services. Not since the first Gulf War had the regiment been deployed anywhere other than Northern Ireland and, though they'd become experts at handling the province, they'd watched enviously as the nineties and noughties had thrown up juicy deployments and new opportunities that always fell to someone else.

Finally a Christmas not spent in Belfast or Buckingham Palace and three new platoon commanders to tease for good measure. Fergus, befitting a twenty-five-year-old of his unusual dignity (not for nothing had he been known throughout Sandhurst as the Colonel) and fine head of blond hair, was sent to join the smart and tall men of the Queen's Company, the Sovereign's own unit of 110 men standing at an average of 6 foot 4 inches and as smart (as the saying went) as carrots (although the effectiveness of the carrot on combat operations had long been questioned by those outside Sandhurst and Horseguards); Mark had been sent to join the short, scruffy, taggy 2 Company, which would suit his generally chaotic admin and equally chaotic hair, and I had been posted, possibly for vague and spurious naval connections but more likely with a sense of mischief, to the Inkerman Company, the 'fighting Ribs'.

The Inkerman Company was named after the famous battle of the Crimean War, one of the regiment's proudest honours and, as I was told in no uncertain terms by the sergeants' mess members on my arrival, the 'soldiers' battle'. It was so called because the Guards had fought with exceptional steadfastness often without their officers (although not, as the sergeants' mess mythology had it, because they'd all run away but because they'd mostly already been killed), and the historical lesson was obvious to me: a young and clueless second-lieutenant straight out of the factory, I was very much surplus to requirements. My expectations of Bosnia had been formed by the horror stories CSgt Coates had enjoyed telling once he'd found out that was where I'd be going on leaving Sandhurst; the curious relish in his voice as he'd fondly recalled his months spent in the mid-nineties sorting mutilated Serb bodies from unmutilated Bosnian ones: 'You had to leave the Serbs out in the sun, so they'd go off, and the families wouldn't notice, and you'd have to keep the Bosnians in the fridge, so the families could make sure that they were all in one piece – happy times!' When I'd worried that was a little bit grown-up for me I'd taken assurance from reading General Sir Michael Rose's *Fighting for Peace* and imagining myself in front of a thin green line, my platoon and moral courage the only thing standing between some vicious neo-Nazi thugs and the next Srebrenica.

I hadn't expected to be straight on duty; camp orderly officer for the Banja Luka metal factory – home to the battalion and the various other nations who made up the multinational HQ controlling north-west Bosnia. Doing the evening checks around the Task Force headquarters was exactly the same as when I'd been duty cadet at Sandhurst a few weeks before, only then I'd carried a stick and now I had a pistol. The metal factory itself was like a movie-studio hangar that no one had cleaned up after shooting *Terminator*. Sprawling compartments of reinforced corrugated iron and improvised stop-gap measures keeping up the walls. Military hardware everywhere among the hulking wrecks of plant machinery which loomed like dinosaur shadows after dark in the Natural History Museum None of which was more unnerving than the huge, smart soldiers suddenly saluting us round every corner. Each evening the boys would retire to their iso-container cabins with the cricket (or Dutch porn if one of the guardsmen had sorted the aerial on the TV); in the background somewhere out of sight Fergus, Mark and I would compare notes over pint-sized gin and tonics – we certainly weren't on a Sandhurst exercise any more.

When we did get out on the odd patrol (lest we took

ourselves too seriously called things like Op Stable Door), some operation targeting the gangsters who cruised around in black-windowed BMW 7-Series, organized crime the real power which had rushed into the chaotic vacuum the conflict had created, we mostly just took photos of ourselves posing in missile silos. It was good, clean fun, and we got to compose exaggerated e-mails home, but it wasn't *magnifique* and it certainly wasn't *la guerre*.

But the Grenadiers were enjoying Bosnia, enjoying being away, putting themselves through their paces in the snow, the perfect blend of operational realism to sharpen professional skills without anyone seriously thinking that everyone might not come home. A regiment in peacetime trains for war; the maxim was all well and good, but unless a regiment in peace-time was on the verge of being deployed the reality wasn't quite that simple. A regiment in peacetime is effectively undermanned: people away on courses and compassionate cases and sorting things out, companies detached on exercise, platoons supporting other Army activities and bods flung all over the place. A Guards regiment in peacetime was also invariably marching around London in tunics and bearskins, which meant that the one time you could really get a feel for a 'regiment', that vague but oh-so-real concept of men and steel which supposedly made our army the best in the world, was when it was 'on ops'. On ops an Infantry battalion, like ours, became a 'battlegroup', and although we had a notion of how things worked in theory, out in Bosnia we were introduced to the practice.

The subtle nuances of who actually holds power where, the long reach of the commanding officer, the lieutenant colonel, the senior officer in charge and his relationship with his regimental sergeant major (abbreviated to 'RSM' by many but for Grenadiers strictly 'the sergeant major'), the senior soldier of the 650-man unit. Maybe twenty years ago you could have drawn an anology between a battalion and a big factory – the commanding officer the boss, the rest of the officers management, the sergeant major I suppose the senior shop steward, and then everyone else – but there was nothing comparable any more. For junior officers, used to creeping Sandhurst corridors in fear of the colour sergeants and even company sergeant majors who now saluted us, the men to really fear were the late entry officers (the LEs), salty veteran majors and captains who'd joined the Army before we'd been born and come all the way up through the ranks. They remembered second-lieutenants from back in the day as the idiot Ruperts who'd got them lost on patrol in South Armagh and nearly killed and still expected them to clean their boots for them when they came back in. The LEs ran parts of the battalion we'd never come across at Sandhurst, the 'G4' world of the stores and logistic chain, bullets and beans, all very dull but you couldn't do anything without it, and therefore them, and they knew it.

If they didn't pick us up for something, the adjutant would. A captain, probably only six years or so older than we were but the right-hand man of the commanding officer and responsible for all junior officer discipline. Mounting duty to him first thing in the morning would involve an extraordinary flurry of banging doors, shouting and running on the spot, invariably conducted incorrectly, or if done right, done in kit which wasn't smart enough, and either way extra duties would beckon and you would lose a leave pass or, back home, a weekend.

Faced with such a bamboozling new workplace – the scarily senior headquarters where you knew you'd either salute the wrong person or forget to salute the right one; the foreign G4 world and its strangely hostile old veterans, and at the other end of the spectrum, Support Company, a whole company of recce-trained soldiers and snipers and anti-tank weapons operators and mad mortar men, all senior captains and improbably elite soldiers we could only coyly admire from afar – we didn't so much join the battalion itself as our respective companies; 600 men were too many to know at first but the 100-man companies quickly became familiar. And I loved the Inkerman Company.

The company commander had recently got back from a UN tour in Africa and had a cheeky sparkle in his eye and a strangely crooked finger that even before you knew he loved nothing better than teasing the crusty LEs and organizing midnight booze runs, you knew he was fun. Seb 'Gaiters' Wade reminded me slightly of our Aussie platoon commander at Sandhurst: he gave off that same air which seemed to say: 'I don't care how you get something done, so long as you get it done well, preferably better than everyone else,' and it suited me fine. His company sergeant major was a fearsome giant called Daz Chant, a proper soldier who'd spent time with the Pathfinders and whose favourite word was 'cunt' but who projected a similar vibe: *look after my boys and I'll look after you*. The other platoon commanders, Gabriel and Sidney, were a thinker and a joker who couldn't have been more different or more similar, and were both well liked by the guys, if not always by the sergeants and the company sergeant major. Only a couple of years older than me but with a worldliness which seemed ancient, Gabriel had been crowned the world shin-kicking champion at some spurious village fête in Devon and Sidney probably the champion of a dozen other sports that only he and his crazy friends had heard of, or else invented. They had hair that would have given a Sandhurst instructor a heart attack and were in the middle of a bad moustache competition – I was in heaven.

So it didn't matter that we got sent home for a course within weeks, grumbling because we weren't being allowed to stay long enough to get the medal which would have been our first, and the first of any of our Sandhurst contemporaries. It didn't matter that the most nerve-racking thing that had happened had been when the hot water failed during my stint on duty and unless I'd managed to get hold of the plumbers in time the whole battalion would have been rioting as they stood freezing in the snow in flip-flops and towels waiting for the warm showers. It didn't matter that our first 'operational' patrols carrying weapons loaded with 'live' ammunition had been to inspect the same site inspected the week before and had degenerated into giant platoon snowball fights. What mattered was we were getting to know our boys and they were getting to know us. We were becoming Grenadiers.

Unfortunately, becoming proper officers and then proper Grenadiers wasn't enough, we still had to attend the fourteen-week course at the Infantry Battle School and become proper platoon commanders.

***

It was difficult to say what was most depressing about the long, Sunday-blues drive to Brecon; the horizontal rain, the four p.m. dark or having to pay to get into Wales. It had been hard to leave the companies and guardsmen we'd been working all year to join and, even though we knew we were only being sent on a course, even though we were still Grenadiers and even though we had rank, that paltry but significant lone star on our chests that meant we were officers and could hope to be treated as such, January 2005 felt like January 2004 had – starting Sandhurst, cold, nervous, in the rain, a long way from home.

Brecon was the home of the legendary platoon sergeants battle course ('seniors'), the SAS's own back garden, and our only memories of it were the nightmare flashbacks of Ex Long Reach and Crychens Challenge that had been too traumatic to suppress. The place was the Infantry Battle School and was all about running, big hills, heavy kit and killing – the best sergeant on seniors didn't win a plaque, he won a bayonet. The classrooms and corridors were plastered with slogans like 'pain is weakness leaving the body' and laminated credos which, when we read them, had us feeling like unsuspecting punters who'd signed up for the whole Infantry thing without the full facts and could we have our money back please and go and join the Cavalry so we could spend the next three months down in Dorset getting drunk and crashing tanks:

Let us be clear about three facts: First of all, all battles and all wars are won in the end by the infantryman. Secondly the infantry-man bears the brunt of the fighting, his casualties are the heavier, and he suffers greater extremes of fatigue and discomfort than the other arms. Thirdly, the art of the infantryman is less stereotyped and harder to acquire than that of any other arm.

It was hardly a great sell. Weeks of getting comfy and well fed in Bosnia had allowed us to bond with our guys but it had blunted the edge we had acquired towards the end of Sandhurst, and we definitely needed it on this pointiest of courses. All the buildings at the Infantry Battle School were named after VC winners, and we would trudge from our accommodation in Watkins (named after the implausibly softly spoken little Welshman who we'd thought quite fey when he came to open it until we'd looked up his citation online and read about the bayonet charges he'd led against fifty Germans in northern France in 1944) to classes in McKay, never escaping the symbolism that we had our lessons in a building named for the 2 Para sergeant who kick-started the Battle of Mount Longdon after his company had been stalled by a murderous hail of machine-gun fire and grenades on the front slope: found face down in the machine-gun pit he'd charged single-handedly, surrounded by the Argentinians he'd taken with him on a night when everyone who knew their Falklands history remembered that elsewhere on the mountain his platoon commander hadn't exactly put in a textbook performance.

There was definitely a cultural element to the tension. We were at the home of Infantry non-commissioned officer (NCO) training, and the very classrooms bristled with a focused aggression that our post-Sandhurst mindsets were tired of and our student backgrounds resistant to. The officer vs. NCO politics hadn't existed back when the platoon commanders course had been a gentleman's affair down in Warminster with London in easy reach up the A303 for dinner. Some far-sighted but misguided entrepreneur had even opened a 'trendy wine-bar' to cater for the influx of officers. The popular joke at the time as the locals in 'the Welly' got used to a few more chinless chino-wearing punters was about the local bird who pulled one of the new officers and took him round the back for a quickie. Asking politely (as no doubt befits a Sandhurst man) if she wanted to see his 'member', he drew her up: 'Your what?' she demanded. Upon which he had dropped his cords to show her, and her face lit up, recalling her similar encounters with the sergeants course; 'Oh, it's like a dick only smaller.'

The old ones are the best.

★★★

So, like last time I'd found myself in Wales and channelling aggression and bayonets, there was nothing for it but to give

99

in. Hammering the treadmill in the camp gym in Banja Luka with the i-Pod playlisting aggressive metal and running through all the massive improbables that would have to occur to fulfil my idle dreams of unlikely adventure, I had known Bosnia was not what 'it' was all about. Exciting, yes, with puppy-dog enthusiasm, and maybe even the sort of noble venture I'd imagined when I'd first decided to join the Army; something constructive and a bit different somewhere remote and, to civvies back home, a little dangerous. But, I'd lost that innocence on the ranges and assumed that the sense of impatience for what was next and better was simply to do with being in training.

Out in Bosnia, however, the guys who'd wanted for so long to get out there were chomping at the bit to get back and start training for Iraq, which was where 'it' was at. Out in Brecon we'd exhausted Bosnia stories by the end of the first week, and our peers who'd spent Christmas by the fire at home but who were definitely headed to Basrah on the first flight after the course finished had more kudos than we did. Even the shamelessly fished-for but nonetheless thrilling replies to Bosnia e-mails from long-forgotten exes signed off with lines like 'be careful out there' were forgotten at the bottom of inboxes. At Brecon we climbed back on the dangerous escalation elevator and got back into 'it'.

'It' was psyching ourselves up for the agonizing 'Fan Dance' – the gruelling 24km race up and over Pen y Fan, where we pushed the floppies to the point of collapse and still got sick enjoyment out of our stint carrying the extra weight of the machine-gun because 'the general'* was what 'it' was all about. 'It' was me and Fergus (although obviously not Mark

* As the general-purpose machine-gun (the GPMG) is universally known.

because he was already too fit) pushing out for runs over the hills in our free time and taking hour-long PT breaks in between episodes of 24 so we could be as fit as Jack. But more than anything else, 'it' was having the Y Company PWRR (Princess of Wales's Royal Regiment) tour video played to us again and again in lectures and never getting bored.

I suppose it was appropriate that we were the 'video' generation. Half the lecture theatre must have been born in 1982, same year as MTV crackled on to the air with the moon landings and *Ladies and Gentlemen, Rock and Roll*. It was only natural that we'd graduate from mix-tapes and mini-discs to full-blown multimedia. It was one thing jogging through the woods up to Ashley Green back home to try and keep fit in the Sandhurst vacation, schoolboy memories on mini-disc to stave off the boredom of running. It was a different matter once we'd seen the first home-made music vids, little mpeg montages of the high-octane destruction of the American invasion of Iraq set to 'Die Mother Fucker Die!' and then been endlessly exposed to the famous PWRR video.

The Y Company PWRR video was a work of pure genius. They'd created an MTV diary of the weeks they'd spent under siege in Al-Amarah in August 2004 and set the bench-mark for all the future Army video compilations. The Lost Prophets' 'Last Train' was the perfect backing track, a poig-nant enough ending for the obligatory lingering shot of the guys who didn't make it but with enough heavy guitar in the mid-section for the action scenes. The synching of the drums at the bridge with the first crackle of rounds recorded on mobile phone and digital camera video became standard, as did the eerie green 'through the night vision' shots, the slow zoom-in-and-out effect on grainy greyscale stills photos and the spinning, spurious factoids – '86 SA engagements' – which lent the video its credibility and its appeal. Montages, the work of a few hours on any standard piece of laptop software, changed the way soldiers went to war.

Previously the mini-epics had been exclusively in our heads. The jogging playlist flicked to something suitably gung-ho (a bit of Guns 'n' Roses usually saw you through a quick 3-mile circuit of the Academy grounds), and your imagination was the limit. But the problem was always how to stream these heroic images back home into the astonished living rooms of all the guys you wanted to silence and girls you wanted to fancy you. The scenario always had to involve an embedded news team (usually hot young reporter, romance blossoming against all the odds to add some spice to the run) and then things got implausible (as if they hadn't been implausible the moment you pulled your trainers on and started the warm-up).

Once we'd seen the PWRR video, seen how simply Windows Movie Maker fused the images we wanted to take and the music we listened to to psych ourselves up for it, and then gave us the medium by which we would show our efforts to everyone back home, we'd seen the perfect art form. I didn't know a single guy in the Y Company video, but they were the heroes of the new wars we were fighting, and their video was more vivid, more real and more motivating than all the reportage and training and lectures in the world. E-mails were fun, but as we got back into 'it' we realized nothing was going to trump the glorious montages we'd play back on our laptops, immortalizing ourselves as the heroes we had obviously always wanted to be.

★★★

But there had been no photos and no excitement in Bosnia which would have warranted making a movie and there was even less in Brecon. I found myself as tired as I'd ever been on one of our endless long exercises, staring across a fence line at a herd of cows, gentle chocolate brown and retro black and white, chomping away in the field with their silly long eyelashes. I was recceing the stag positions, taking it seriously even though no one was watching or would have cared because we were into 'it' by then, furious when one of them saw me, so I dropped into a ditch and observed them through my sights.

A field of what appeared to be animals grazing at a distance of 100 metres. (Being careful not to call any of the bleeders 'cows'.) Their lead scout had alerted the rest of the platoon with the codeword 'moo', and slowly but surely thirty cows were staring through the trees at me, on stag, staring back. And I've always liked cows, so my spirits were lifted, and between us – the muzzle of my rifle and the wet tips of their noses – was just the thinnest of wire fences.

And once we were back in the mess a week later, warm and dry and cramming down thirds of issue cheesecake, I looked back fondly on these slightly surreal moments – behind me thirty grown men scrambling around in the mud, practising how best to kill each other, and in front of me thirty pairs of soft eyes staring with an intense curiosity and myself in the middle, unable to work out on which side of the fence were the dumb animals. But these weren't the moments which would be played endlessly to Sandhurst cadets when we were boastful 'voice of experience' captains and it grew frustrating that, for us Grenadiers, those moments didn't seem to be likely to come any time soon.

By the end of the course, fourteen demanding weeks which hadn't been as bad as we'd psyched ourselves up to believe because we'd learned by then just to go with it, we were probably as good a bunch of soldiers – by the book, know the right answer, run 50 miles a day over the mountains with our wounded friends on our backs soldiers – as we'd ever be.

Getting into 'it' on PCD, not relishing the extra ammunition for the machine-gun section – Malawi, March 2005.

We spent a month in the jungle in Africa, making up for all the nights we'd spent shivering on Salisbury Plain tracking hippos through the night-sights, drinking in enormous skies and picking out the Southern Cross. There was no doubt living and training in the jungle (even the soft Malawi bush, which, deep down, we knew was to the 'real' jungles of Borneo and Belize what 'urban' Fulham was to Brixton) honed your skills, completely melted the outside world away, the longest we'd spent without mobile phone reception in years, so not even the distraction of a bored text message home to pass the time on day-long ambushes, just a copy of *Heart of Darkness* hidden in our Tactical Aide Memoires.

It would have been the perfect preparation, should have been the perfect launchpad to rejoining our regiments with a few more skills and a bit more knowledge and a lot more hunger and launch off to war with machetes still sharp in our webbing, but for the Grenadiers, something else lay in store.

On the Square and in the Night-tray

In Bosnia the Inkerman Company young officers had amused themselves winding up the Senior Major – the silver-haired battalion second-in-command with a passion for the Queen's Company – by compiling historical evidence that his beloved company hadn't actually fought in any of the key battles in the regiment's history.

Every good Grenadier knew (and every good Coldstreamer hated) that we had earned our name on 18 June 1815 for the role the First Foot Guards played in the defeat of the French Imperial Grenadiers at Waterloo – the only regiment in the British Army to have won its name in battle. Forty years later the legends and heroes of Alma and Sevastopol and the Inkerman had covered that name in glory, won the regiment's first Victoria Crosses and become central parts of its history.

We teased the Senior Major with the insinuation that these key actions had been fought by the scrappy men of the regiment, not the tall, smart men of the Sovereign's Company who throughout the spur-winning nineteenth century would have been sat in London or Windsor guarding the monarch and getting fat and bored. As fresh new officers we hadn't quite understood the significance of the difference, the tension that existed in the conflict between the two roles that the Household Division, dedicated to the protection of the sovereign, alone performed, the contrast between the proud fighting history of our new regiment and our own heroic fantasies and the reality of performing Military Task 2.5 – Public Duties and State Ceremonial.

It didn't matter that the crap about the Queen's Company probably wasn't true. The battalion got back from Bosnia just as we came crawling out of the jungle and off PCD, coursed to the max and raring to fight whichever wars were coming our way. Instead we were all sized up for our drill boots and marched on to the square for spring drills.

***

The story behind spring drills was that Queen Victoria had noted with displeasure a less than immaculate performance on one of her Birthday parades. Such slackness was unthinkable and for it to be remarked upon unheard of, and in penance and to ensure it was never repeated, the Guards Regiments vowed to spend a week in spring practising their drill for the next 100 years.

Unless she'd spoken from beyond the grave, 100 years had expired by spring 2005, but history and maths didn't wash with the drill sergeant – the warrant officer whose only consolation at being in charge of the drill square and thus the shoutiest, angriest man in battalion was the chance to thrash the junior officers every morning before breakfast with the rest of the sergeants' mess watching unsubtly at the windows with their coffee – more bloody drill.

In my memory, the London summer of 2005 is almost as sunny as the Iraqi summer of 2006 and the Afghan summer of 2007 would be. It is blurred in a similar way, disjointed and punctuated not by weekends and holidays but by events and places. We came back from Brecon wanting more than anything in the world for our summer to be a blur of battles and deserts, but what we got was a blur of palaces and castles.

We'd done all the mental preparation for facing the enemy, and somewhere I'd missed the preparation for right-wheeling out of Wellington Barracks towards the Birthday Cake (the lavish Victoria Memorial statue in front of Buckingham Palace), already baking in a tight scarlet tunic on a packed Sunday, and suddenly being hit by the cameras. Thousands and thousands of flashes as the thumping of the band echoes and you glimpse the Old Guard already waiting for you and, however much you want to damn it all as the same anachronistic crap you hated bits of training for, you can't because your chest is so swelled out with the surge of the crowd that only as you come in through the gates and on to the forecourt of Buckingham Palace and remember that here it starts to get complicated and a slip-up would be very public do your efforts to keep the right elbow up as you carry the Colour start to ache.

We weren't soldiers that summer, we were actors. Spring drills was our dress rehearsal, and before we knew it our weeks and summer months were no longer days but twenty-four-hour segments of guarding the Tower of London, Windsor Castle and Buckingham and St James's Palaces. Every duty a glorious photo-shoot moment we would come to intimately know as Tower, Windsor, Buck and Jimmy's.

The confusion of the French tourists about summed up the confusion of public duties. They were by far the least respectful, most annoying, which was explained by the fact that they assumed we weren't real soldiers. The Americans just loved it too much to be anything other than Disneyland giddy, the baby-boomers snapping away all baseball caps and bum-bags and the obliging college girls. The Japanese were cute, sent in a terrified, giggling scutter by the slightest movement of the guardsmen or barked word of command. But the French couldn't get their heads around the idea that these were trained soldiers – that the medals shining on scarlet tunics were actually anything more than decoration.

We drew in money, that was for sure, but there was no ammo in the rifles, and whether it was Buck or Windsor everyone knew that it was SO14, the Royal Protection Police, who did the actual guarding. The sceptics asked why on earth it needed to be highly trained soldiers stood still for two hours at a time. The realists replied that highly trained soldiers stood still wherever they were told and it might as well be outside a palace upholding 'the fabric of the nation' as on a freezing VCP in Bosnia or in a Sangar in Belfast. Did it make us better soldiers – the pride and the discipline? Perhaps it did. The bearskin, after all, had been a pretty practical bit of kit for dismounted troops holding the line against cavalry – the curb-chain protecting the face from the downward slash of the sabre and the deceptive hollow height of the caps themselves tempting and disarming the lancers. We might have wondered how likely we were to be facing lances and sabres but were too busy enjoying being the centre of attention as we marched around.

It didn't matter to us that we were invisible under the bearskins, that it wasn't us being photographed but our uniforms and everything they meant. On Tower and Windsor it was our duty to stroll around, stepping out from the officers' flat to an instant buzz of interest and then marching off with a gaggle of snapping and questioning tourists in our wake. Imperiously silent for most of the time except perhaps to smile faintly at a particularly fit group of Americans and invite them up for tea to try on your uniform with their astonished giggles and excited incredulity that you 'actually spoke' ringing in your ears up the stairs to the flat, past the nodding appreciation of the guardsmen who might have resented the lack of freedom to do the same but expected nothing less of their officers than to make up for it.

And my girlfriend Jen was absolutely right when she came to visit the Tower, or maybe it was Windsor, but there were definitely tunics and tourists involved, and they all blurred into one after a while, when she pointed out how unhealthy it all was that after only a couple of months we didn't find it strange. She rose above it magnificently, the fawning attention we got from the try-hard tourist girls, which was maybe as hard to deal with as the six-month tour separations; at war you might die but you weren't going to have a threesome with Texan cheerleaders.

No wonder so many Army boys got married earlier than most – we took for granted the tolerance of our long-suffering girlfriends and then ponced around in front of them. Were miffed if the day clouded over and there were only tens instead of hundreds of tourists waiting as we wheeled in through Henry VIII gate and on to the square at Windsor Castle, wondering what random object whoever it was stood there waiting at attention was going to try and hand over at the handshake – Haribo were popular but the more bizarre the better: swimming goggles, once apparently a sausage, anything other than the 'Golden Key' or whatever crap the tourist were being fed by the clueless guides. That we considered it only right and proper for people to stop and stare as we walked past, or to be able to step out into the road and expect the traffic to stop. Proper London cabbies know that officers in uniform won't, can't wait at traffic lights and slow the traffic obligingly. The problem was after a solid summer of on/off guards and dangerously high levels of residual Moscow Mules (the St James's Palace mess speciality) in the blood-stream, we'd forget we weren't on guard, stride out non-chalantly over the Mall to be nearly run down by the traffic in jeans and a t-shirt and wonder with puzzled disappointment why no one was stirring in the park as we walked through.

The strange attraction of the tunic and bearskin; dressing up was never so much fun – Tower of London, June 2005.

This might not have been what anybody joined the Army to do, but it was dangerously seductive, and all thoughts of guts and glory might have been lost completely among the silver and historical relics on the highly polished Queen's Guard table if we hadn't received the frantic call to switch from ceremonial uniforms to combats and start tactically patrolling the palaces in the confused minutes after the 7 July bombs went off. Suddenly the square at Wellington Barracks was a buzz of activity, and choppers in-and-outing shocked generals and focused 'special' types in jeans and sideburns with the quartermasters worryingly totting up the holding of gas masks as we wondered what might come next and everyone waiting for the call to go and help the police pull bodies out of the underground.

Peacocking across St James's Park in a bearskin didn't draw half as many stares as running through it in combats as we ferried messages back and forth between the detachments at St James's and Buckingham Palace and checked up on the guys on post who were taking it seriously for once and stating with meaning rather than just repetition that 'all was well'. I was briefly reminded of the favourite regimental story about the guardsman who had been on post on the corner of the Mall when the IRA had bombed the Carlton Club and who had sprung to attention when the officers had run out to find out what was going on and despite the smoke clouds billowing and the debris lodged in his bearskin had stated as he always had that 'all is well'. When the decision was made the next day to go ahead with the full ceremonial mount, the crowds were enormous, and the atmosphere was electric. There had been grumbles that you couldn't police the mount, that marching behind a ruddy great band in bright red tunics down the public streets of London was an invitation to a follow-up which couldn't be adequately protected by some barriers and a few mounted police. But that was the whole point, that was why it felt so good and why chests were more than usually puffed out, the bayonets of the escort to the Colour more than usually shiny as a gesture of defiance that said 'This is what we do, this is our way of life, this is why more people from around the world come to this city than anywhere else, and you're not going to stop it.'

★★★

One of the few bits of relevant wisdom that my grandfather had passed on to me when I was deciding to join the Army was that mostly the Army is about boredom. A few live-fire exercises and a couple of weeks in Bosnia under my belt, I was in no position to say what 'war' was or wasn't like but I was starting to get a sense of the strange rhythm of Army life. There were bursts of sustained intense activity, Sandhurst and Brecon had been unusually extended examples of these, although even those courses had been punctuated with moments of drifting calm, but these came at odd and inopportune moments, and the rest was, well, the rest was extraordinary.

Friends in offices may not have had early-start Friday-morning battalion PT sessions, tabbing out 8 miles under enormous bergens past perplexed herds of deer in the Windsor Great Park, but neither did they have the long days of nothing. Pulling on a tunic and marching around for an hour and half in the morning was all very well, but then we would sit around in the mess in St James's Palace and count scampi fries, literally doing nothing.

Now the learning curve was steep, but downhill. After the hustle and competition of course culture, everyone being watched and watching, we now embraced the mess life, which began with a full cooked breakfast, coffee and biscuits squeezed in for an hour or so at ten-thirty and then everyone back in for ginger beers and crisps with Worcester sauce before lunch. A good long lunch and a healthy cheeseboard would just about see us through to tea and toast at four, by which time we needed a token run to clear space for a big supper at seven-thirty. Whatever the starter was it was always in a glass, and if we didn't like pudding, which we didn't, there was always the night-tray.

I learned to love the night-tray that summer, the idea of the night-tray, the reality of the night-tray. One of my appreciative friends, up for a boys' weekend when I was on piquet duty, confined to camp and on call but playing long evenings of poker in fancy dress, even passed out and spent the night in the night-tray. I suppose the night-tray symbolized everything that was suddenly good about life, everything that, when we put our thoughts of war to the back of our minds where they belonged, we had pushed through the last eighteen months for.

And the night-tray, of course, wasn't even a tray, but a room.

***

They liked to say at Sandhurst that the Army wasn't just another job, it was a way of life; a battalion was not the company you worked for, but your family. I wasn't sure this was necessarily the right way to think about things, was pretty sure it fostered the insularity and sense of superiority which characterized some of the cocks at Sandhurst and the cockish instructors they would no doubt become, but in an idle mess you could see that it rang true.

The Guards didn't have bars in their messes, another example of the sort of inclusivity which no one imagined of us. Bars meant rounds and rounds might have meant embarrassing someone who didn't necessarily want, or couldn't necessarily afford, to be involved. During the day the mess orderlies discreetly noted who had ordered what and chalked it up against our bills, which meant that, once the mess staff had gone to bed, the night-tray was opened. A room with a fridge well stocked with all the booze we could possibly need and the other essentials: fags, Smarties, crisps and Worcester sauce. The piquet officer signed for the key and in theory was responsible for the stock, but everyone signed, or at least just about scrawled, for whatever it was they took, and the door was never closed. Coming from offices in which they had cubicles in twenty-man rooms, e-mails monitored and websites blocked and billed, their days in six-minute chunks, whispering in reply to my calls that they couldn't be seen to be talking on their mobiles at work, my friends were envious of the laziness of our days and the fact that even at the bottom of the pile I had an office and an orderly, but more than anything they were jealous of the easy-going trust of Army life.

The paradox of the night-tray was that, after a year and a half of being treated like a child, once we'd got through it all we were treated more like grown-ups than any of our peers and for all the distinctly ungrown-up marching around in fancy dress and the eighteenth-century lifestyle, it was because, when we were actually doing our jobs, we had more responsibility than anyone else.

In fact, we were primary-school teachers. Sure, teachers with guns, but a platoon commander was, nonetheless, the guy who sorted out the waking day of the thirty men under his command, taught their lessons, helped with their home-work, sorted out their petty squabbles and put plasters on their knees when they fell over in the playground. 10 Platoon, the Inkerman Company, 1st Battalion Grenadier Guards were ten to fifteen years older, granted, than your average primary-school class, a lot bigger and uglier and only a little bit better at maths, but they were my completely my responsibility.*

And even in peacetime, this was terrifying. Terrifying when guardsmen came to me with their money troubles, not understanding why, when their banks were telling them

---

* To those who found the useful generalization patronizing, we pointed out that the banter went both ways – all junior officers were floppy-haired, brandy-quaffing, huntin', shootin', fishin' inbred imbeciles who'd spent their year at Sandhurst learning to use a fish knife.

they were overdrawn, they wouldn't accept a cheque for the money owed. Terrifying when guardsmen fell in first thing in the morning in paper suits because their clothes had been sent to forensics, still a bit too drunk to remember what they had or hadn't done the night before but touchingly confidently putting their arrest reports and the conduct of their defence in your clueless hands. Terrifying when guardsmen came to see me because they shared a girlfriend who was pregnant and couldn't work out whose it was and didn't really care and didn't want to pay for paternity tests so could I witness a coin toss. Terrifying most of all when a wincing Monday-morning guardsman would ask to report sick and drop his trousers to dispense with explanations; as we were always saying, in the Army a picture paints a thousand words.

The most basic training modules the Army conducts, the lessons that must be delivered annually to keep any soldier current, were the Military Annual Training Tests (MATTs). MATT 1 was shooting, MATT 2 fitness, MATT 3 first aid, MATT 4 chemical, biological, radiological and nuclear (CBRN), MATT 5 navigation and MATT 6 values and standards. One to five were pretty straightforward, bread-and-butter Army stuff, but values and standards incorporated the law of armed conflict, security, health and safety, substance misuse, and equality and diversity. I was supposed to be a personal trainer, lawyer, doctor, social worker and padre, and, looking around my peer group, we were on some pretty shaky hypocritical territory there.

So what did I actually do for a whole summer? What did we actually do full stop? Aside from the marching and the eating and drinking and the museum living and the entertaining and the running and the shooting and the financial advising and the legal advising and the medical advising and the drugs lecturing and the relationship counselling, I don't really know. But we were no closer to seeing the enemy, whatever that was.

And in the Army way that I was learning, the counterpoint was suddenly a spare fortnight in the training programme and the whole battalion off to Dartmoor for a horrific exercise. So while everyone else was watching England finally win the Ashes we were hauling ourselves over the babies-heads with the heaviest bergens we'd ever lifted.

Guard duties were great for conducting interviews with all the blokes; getting to know that Gdsm X was a keen artist and wanted to join the recce platoon or that Gdsm Y was dating a fifteen-year-old, but it was all right because her father liked him and she looked older. They were perfect for joking in the company bunk with Sgt Childs, my ultra-competitive but ultra-competent young platoon sergeant (a new platoon commander's nightmare: an all-round better second-in-command. Sgt Childs could out-run, -bench and -shoot me, but I nearly killed myself beating him in our marathon first encounter on the squash court, and we were an unstoppable team thereafter). Public duties were fine for dreaming up idle adventures to fill the gaps between guards, taking the boys off for an afternoon water-skiing or recceing low-level training areas with the best pubs near by, but it wasn't real, it wasn't testing.

★★★

Exercise Dartmoor Dash was testing.

A race between all the platoons in the battalion, hundreds of men in little teams across the sodden moor. By the morning of the first day of the exercise half the company had disappeared into the medical tent with ankle injuries and lower-limb injuries and back injuries and many, many spine injuries (not actual back injuries, but lack-of-grit-and-backbone injuries, also known as 'upper-head injuries'). Those patrols that had made it had cut down on to the roads and hitched lifts on the back of tractors, and only poor old Sgt Barrett's boys were still unaccounted for, plodding gamely on in completely the wrong direction after he had programmed his brand new GPS upside down.

When the Dartmoor rain closed in the summer really ended. Sgt Childs and I could only giggle as we shivered uncontrollably, vainly trying to dry off after the river crossing and watching the heartless senior visitors chowing down on warm bacon rolls behind the safety Land Rover. We might or might not have been hallucinating when a lone figure appeared through the six a.m. mist, eighty if he was a day and dressed like he'd run all the way out of *Chariots of Fire* with a dripping moustache and a dripping spaniel in his wake, and shouted a cheery 'Pongos eh? Nice morning for it!' as he disappeared again. It was that sort of exercise.

What we should have stopped to consider was that the Paras and the Marines and the Jocks in the Falklands had basically done exactly what we'd just done, with real bullets. That might have woken us up for a few seconds with a sharp slap, but we were so far gone in public duties and desert yearning that we couldn't make the link, wouldn't make the link until two years later when someone would remark in the shattered shell of a compound somewhere in Rahim Kholay in the middle of the Battle for Adin Zai that the last few days had been 'almost as bad as Dartmoor Dash'. Almost.

For all the relief to be loading up the coaches, stiff and blistered but sedentary and already looking forward to Burger King at Membury Services on the way back, I felt hollow. For all the congratulations that somehow we'd actually got the best time, I couldn't help but gaze out of the window at the murky hills as we moved off north up the M5, thinking that this was pump.

Somewhere, as I was snoozing on the coach, aching from lack of fitness after a summer of stamping and twirling swords, friends were doing things for real. Somewhere, as we overdid the nuggets and got hit by the instant post-MSG-rush sickness of the junk food, guys I'd slogged through Sandhurst and Brecon with were adventuring in Kabul and posing for iconic snaps on desert patrols in Iraq. Strolling back down the Mall after a swim, trunks hidden neatly under the bearskins and enjoying ignoring the astonished gasps of the queues outside the sandwich shops was fun, but it wasn't what we'd joined to do and it certainly wasn't what we'd just humped across Dartmoor for.

Marking Time and Treading Water

We'd joined up and humped across Dartmoor to fight the three-block war. Bosnia had been the perfect start, classic low-level peacekeeping, help the police, paint a school, build a bridge and boost the local economy by stocking up on pirate DVDs and porn, but it felt like we'd gone backwards: not the next block uptown towards moment-of-truth warfighting but back into the leafy suburbia of an idle peacetime army.

When we weren't marching through London like the soldiers of the 1870s, we were boozing and 'exercising' like the soldiers of the 1970s. Old-school British Army of the Rhine style junkets and back to Windsor to compare the price of beer and whores around the world. As if in subconscious tribute we even organized our company adventure training trip to Germany, where the new platoon commanders, fresh off Sandhurst and Brecon themselves – horizontally laid-back Harrison and 'goldenballs' Marlow – got their first taste of 'real' platoon command diffusing the situation at the *Biergarten* after LCpl Redgate had upset the owner by eating the microphone during karaoke night.

Our planning 'exercise' in Malaysia probably took the biscuit: three weeks with the Aussies, Kiwis and Singaporese testing contingency plans for an Indonesian play at Malaysia's strategic oil reserves dressed-up as 'Command and Staff Training'. We were supposed to be testing the new BOWMAN (already well known across the Infantry as Better Off With Map and Nokia) radio systems which the guardsmen whose only job was to push cubes across the giant map board could have told you wouldn't work as soon as you actually got it out in the field but was fine for playing solitaire in the comfy gym where we were 'exercising', so we didn't mind.

If we learned anything from a year of very much *not* being on operations it was the ying-yang nature of the Army. From sipping Moscow Mules and doing lines of snuff at St James's

The company commanders hard at work 'testing' the new communications systems – Malaysia, September 2005.

Palace* we'd found ourselves slogging across Dartmoor, and within days of getting back and dry we were out lying on a beach in Malaysia and trying to explain to the soldiers from the Corps of Drums that the nice girls they'd 'met' in Singapore's infamous *four floors of whores* weren't necessarily 'girls', to which they would respond with a grin and shrug: 'Did it anyway, sir!'

Spiking the LE's morning coffee with Viagra substitute we'd bought from the dodgy shop where we found the 'guardsman' vibrator, which we just had to buy (not to mention the 12-inch chin-mounted 'Facilitator', which we didn't) wasn't *Platoon* or *Apocalypse Now*, it was pure *Buffalo Soldiers*, and the only thing which brought us back to earth was visiting Singapore's huge Commonwealth war cemetery. The padre told us all to find someone with the same birthday as us, which was all too easy among the row upon row of serried white stones which were only further reminders that we'd left Sandhurst wanting and expecting something more profound.

From Malaysia, after a bit more marching and guarding, I took my boys on a visit to the Royal Navy, spent a month on an aircraft carrier and marvelled at how tiny and insignificant the little grey box with more than a thousand people living and working in it was against the expanse of the ocean. A change is as good as a rest, and the lucky hand-picked few

* The pride of the officers' mess at St James's Palace was the snuff box crafted from one of Marengo's (Napoleon's horse at Waterloo) hooves. I was never more embarrassed than when one of my guests, as innocently as I suppose he could, forwent the usual pinch between finger and thumb and started to rack up a 'line' of the stuff. Like a modern Queen Victoria and her famous bowl of soup, with barely a raise of his eyebrow the captain of the guard proceeded to hand him a neatly rolled-up fifty, and we all joined in.

guardsmen were delighted to be on board, would have taken the sea-sickness over more public duties every time and loved the laid-back atmosphere on board the ship.

We had a wonderful time living out *Top Gun* fantasies on the flight deck, teasing the sailors for how they carried rifles when they had to and burning 200 litres of fuel a minute through the Mediterranean. We were joined by a Korean war veteran, a friend of the Captain who recognized some fellow landlubbers and regaled us with understated and moving anecdotes of how he'd found himself, a nineteen-year-old National Service second-lieutenant, leading combat patrols through the same Malayan jungles which weeks before we'd been frolicking through like gap-year teenagers. He'd got on what he thought was the boat home from Hong Kong and found himself sailing up to Korea and then winning a Military Cross and burning crypto with the Gloucesters at Imjin River as whole Chinese divisions swarmed the position. Divisions at nineteen for fuck's sake, and we'd never so much as made our rifles ready in anger.

We consoled ourselves upstaging the crew in our red tunics when the Queen came on board in Malta, and then rushing to put them back on after she left and the *Sun* arrived with Danni, nineteen from Coventry, and Nicola T, twenty-one from Bournemouth. As we made our way back towards Portsmouth I smuggled the golf balls I got from Gibraltar up on to the flight deck and spent an awesome half-hour smashing them out off the back of the ship with a five iron, gloriously liberating hooks and fades out into the Atlantic. It was all harmless fun, but that was precisely why it bored us. They teased us on board and referred to us as 'the trees' because we stuck out in our combats – but we'd chosen to wear combats for a reason, and we didn't want our fun to be harmless.

Harmless fun, driving golf balls off the flight deck of HMS Illustrious – *Bay of Biscay, December 2005.*

And what really brought home how far we hadn't come was when we got back into port and my phone came back to life and there was a message from my father in the inbox: 'Greetings from Baghdad the Mother of all chaos. A certain amount of incoming in the IZ but none on us. Kurdistan was more stable and able to lose body armour and helmet for a couple of days. Shortly flying to Basra then back to BZN tomorrow. Love Daddy.'

Unbelievable. He'd had his go in the Middle East in '91, slamming missiles up from HMS *London* to convince another few hundred Iraqi conscripts to surrender to the armoured divisions roaring up from Kuwait. It was my generation's turn now, but he was still first with the snaps of Baghdad, the adrenalin shots of the Pumas skimming low over the iconic Crossed Swords, the toppled statues of Saddam and rubble J-Dam-ed remains of the Believers Palace and other vainglorious landmarks of the broken city.

★★★

The thing about the Telic medal for Operational Service in Iraq was that it looked so good on a tunic. Bright yellow and the scarlet underscored by the lines of black which made a change from the subtle distinctions of widths and shades of UN and NATO Balkan and peacekeeping blues and whites, and the almost ubiquitous purple of the General Service 'I lost my twenties in Northern Ireland' Medal.

Leaving Sandhurst, there was no doubt where everyone wanted to go for their first medal, where the Micks had won their rosettes and MCs, where the PWRR had made their videos and where Beharry had won the first Victoria Cross in our lifetime. And, if possible, it was killing the rest of the Grenadiers that they hadn't been to Iraq even more than it was killing us.

For the battalion it was personal and had been since the first excited invasion whispers had gone round and the word had been that the Grenadiers would be there at the start like we had been in '91. For those with long memories it probably went all the way back to 1982, sat in Chelsea Barracks and toss a coin to see if it would be us or the Jocks to go down and write new chapters of military history in the Falklands. Heads we lost.

Since coming back from Granby we'd been Northern Ireland commuters and watched others fighting the new post-Cold War in the Balkans and Sierra Leone, which was easier to stomach as, for all the pot-shots and hairy moments, no one was sewing new battle honours on their colours. But in 2003 there was only one place to be if you were in the armed forces and it wasn't on Horse Guards putting on the immaculate birthday parade the Major General had demanded; showing the country that we weren't being over-stretched, which of course we were, it was just that they didn't need the new light machine-guns (LMGs) and Warriors on the Mall. The Grenadiers had taken the disappointment on the chin and looked pretty smart on the square and as a reward had trooped off to Bosnia (only nine years after the interesting stuff had stopped, but at least we were there for the transition from a NATO mission to an EU mission, so got two medals for the price of one, even if the EU one was gopping). However, Telic had become Telic II and III, and by the time Mark had managed to get out attached to the Paras it was Telic VII, and every battalion in the British Army had been to the Middle East, except for one of the Green Jackets. And us.

All we wanted for Christmas was to go to Iraq.

★★★

I didn't even get to spend Christmas at home, sat up in the officers' flat in Windsor Castle and playing poker with the equally unimpressed guard who'd opened all the presents and eaten all the chocolate before we'd even got to lunch and were realizing for the first time how crap Christmas telly was.

But when we got off guard, as if in answer to our unspoken Christmas wishes – *Santa I've been so good, please send me to the desert* – the battalion was alive with excited rumours. The rumours had started, of course, with 'Sidney'. Notching up his third season captaining the battalion ski team to ever-greater feats of drunkenness in Val d'Isère. It could only have been Sidney who would have insisted all the visiting generals join him in a round of gas-chambers in Bananas before mounting the bar for a hearty chorus of 'The Wild Rover'.

Sidney oozed a beguiling, privileged charm and was bound to be the first person that the heads of the Army would take into their confidence, and so, when Gdsm Quinlan told me that we were going to Iraq because he'd heard it off Captain Allan who'd heard it off a general on the way to Dick's T Bar, I didn't dismiss it out of hand.

We'd have asked Mark to confirm it if he wasn't already out in Iraq being a hero* but we knew he was too honest and disciplined to have told us even if he'd known and even if we could. Marlow and I jumped around the mess like excited children pestering the company commanders, but they were all being uncharacteristically enigmatic, so we went to find Faulks. Gdsm Faulks was the commanding officer's driver and as such usually the second man in the battalion to know anything important. He stonewalled us like a pro, pretending to concentrate on the copy of the *Sun* which the mess staff thought we didn't realize they stole every morning before we got down to breakfast. All he would let on was that maybe Sgt Smith, the battalion PT instructor, might know something.

Rushing off to the gym, we wondered what Sgt Smith might know, given that his only job was to plan our Friday-morning PT sessions, when invariably something would go awry and our 6-milers would become 8-milers and our 8-milers agonizing 12-milers with the entire battalion mutinous and certain we'd passed that particular tree three times already. What Sgt Smith did know, and for which precious information we instantly forgave him every lung-bursting extra mile and nasty end-of-run surprise exercise of the last year,

---

* Mark had been Mentioned in Dispatches for his bravery and leadership in extracting his patrol from a gnarly ambush – by all accounts he deserved more.

was that the whole battalion was to muster in the gym that afternoon.

So by the time the officers trooped in after lunch and the rest of the battalion was waiting in the gym, the tingling sense of anticipation in the air was electric. We stood on one side, trying hard not to grin like idiots while we watched the sergeants' mess members' eyes light up with a fire that had burned for three years as resentment that they spent the summer of 2003 on Birdcage Walk instead of the Basrah highway; as the commanding officer announced what everybody already knew there was a roar like a penalty shootout, and guys punching the air and hugging each other with delight.

We were going to Iraq.

Not back to Dartmoor or Wales or out for the scheduled big exercise in Canada which we'd been trying to pretend we were excited about so the blokes weren't as disappointed as we were, fucking Iraq. Iraq, where it was kicking off again after the post-invasion honeymoon that it was becoming increasingly obvious the British Army had squandered down in Basrah. Iraq, from where I'd be able to send back the tantalizing and heroic e-mails I'd already started composing as I sped down to London that evening with the good news; careering around the Hammersmith roundabout imagining with glee how much easier it would be in a Snatch with a top-cover gunner firing warning shots at the cheeky Vauxhall Vectra trying to cut me up at the lights. I was so excited I was practically winking at the model-fit door girl as I swaggered into whichever over-priced bar it was where someone was having a birthday – *don't worry whether or not I'm on the list, babe. I'm off to war!* So excited that I didn't get it when I broke the news to Jen and the girls and they didn't share my ecstatic grin. Didn't get it that she'd be upset, that she read the reports in the papers not as grizzly invitations to come and prove yourself but as ominous threats from a malign force that wanted to seduce her boyfriend away to his idiot death. Didn't get it that this was news to be broken sensitively and apologetically to those more patient and loving than we deserved.

Turned out no one got it. Bemused up in Windsor the next day, we compared stories of horrified families and tearful girlfriends and strangely nonplussed mates. Surely the frustrated bankers who could all quote *Full Metal Jacket* by heart would have got it: the boys who'd gone out on high-spending corporate weekends to Vegas and had admitted to having more fun firing a couple of guns on a desert range than dropping thousands in the Bellagio, surely they 'got' our excitement. Mostly, they didn't, and for all the encouragement and support that would follow, the first subtle barrier had come down between those who were going away and those who would stay behind; the first hint that things were different when it was all happening for real, that we were no longer 'mates in the Army' and they no longer mates we normally saw except when on exercise. They were suddenly 'civvies', while we were on the verge of being soldiers.

Three Years Too Late

They sent a US 'Full Bird' colonel from the First Infantry Division, the famous 'Big Red One', to brief us at the start of our new and hectic training regime. He casually stood in front of the most attentive Army classroom I'd ever seen and carefully explained the concept of 'huah'. 'Huah' was the noise somewhere between a retch and a burp which first the US Rangers, then the US Marines and then with slight variations of tone and emphasis everyone else in the States made all the time. 'Huah' was anything from a battle cry to saying good morning to an officer. But 'huah' was also a concept, a mentality. 'Huah' was apparently holding off 4,000 Zulus at Rorke's Drift; 'huah' was founding the SAS and yomping across the Falklands. As he quickly rattled through a capabilities brief of the US Army and which bits of it we might come across out in Iraq, it seemed to all of us that 'huah' was having an army so big you had more guys sitting in Korea *just in case* than we had full stop. Apparently we would have to train hard, it was going to be a tough few months, and 'huah' was not sitting in a warm Land Rover enjoying a fag while your guys were out on a night exercise.

As it turned out pre-deployment training wasn't particularly 'huah' at all.

With all the earnest enthusiasm you would expect we rushed off to the library to get out Teach Yourself Arabic books and histories of Iraq too heavy to ever be anything other than extra weight in bergens for Friday marches. Hours were spent balancing platoons and companies, the right number of medics per section, who was best on the venerable but brutally reliable GPMG, who would be the drivers, the signallers – in those early months of excitement the atmosphere was terrific and the motivation to work hard only increased by the continued grumpiness of the wives and girlfriends learning that a 'six-month tour' didn't include the two months before that we would be permanently away on exercise.

Our enthusiasm didn't seem to be matched, however, by those who were supposed to be training us. Operation Training Advisory Group had sprung up from the old Northern Ireland Training Group, where they had been pretty slick at delivering essential pre-deployment training – they had thirty years' experience. But when the law of armed conflict instructor forgot himself he'd lapse back into talking about what to do out on patrol in Armagh not Al-Amarah.

We laughed off the slips of the tongue and the comedy mapping of Salisbury Plain, turning Warminster into Baghdad and Somerset into Iran. At least in Copehill Down Village an approximation of an Iraqi village had been created out of iso-containers so that the more clueless young guardsmen wouldn't imagine that Azubyar looked like an East German town, all gabled red roofs and three-storey brick buildings which we nonetheless practised searching through for the Duke of Wellington's Regiment boys playing enemy and civilians in Adidas trackies and Camden-market schemaghs, running around shouting 'Ali Baba'. Not that we attacked it in the end, someone in their wisdom choosing instead to test our suitability to deploy by launching the battalion in an enormous forest assault, our tactical effects system vests beeping all the way into a woodblock as the Plain was turned into a giant game of Quasar Laser to inject realistic (and terrifying) casualty play into the exercises.

Leading the Inkerman Company over the line of departure, groggy at dawn after the stumbling night insertion, we'd been chuckling with Seb at the fairy-light farce of the Queen's Company in the forming-up point, lit up like Oxford Street at Christmas with glo-sticks on their helmets because they'd all got lost. We weren't chuckling ten minutes later, my break-in platoon massacred before we'd breached the wood line and the little screen on my vest informing me that I had a gunshot wound to my lower back. Propped up against a tree, remarkably calm for a dying man, I directed the incoming sections up the slope into the murderous enemy 'fire'. Grinning guardsmen sprawled all over the forest floor, pointing delightedly at their beeping screens when told to get up off their fucking arses: 'I can't, Sergeant, I've been shot in the lung.' As I was tossed over someone's shoulder and alternately dragged and bounced the long kilometre back to the make-believe aid post, I took solace in the fact that, as far as I knew, there were no woodblocks in Iraq.

At Sandhurst the frustration that our training had seemed irrelevant had been a mere irritant; we were, after all, training for 'a war', and one model was as good as another. The DS loved to repeat the mantra 'train hard, fight easy', which seemed to lack optimism to those of us who hoped to 'train easy, fight easy' but probably recognized the more fundamental truth that, whatever else, you wanted to avoid fighting hard (as if there was such a thing as 'fighting easy' anyway). As the yanks put it with all the unironic schmaltz we would have hoped from them, 'Let no man's ghost say: "I wish I had been better trained."' What pissed us off, as we shared six Snatches throughout the battalion, stood for hours on cordons, looking out over Salisbury's rolling green hills, lush with spring, and squinting out at the Stonehenge crowds towards the A303, was that surely now, with weeks not months to go, we were training very much for 'the war', and it was a war with a lot more sand.

★★★

We moved from Salisbury up to Thetford, everyone by now exhausted by exercise after exercise, days when we were in scenario, days when we were on stand-down and snuck into Tillshead in stolen Land Rovers for newspapers and sweets; fully tactical, non-tactical, gloriously illogical 'semi-non-tac'. In a desperate attempt to focus flagging minds and raise flagging spirits, we changed into our desert combats.

For the first day this worked, and we got a lift from the thrill of finally putting on the combats that meant something.

Then the weather closed in, and after mild weeks on Salisbury Plain in windproof smocks we shivered in the lightweight desert gear and, as the rain came down, we looked ridiculous in green Gore-Tex jackets with damp yellow legs sticking out of the bottom.

Real progress wasn't made on serials or under the instruction of stuttering OPTAG NCOs, who admitted that they had only been on a weeklong visit to Iraq, *sirs, gents*, or the bullish SO2s, passed-over majors who'd done a whole tour so wouldn't take any questions at all *and fuck you for asking*. As I realized was often the way in the Army, whether cleverly, intentionally or happily by accident, progress was made in spite of the training that was being done. The time we were spending with our platoons, how intimately we came to know our boys, their strengths and weaknesses, how much closer we became as a mess when the mess was no longer a building to be dashed from as soon as possible down to London, but a dripping tent in which we snatched quick hands of bridge during hard training.

Mates became comrades; Harrison and Marlow no longer a surfer and a boxer with whom to take it in turns to wind up the LEs but the guys you depended on, and who depended on you; the new CSM, Scully, a sarcastic legend of Sandhurst days, no longer someone to argue with over haircuts but the man who wouldn't, couldn't let you down; Seb no longer the ever-green, good-time boss but the commander you loved for standing up for his company, shouting down battalion HQ as they made improbable, impossible demands.

Which, I guess, made up for the holes in the training, the always 'notional' enemy, or air-support or medevac team. I thought of how soldiers interviewed after a fight would always say the training kicked in and wondered how as I argued with a fat Yorkshireman (notional tribal elder) through a Gurkha (notional interpreter) about who would get on the back of the four-tonner (notional Chinook). It wasn't that we wanted to be thrashed. We were more than happy to sneak off to the Angel for a few jars (which, if we'd been smarter, we'd have just explained to the exercise staff was the 'notional US dining facility'), but you couldn't help but wonder what we'd do when the enemy weren't notional.

There was something wildly indulgent about the build-up to a deployment, the morbid pleasure of drawing up a meaningless will, working out who gets your CD collection and taking advantage of the subtle emotional blackmail of 'going away' parties. I sent out an invite which promised 'like the wedding from *The Deer Hunter* but with better hair'. It was an iconic snap of two squaddies marching some detainees down the road – too good an opportunity to miss, knowing that most of my friends, if pushed, probably had questions and qualms about the whole Iraq thing anyway. 'Goodies,' said the arrow pointing at the soldiers, 'Baddies,' said the one pointing at the prisoners, 'it really is that simple'. But all the time 'the real thing' was in our minds: documentaries on the news, the inexorable press build-up to the hundredth soldier to die (which had the morbid tabloids cheating and counting the poor guy who had a heart attack and died of old age tucked up in his bed in Basrah). We should have paid more attention to Mark's real-life reports of life 'down there' – he'd lived it after all, and his measured refusal to share in our gung-ho enthusiasm was telling, but our minds were elsewhere.

Good soldiers don't plan ahead. We spent every penny we hadn't yet earned on extravagant, teary girlfriend trips abroad and badly behaved lad-weekends to Eastern European capitals because at the back of our minds was always the thought, you can't take it with you.

It might have been hard on mothers and wives and girlfriends, but as the late-night doors and gates closed and we drove off with waving hands still looking out of windows, our thoughts were already in the sand.

IV

Welcome to Fucking Iraq

Twenty-seven long months and nineteen days after I had sent my first snivelling e-mails from Sandhurst, I could finally send a dispatch from 'the front'.

> *07.v.2006 – 'Welcome to Iraq'*

whoops-a-daisy!

i guess I shouldn't have shouted 'COME ON THEN' out of the back of the chopper as we flew hard and low over the Southern Desert out of Basrah on Friday . . .

it looks like they did.★ but then how could I not have done with the tailgate down and from the rear seat the iconic hulks of burnt out wreckage of '91 framed perfectly by the rear gun and the loadie watching his arcs with his feet dangling down as we hammer along at what seems like just yards above the dirty sand?

it's all I can do to stop myself expecting him to turn around with a grin and a packet of Marlboros in his helmet and drawl about giving women and children '*less lead*'.

★ Two days after we arrived in Iraq a Lynx helicopter went down over Basrah with the loss of the four service personnel on board. The ensuing chaos gave some rather sharp focus to our arrival and, although we watched the whole thing from the sidelines, our anxious mothers were not to know, and the strained answerphone messages contrasted eloquently with our frustration at sitting idle in camp.

the rows and rows and rows of blue cyalumes marking out acres of hardware in Al Udied and the sudden plunging of the Hercules into darkness as we cross out of Kuwaiti airspace and begin the jerky corkscrew and roller coaster blackness of the tactical descent into the APOD have combined with the lack of sleep and the Star Wars dusty nothingness revealed by the dawn to numb our ability to distinguish between the films and the books and the so long anticipated reality.

there's a part of me that knows we could have done without what's been going on in Basrah over the last few days almost as much as our mothers and girlfriends could have done without the agonizing wait of the Op MINIMIZE which was immediately called.* Certainly the poor guys who died could have done without it, as could the boys who stood on the cordon for eight hours while bloody violence unfolded in the city which we used so famously to patrol in berets.

and I've nothing but envious respect for the now legendary platoon commander who had been first onto the baseline and was still there holding the crowds at bay hours later when the General came up on the all-informed net to give

* In any operational theatre, as soon as a soldier is seriously injured or killed there is a blackout of all communications back home. The welfare telephones and internet are shut down, and in the few bits of Iraq and Afghanistan where people have working mobiles they are expected not to use them. This ensures that the family hear the bad news first through the correct channels and not, as had previously been occurring, from friends back on the patch who had already got word from their own husbands that they were fine but that poor old Mitch had died, or in one shocking case from the first reporter who made it to the door. Knowledge of this system and the magic words 'next of kin have been informed' somehow apparently never comforted folks at home when 'incidents' and 'casualties' filtered through on to rolling news.

encouragement and reassurance and explain the delays were *'because there were many things to be factored into the extraction plan'*. Crackling from the ground and with the angry pops in the background, he cut in with a curt: *well I've been here five hours, I've got a T2 casualty, four T3s and a broken down wagon – factor that into your fucking extraction plan.*

he could have done without it, his casualties could certainly have done without but we'd be lying if we didn't admit that it sharpened the mind.

apparently it's all about hitting the ground running.

it's just a shame that for us, that running currently consists of once round the airfield for morning PT and not off the back of the choppers to reinforce the beleaguered Shaat Al Arab.

what was kind of sweet was the apparent surprise and shock of the public back home as we sat in the DTDF watching the rolling hyperbole and outrage on Sky News. Why was everyone surprised at the attitude and celebrations of the crowd? How did you all imagine things were normally down here? It's not exactly as though one just strolls into town to buy fags and a paper from the local mini-mart.

so, as long as we don't walk anywhere (landmines), drive anywhere (roadside bombs), stand still anywhere (snipers and mortars) and now it seems *fly* anywhere – it's perfectly safe.

as for all this famous Arabian hospitality I've been reading about, I'll take my chances with the petrol bombs and IEDs. It seems unfair as I desperately try to educate myself so that I

'Chalk 3' don helmets and body armour in the back of the Hercules as we cross into Iraqi airspace and begin our descent into Basrah – May 2006.

can wage war with cultural and religious sensitivity. Rest assured you won't find me accidentally baring the soles of my feet to a woman as I shoot her husband and heaven forbid I knock over a Quran in the house of the man I'm arresting and detaining for three years without trial.

hearts and minds people, hearts and minds.

welcome to fucking Iraq!

The first thing I can clearly remember beyond the fug of the heat and the jet-lag haze of Reception Staging and Onward Integration and endless processing through South Cerney and

Brize Norton and Al-Udied and Basrah Air Station and Transit Camp 2 until none of us had a clue where we were or what day it was, was a pog. Sat in the Shaibah NAAFI, the Navy, Army, Air Force Institute cross between a café and a corner shop and which had the look and the feel and the smell of a dry Wetherspoons, as the last dregs of excitement from the lights-out steep pitching of the Hercules as it crossed into Iraqi airspace and landed hard at Basrah and then the iconic chopper ride low across the desert seep away in ennui, I realize I am staring at a pog.

The currency was dollars for iced-coffees from the 'Oasis Café' and pepperoni passion from Pizza Hut or meatball deluxe and a Snapple from Subway, and change is not in coins but little cardboard discs with pictures of hardware on the side; Apaches for a dime, M1 Abrams for a nickel, waving Iraqi kids for a quarter – we didn't cover any of this in training. Outside the Welfare Village, air-conditioned SUVs ferry staff-officers back and forward from National Support Element, parked up alongside steaming Warriors, mini-tanks just back in off patrol or Snatches stocking up with Gatorade before pushing out on convoys. Fergus made the point, pretty spot on, that if Al-Udied with its rows and rows of cyalumes and vague shadows of endless USAF jets and presumably a token RAF Tornado older than me parked up somewhere near the back, was *Star Wars*, then Shaibah was pure *Blade Runner*.

Trying to get our bearings, we queued at the bar between blanket-stackers in Bermuda shorts and flip-flops and stinking guys still in their body armour with rifles slung. We're all in hysterics when we find 'Dell Boyz Gift Shoppe', where you can buy towels with pictures of the Virgin Mary on one side and Islamic blessings on the other, not to mention every pirate DVD you can imagine and even fake Balkan Sobranies, which we just have to get because nothing will upset the old crusties more than junior officers smoking pink, gold-tipped cigarettes.

The first e-mails home should probably have told tales of pogs and discounted Oakleys and the uneasy side-by-side of the Welfare Village and the helipad, thundering Merlins in and out of Basrah with people actually working or worse still injured, while life in 'Shaibiza' ticked on to the beat of cruel British Forces Broadcasting Services (BFBS) radio programming throwing out dance anthems as if it was a normal Friday night. They should have told of the sense of being in the foreground of Bruegel's *Fall of Icarus*, there was a war going on somewhere, but we were watching it on Sky News stuck in the DTDF or on picnic tables in the Welfare Village, not even getting to see, let alone be part of, the action. They should have told of the frustration of being Rear-Operations Battlegroup, but they couldn't, so we just stayed quiet and waited for something to happen.

As Rear-Operations Battlegroup (ROBG) the chances of that were fairly slim. Broken down into company groups tasked with running the Detention Facility (DTDF), guarding Shaibah itself, patrolling and securing the routes in and out of Basrah with one lucky bunch up in Baghdad, it was clear that most of our jobs would be pretty steady. We'd been ecstatic when it was announced that the Inkerman Company would rotate through Baghdad, but would have to do its share of time running a glorified PoW camp to earn it. After all the infantry indoctrination we'd got out on operations we were just another bunch of Rear Echelon Mother Fuckers, watching enviously as the reserve battlegroup saddled up in Warriors to push out on strike ops in Basrah itself.

I think it was resentment against our REMF status that made tempers short in those early weeks, the Senior Major snapping like a wind-up dog at everyone, late entry officers busily feathering their own nests while we crammed ourselves into bursting tents. Well-connected corporals would glide by in pick-up trucks while the intelligence officer had to beg for a bicycle, and in the absence of having anything real to do and the frustration at being surrounded by other units who did, silly regulations and duties flew all over camp. Flip-flops and shorts were banned amidst howls of protest from the fatties who hung around all day tanning and the more legitimate protests of the guys who came in off twenty-hour sweltering patrols and wanted to relax.

★★★

Rear-Operations Battlegroup was a shit job, but it was the making of the Reading Club, and in the same spirit of defiance with which we had sacrificed sleep and ease for the principle of darting back to London from Sandhurst for civilized food we foraged for chairs and books and set up round the side of the Crow's Nest, our little haven for reading, tanning and purging. For our task in the DTDF the normal three-platoon structure of the company had been abandoned, and we were now two half-companies. Harrison and myself in one, which meant I did the night shifts and Harrison – not known as 'straight eight' for nothing – could get his fat head down and then make brews for Seb during the day. Marlow and Bysshe in the second. Bysshe was attached for the tour with his fellow Coldstreamer, 'the Amazing Sugdini', both Sandhurst contemporaries of mine, so the desert was beginning to feel like a bit of a reunion. Marlow was strictly junior, but Bysshe was attached and had an unnerving habit of looking more stressed than he actually was, so they probably shared the duties out more evenly, but it never bothered me, I liked the cool nights and the rare solitude.

Fergus and the Queen's Company had deployed straight up to Baghdad, and Mark and 2 Company were training Iraqis in Dhi Qar, which meant, to our sadness, that the three of us who commissioned together would miss each other on our first tour. As it turned out, Fergus was fine, putting in good performances in the 'manly drinking competitions'* he staged by the pool with Reynolds, the other Queen's Company platoon commander. They must have had enough time on their hands because every so often we'd get a fax or e-bluey which read simply 'COCK'; it was good to know there were some constants. Mark wasn't so lucky, busy getting his company commander out of ill-advised fights with large American contractors, but then he'd done it before, so it wasn't really his first time.

The rest of the Reading Club was whichever young-uns were around. Barty, the brand new officer out of Sandhurst yesterday and wide-eyed with it all, had somehow found himself with Support Company, who resented such a junior imposter and worked him like a guardsman. I was delighted that Big Nick Tobin, a veteran of the mighty XV Platoon at Sandhurst no less, was in the squadron of Queen's Dragoon Guards (QDG) attached to us for the tour, and when they weren't out patrolling – which given that they had tanks and we had Land Rovers was most of the time – he would join us.

Despite living on top of each other, we barely saw each other, but for an hour or so every other day as one patrolling multiple came off shift and the DTDF handover phase was ongoing, we could lie out in the sun, hidden by the canvas,

* Points were awarded for the manliness of approach, ripping the bottle cap off with your teeth and pouring as much water as possible over your head – no wonder the Americans thought we were all mad.

The original Junior Officers' Reading Club behind the 'Crow's Nest'
tent in Camp 4, Shaibah Logistics Base – Southern Iraq, probably May
2006. Left to right: Harrison, me, a friend.

our little whinges drowned out by the generators, and wonder
how it was that all that we had dreamed and boasted of had
come to this – lying in pink boxer-shorts, sunbathing with
novel in between shifts as a prison warder and episodes of
pirate DVDs.

We needed a neutral space. On tour you were never alone,
never off duty. For six months people wore nothing but
uniform, maybe the desert shorts and a plain t-shirt to really
relax on a slow day, but combat pyjamas every day for months
on end. We'd snuck out civvies with us, hidden in the bottom
of our bergens in anticipation of illicit trysts with sexy journos
up in Baghdad, but they only ever got worn in the tent on a
Friday night just to break the monotony of yellow and brown.
Hidden behind our tent, even if only for half an hour every

other day, we didn't have to pretend to the guys that running the DTDF wasn't monotonous toss, didn't have to assume the serious focus that the sergeants' mess expected of us now everything was 'not a drill', could talk amongst ourselves as friends rather than colleagues. We talked about our expectations, our fears and hopes and whether it was wrong that they remained a little bloodthirsty, even after guys started getting killed.

Out in Iraq there was nowhere normal to escape to except behind the tent, where Harrison could shamelessly immerse himself in surfing magazines and Marlow and I could use the long words we'd learned at university without the boys accusing us of being 'gay'.

★★★

We acquired a 4x4 and wrestled driving clearance from the Mechanized Transport Platoon ('Because officers just don't drive, sir!') and trundled to and fro from the Crow's Nest in Camp 4 to our new office, listening incongruously to Johnny Cash and Elvis. The warden may have thrown a party at the county jail, but I was suddenly the junior warden of the Shaibah jail and I don't think we could have got together much of a prison band.

There was a peculiar calm in the peace of the exercise yard; the holding facility for detainees awaiting transfer to the Iraqi justice system was an oasis of tranquil efficiency amid the general bustling chaos of Shaibah Logistics Base. In the initial processing and interrogation compound the scratched Arabic messages on the cell walls encouraged new arrivals to look forward to the 'easy life' that the detainees enjoyed.

Not that it made it any easier to explain to the young guardsmen why the blokes they were guarding, hardened criminals, most responsible for at least the murder of civilians

143

and often of coalition soldiers, had better living conditions than they did back in the camp. Why the prisoners we weren't allowed to call prisoners (detainees, if you please) were fed so well and why the air-conditioning was a higher priority in the cell block than it was back in Camp 4. The delicately balanced legal arguments that supported the fragile legitimacy of the system meant we handled a bunch of villains with kid-gloves to make up for the coach and horses the UNSCR 1456 was riding through quaint notions like habeas corpus. I suppose it was all in keeping with the topsy-turvydom of the place that, handing over to Harrison in the middle of our first night shift, we realized that arguably the most sensitive cog in the whole machine was in the hands of a couple of frustrated lieutenants and a dozen resentful guardsmen. Through the duty shift you had to keep looking at the 'phone' on the desk as a reminder that Seb answered straight up to the two-star divisional commander and that, just before we arrived and someone had accidentally dropped a Quran while moving one of the detainees to a different cell, Number 10 had been immediately in the loop.

Even when on one of our early shifts we were mortared for the first time – grinning under the table during the attack and then strutting around afterwards with self-importance for having been on duty when it happened and we first came 'under-fire', spinning wild hypotheses that the enemy had been aiming straight for the DTDF itself as a prelude to a mass break-out and imagining the accolades we would get for thwarting such an unlikely event – most of the detainees slept through it. The excitement of the lock-down and the soak period and the sirens was diminished when you knew that the Bangladeshi guys working in the Pizza Hut kept on delivering right through the 'attacks'. Anything interesting in our prison we couldn't have written home about anyway.

The most exciting thing was finding a laptop that would accept the dodgy DVDs of *Over There*; watching which while on duty must surely have constituted some supreme form of post-modern irony, but we never got round to it because, to everyone's amusement, the roving sentries caught Detainee 819 wanking in the exercise yard.

After about a week the novelty and sense of false importance we got from screening everyone had worn off. We stole some free weights from someone else's gym, and the boys stocked up on protein shakes and benched and dipped and curled on one side of wall while the detainees prayed and walked and played ping-pong on the other. For all the latent homo-eroticism it was just another sweaty way of passing the time, and we were no freer in our gym than they were in their yard.

Riding Top-cover

Fortunately, we discovered a better sweaty way of passing the time and snuck off on patrol with Tobin and his boys. With all their experience it was the attached squadron from the QDG who were doing the bulk of our patrolling. Laid back and swept-up officers and wise-cracking valley-boy NCOs, they were an easy bunch to like, and as soon as we got the nod from Seb we were begging them to take us out on patrol. It would have been wrong for us to have commanded them on our own, and no one wanted too many chiefs, but we were so desperate just to get outside the wire by that stage that we were happy to take off our rank slides and muck in on top-cover.

Most soldiers after a few weeks of bouncing around every day perched vulnerably out of the top of a vehicle waiting to be blown up would readily say that being a top-cover sentry is a pretty thankless task. It wasn't exactly what months of leadership training had been invested in us for either, but the troopers on a busy and nerve-racking schedule were only too glad to have a night off if some idiot Guards officer wanted to do their job, and, as it turned out, I liked 'top-cover' about as much as anything I'd ever done in my life.

19.v.2006 – 'Finally . . .'
so, after weeks of boredom, a little something

if being mortared was like drunkenly losing one's virginity – slightly blurred memories of archers/baileys tipsy party and excited giggling story swapping the next morning with all your friends and Friends in the background – slightly painful and slightly disappointing, saying you hope he won't say anything but secretly hoping he tells all his friends etc etc – then getting out on a first Op took things to another level

i have never been so scared and excited at the same time, extreme sports can piss off, freefall is about as gnarly as hung-over Sunday brunch at your local gastropub

Op SHAIBAH EAGLE was a little heli-mission to drop down towards the Iranian border and have a peek at a self-styled commando unit of Jaish Al Mahdi who've been busy lining the streets with IEDs and firing in last week's rockets. A couple of dummy drops onto local corrupt DBE (depart-ment of border enforcement) posts, just to keep the dodgy bastards on their toes, before putting down on the high-threat IED route and doing a foot patrol clearance, long haul through the night back up to our base location.

of course, midnight, waiting on the pad – adrenalin shaky and immobile under the weight of new robocop-esque body armour, great at stopping the rounds but not much chance to run away – news comes in that the threat level has just upped to HIGH (G2 report increased likeliness of kidnapping) and so the bird has been tasked elsewhere – not enough choppers to go round as it is without them getting shot out of the sky.

in classic army style, we'll go anyway, in the vehicles

so it's all change and suddenly riding top-cover in a Snatch, the world illuminated bright green through the night sights and the midnight breeze still hot blasting against the sides of your face. gulping down great lungfuls of clammy, diesel air as we fly out of the main gate and into the real world, passed the blown-out shells of old suicide detonated car bombs and even a downed Iraqi fighter jet, still sticking nose first out of the desert

now headlights on, charging at a forty that feels like eighty, zigzagging across either side of the carriageway with what little traffic there is around getting the hell out of the way as we take aim through the night sights just in case.

two years ago, after the initial war, we could drive these roads in soft-skin vehicles, now i'm straining my eyes with incomprehensible levels of concentration, scanning the mountains of crap that unhelpfully line every possible route and the palpitations are real because the huts and the dogs are moving too fast to take in properly and this is the real thing, top-cover, lead vehicle. The ambient light from the oil-flares works perfectly for the CWS and then the split second heart beat skip – a mortar surely looms into view, a glinting sinister round metal tube pointing directly at the driver door sticking out of the bank and there's a lifetime long pause which lasts a second before I'm screaming down the PRR *'where's the fucking command wire, where's the FUCKING WIRE?'* until a last minute familiar font presents itself and we carry on zooming past a discarded Coke bottle

it's an exhausting, surfing, balance experiment, fighting for position and a decent view but trying to stay low from the threat as the Snatch bounces from one carriageway to another with fractional warnings before crashing over potholes with a dull hammering of knuckles and elbows bruising and bleeding in the dark.

and then silence

lying-up on the fringes of a village, lots of activity, maybe too much for 1 am, Tobin and team push forward while Hennessey and Co. keep rifles trained on the huddle around the bicycle in the town square. clear as computer game daylight i flick the cross hairs on and almost without realizing I'm doing it, i take up the drop on the only adult male in the centre of a group of children and, him not knowing i'm even there, i scan his robes for any concealed weapon while the boys push forward.

breathing calm and regulated now, finger almost indecently flirting with the safety catch, tracing light and teasing circles over the small bud, feeling every detail of the slight indent F for fire and ghosting now over the cool metal of the trigger – an incredible and unplaceable feeling of responsibility, sinister and strangely ecstatic, bewildering calm and almost elation to have this stranger perfectly lined up, a fraction of a second – two silent fractional movements and one 5.56 mm tracer round away from me and eternity and slowly from under his robes he pulls out another bottle of Coke and takes a swig.

and then nothing, and we're off at top speed, no need to stay around, we're back into camp and the sudden wave of vomited release and euphoria, all the bundled up stomach knot of nerves and concentration and suddenly noticed ear-burning knuckle-bleeding elbow-bruising from hammering around in the metal shell of the Snatch – slow pain and dull ache of huge body armour and the burn of a shoulder that's held the rifle up for far too long, ripping off of helmets and peeling off of sweat drained shirts and stinking armour and sparking up of fags even though we know that smoking kills

and funny, but it's very difficult to go straight to sleep

The fun should have gone out of it pretty fucking quickly when the first patrol from the battlegroup got hit, when Lt Tom Mildinhall and LCpl Paul Farrelly, who'd been scoffing at the same tables as us hours before, were lying broken in the morgue on the other side of camp. It woke everyone up, how random it was, how two nights before Tobin and I had patrolled the same stretch of road, how the next night it would have been Marlow's turn and as it was there we all were in shorts, too shocked to read or even talk it through, all trying not to look in the direction of the thin canvas the other side of which was Tom's empty bed.

The fun should have evaporated in the hot grief and anger we felt, but I knew deep down the two were inextricably linked. The buzz of getting out was in the danger and its startling unpredictability. We reserved our anger for the officious pricks who tried to bollock us for wearing incorrect headdress on the training range, but we wanted to get back out. Charging broad daylight this time down the Iraqi highways, running the traffic into the hard shoulder with nervous deployment of the laser-aiming dot to keep the suspicious-looking locals a safe distance, escorting enormous vulnerable convoys of water and other essentials, we tried not to think about the guys who had been blown up. I was glad to be on top-cover, whizzing past the shell of Chemical Ali's palace – the only thing higher than one storey in the *Mad Max* wasteland of rusting twisted metal that still lined the infamous Basrah road. Down on the Kuwaiti border the kids ran to the sides of the road to wave enthusiastically, which gave us a brief shot of euphoria until we slowed down at the entrance to the US camp and crawled past poignant long lines of ripped-up Humvee carcasses waiting to be shipped back to the States.

We rode back up sat on the huge boxes of Gatorade we stole from the awesomely stocked US Camp Navistar, but were far from comfortable as thoughts turned to the ceremony we were rushing back for. Sunset and the slow march of the draped coffins, the powerful low dirge of the Fijians muttering their own mourning hymns in baritone line and powerful bass response, which dignified even the muffled epiphany of someone fainting as we waited for the chopper to come in and the gratuitously mating dragonflies that hovered around the padre while heads were bowed in silent reflection.

The 112th and 113th soldiers to die in Iraq began their journey home, and no one wanted to watch war DVDs on stag that night.

So we got *The OC* box-set instead and played paper scissors stone to determine who had to go between episodes and check on the detainees.

★★★

It was strange to think that the IED attacks on our guys were probably being planned and coordinated by the very guys we had in the DTDF. Twice a week as per Red Cross guidelines we held visiting afternoons when hordes of relatives trooped in with cake and watermelon, and we'd keep a close eye on the heavy-bearded bastards whose 'families' always consisted of tight huddles of young men in black. Perhaps, if the tables had been turned, we'd have sat in tight circles with incarcerated friends in Wormwood Scrubs plotting death on the occupying oppressors but I liked to think we'd have fought a little fairer.

Fairer certainly than the Supreme Council for the Islamic Revolution in Iraq (SCIRI). The Iranian-backed SCIRI were murdering people in Basrah in horrifying numbers and then, just as the French Open started and we were looking forward to watching a little tennis during our long shifts, the news came down from Baghdad that the fledgling Iraqi tennis team – training for a qualifying slot in the Davis Cup and the national rehabilitation of international sport – had all been 'executed' by the side of the court they were practising on. Despite repeated warnings – so the SCIRI said – they had continued to train in shorts.

Things like that fired us up, made us glad to be out 'defending freedom' for the few minutes it took us to wonder what freedom we were defending sat in Shaibah arguing over whether or not rap was the most appropriate soundtrack to this particular war. *Jarhead* was right, everybody needed to move on from the whole Vietnam-rock thing, and it seemed to us that the rampant consumerism of gangsta rap struck a chord with our little oil war, so we cruised the airfield in our own hummer blasting out Big Pun and the Terror Squad and Busta and scaring the hell out of the Danes, who thought it was a drive-by.

Mostly the guys just got on with things, grumbling and purging with the caustic humour which is the right and duty of every soldier but only really getting angry when the camps were plunged into silent darkness by the sporadic crashing of the generators and we couldn't watch the World Cup.

Having to stumble around the dimly lit base, the oil flares brighter than ever on the night horizon and everyone with glo-sticks in their pockets like an off-key rave, eerily silent with the generators which we hadn't heard when they were going down and stifling hot with no air-con and water, was tolerable. What wasn't was the occasional roar from the other side of the camp, which meant someone had power some-where and was watching Peter Crouch miss another bicycle kick.

The really dedicated football hooligans were forced to reassess their tactics the night Iran lost to Mexico, and the really disgruntled districts of Basrah erupted in running gun battles. Millwall–Leeds had nothing on that. Perhaps the locals were just worried that Shaibah had suddenly become a sea of patriotic English flags – free from tabloid newspapers stuck to windscreens of vehicles, huge towels on sale in the NAAFI draped bright over the tent entrances. The locally employed civilians who emptied the portaloos by day and adjusted the mortar fire on to the base by night must have thought we were about to launch our own grand offensive, march straight across the desert and on to the Holy Land under our crusading banners of St George.

When the football wasn't on we would climb to the top of the water tower and sit looking out at the desert, the candle-flickering oil flares and the distant shimmer of Basrah in the north and Kuwait City in the south. Legs dangling over the sheer drop and the slight anxiety atop the weakened rusting structure a sort of methadone for the adrenalin junkies who couldn't get out on patrol, we would chill with Cokes as if we'd climbed high enough to get above the bullshit and politics of camp and the confusion and frustration of the tour.

★★★

If we were lucky we'd chopper up to Basrah City on Kafka-esque missions taking our detainees to 'trial', holding them in the lion den of what had been the zoo in the Shaat Al-Arab Hotel while we waited for the Warrior tanks which would taxi us to court and marvelling at what was left of the once-glitzy hotel, the bullet-pockmarked marble and glitzy chandeliers supported by sandbags and barbed wire.

From the back of the sweltering Warriors, clanging with the odd brick thrown but no one really stupid enough to take on the 30mm cannon and the bored and trigger-happy PWRR, we got a through-the-slit glimpse of 'the Venice of the Middle East'; long queues for petrol marshalled and abused by the fat Iraqi police, more donkeys than cars on the roads (one even pulling an ancient cart loaded high with TVs through the rubble-strewn, Bruegel-meets-Warhol streets). Outside houses and in markets the looted bathroom fittings of Saddam's palaces were for sale, and outside the court itself, beneath a towering papier-mâché purple dinosaur which gave the whole thing a surreal theme-park vibe, someone optimistically flogging a jet ski – welcome to Disneyland Basrah. Once in court we'd argue with the bullying policemen who wanted the detainees handed over to them so they could head out back and administer their own Glock 9mm to the back

The only safe view of Basrah, from the back of a Warrior – Basrah, June 2006.

of the head justice. Nervous stand-offs with our supposed allies; former Ba'athists who'd slipped under the radar and kept their moustaches spitting rancid breath in our faces and the tables now strangely turned as the terrified detainees clung to the imperialist infidels for protection from their own countrymen. Farcical process trials in which guys we knew were guilty were confirmed as being guilty by Iraqi judges so they could return with us to continue indefinitely in the same cells we'd got them out of at the crack of dawn that very morning.

What the fuck did we do all summer?

***

After a couple of months we moved to Baghdad. Most soldiers who served a tour in Northern Ireland never fired their weapon; that's probably true by now of Iraq as well. The Southern Desert had its moments, but the only footage of rifles firing we'd be able to put in our video montages was taken on the range.

The early thrill of just getting out on patrol, getting mor-tared, riding top-cover, the early lessons of losing comrades and living out of stinking tents with the same thirty guys for company, days that lost all meaning, weeks measured in snatched units of tanning and banter with the Reading Club, playing politics with the Secretary of State and the Red Cross in our little prison, playing Rumpole with our detainees and charging round Basrah in the Warriors, riding Snatch up and down the deadly motorways and lying nights in the hard sand poised like coiled springs on ambush – all this was for real. We'd always wanted to do these things 'for real'; no one ever promised for real would involve pulling the trigger.

Even so, Shaibah became my default impression of being on ops. From what I could gather from the company com-manders it had more in common with Northern Ireland than we might, at first, have thought: fatigue and boredom, frustrating stags and the occasional tense moment, maybe slightly more tanning. Perhaps wherever you go first is what you judge everything else by, perhaps the guys whose first tour was in the Falklands found everything else tedious and comfy by comparison. But I liked to think there was some-thing more fundamental, that Shaibah was 'ordinary' because there was still something else 'extraordinary' out there, some-thing that would test us in ways that, for all the adventure, Southern Iraq hadn't. Something like Baghdad.

It helped that Baghdad was where everyone's attention was focused, where the Americans took casualties in days that we took in bad weeks.

Baghdad was going to be the real deal.

It starts just as we'd want with a twisting, gut-wrench big-dipper drop into Baghdad airport and everyone on edge because the threat is that much higher so the sweat might be the heat but it might be the fear and either way distant thoughts of humid London not-quite-the-world-record-hottest-day are banished.

Then there's no doubt about the sweat on the helicopter ride from the airport to LZ Washington, the landing zone in the heart of the infamous Green Zone. On the Pumas it's just raw, wide-eyed fear and admiration for the pilots as they dart like wasps too too low and too too fast over the city, spitting out chaff in all directions as we prayed that the incoming flashes were an illusion not the Katyusha rockets being fired at your noisy, hulking, flying metal whirligig coffin by school kids on their lunch break that they probably are.

The strange thing about Baghdad wasn't the danger, it was the familiarity. The Southern Desert and its sprawling camp was as unfamiliar as it was hostile. Baghdad was a city of roughly six million souls, plenty of green spaces with a winding river and a skyline marked by religious buildings and the memorials of past glories and bygone wars. We hadn't known it, but we knew Baghdad all along.

And suddenly being in uniform in what you could discern was someone's town, someone's home, made it all the more startling when the cigarette-warm nights are punctuated by the music of automatic fire and sirens and boom. Double-taking as we drive through because every other public building has had the j-dam treatment and lies wounded on the streets – lavish, jerry-built, marble-façade palaces spilling their brick guts in rubble into the road, hideous open architectural wounds exposing their very innards and everywhere everywhere EVERYWHERE you look everyone has guns guns GUNS.

It was exciting because the names and images were familiar and the chaos felt like history happening. This was the sack of Rome, Saigon in '75, Beirut when we were toddlers, Berlin when the wall came down, and we were slap bang in the middle of it. The CIA Little Bird helicopters whirring overhead, the traffic all up-armoured Humvees and every uniform you can imagine – seemed like everyone wanted a piece of the action.

Even the first night the bangs were just out of sight and the shots only just across the river. The RAF crew as we'd landed had capitulated to the yankeeism that's everywhere and played The Killers over the C130 intercom, and it was still playing in my head, 'boy, one day you'll be a man', as we drank in the city for the first time through the open chopper doors, thinking what difference will it make sitting on my hands but I'm going to do it anyway. I couldn't resist a little *yee ha!*

★★★

The night I arrived we sat out playing bridge on the lawns of Maude House, drinking in the irony that the Americans lived in Saddam's former palace and we lived in his son's former brothel, starting just fractionally with each bang and pop that punctuated the heavy evening. The commanding officer had come up on a visit, so we couldn't crack out the port I'd smuggled past the RAF in a shampoo bottle, but the Stilton – a request from the general himself – was delicious.

After the cards, I wandered round the little camp, too wired to sleep, catching up with the guys on stag. In Shaibah we'd had our ups and downs and little excitements and little frustrations, but we'd been looking forward to this. For three weeks in London I'd marched and lashed with a knot in my stomach like I'd never wanted something so badly in my life. Smoking in the rear sangar with Gdsm Adjei, watching enchanted as tracer snapped back and forth on the other side of the river, I felt at home.

For those of us indoctrinated by the training and filled with professional envy Baghdad was simply somewhere you *had* to have been. Woodstock in '68 for the real cats tuning in and dropping out, ripping up plastic chairs in Marseille in '98 for any self-respecting hooligan. Baghdad was where George Bush Snr had never got to. Baghdad was where the whole world was going to shit because Junior had wanted to get to make up for Daddy. My own father may have got there first on a visit, but he'd had a protection team escorting him. We were the protection team, kitting up for riding out past the KBR-sponsored 'hunting season' sign with weapons FREE – it felt good to be up in Baghdad.

The city itself, at least the bits of it you saw as you whizzed past on top-cover, keeping all traffic out of your 100-metre protection 'bubble' with red-dots and warning shots, was impossible to comprehend. The big-tent camouflage circus of Shaibah had been so strange we had no point of reference; Baghdad was like any city we knew. Green, like everyone always said, with the palms on the banks of the Tigris and the well-cultivated embassy gardens, but everywhere was really the colour of guns and uniforms and armoured cars and the massive convoy which shipped Saddam backwards and forwards to court and pushed even us off the road.

Otherwise, we were delightfully idle. The boys who weren't on guard or on task were busy on Op Massive in the weights room or playing volleyball. The evenings were spent in the 'Duck and Cover' bar, where Thursday night was quiz night and all the ex-Army mercenaries and indiscreet Special Forces boys popped in for a drink and the lance-corporals played poker into the small hours.

Heading down Route Irish, 'the most dangerous road in the world' – Baghdad, July 2006.

Everything was chilled until a tasking came through, and then it was clockwork preparation. Calm but urgent rehearsals of special drills on the Crossed Swords parade ground which the Coalition forces had taken over with deliberate irony as their own real estate and which we monitored from the smashed-up balcony where Saddam had once taken the salute of his army's massive, delusional march-pasts. The boys used to grab shade in the tunnel the generals had built underneath the square so that soldiers who'd already marched past Saddam could get to the back of the parade unseen and march past him again.

Heading out through the Green Zone – or the International Zone, as we were now being encouraged to call it, Green considered inappropriate as it implied that there was a 'Red' Zone, duh! – was warm-up time. Waves from the smiling Puerto Rican and Gurkha contractors outside the embassies, gung-ho thumbs-up from the steroid-pumped mercenaries cruising around lawlessly in SUVs and then out under what the yanks called 'Assassins Gate' and what the boys more poetically referred to as the 'Golden Tit' (probably not realizing that it was a mini replica of the Qabbat As-Sakhrah, the Dome of the Rock, which Saddam had built after his plans to steal it from Jerusalem had failed) and pounding down Route Irish or Neptune, the 'most dangerous road in the world'.

But when we had no taskings, we chilled at the Liberty Pool.

6.viii.2006 – 'A Tale of Two Cities'
it would not be at all too difficult, i think, to contract schizophrenia from too prolonged a stay in this town. consider today, for example.

today (Saturday) is lobster day in the D-Fac (US dining facility which we marvel at and regularly plunder like Bhutanese peasants who have only ever seen a 1950s black and white television receiver, suddenly finding themselves in Comet), naturally, one makes a bit of a day of lobster day so we spent all day – pretty much literally all day – up at the pool trying out new dives (the front flip to dive – painful, the back flip to twist – worse), shooting pool by the pool (nice) munching on free popcorn (not too much in case we spoil our appetites)

and mostly just lounging and waving at the paramedic helicopters coming in every half hour or so.

the lobster was delicious, as was the Baskin Robbins ice-cream
and the cookies we brought back with us.

but then again we earned it after last night which was spent
tensely monitoring the tens of thousands of angry protesters
called up by Moqtada al-Sadr to show solidarity with those
lovely gentlemen of Hizbollah (and you thought the country-
side alliance march was rough and strangely dressed) getting
progressively more frisky on the opposite banks of the Tigris
while we casually sat outside a mosque deep in the 'red zone'
waiting for a dinner party between various coalition generals,
Iraqi politicians and Shi'a clerics to finish, praying they don't
take too long on the After Eights as the collocated US battalion started taking sniper fire and everyone had been static
so long even i could have placed a daisy-chain of IEDs on
the return route.

it's all or nothing as i find myself cutting back and forth,
liaising with the US and the private contractor Ops room in
the British Embassy (which is embarrassingly better than ours)
while the 172nd Stryker Brigade ('the Arctic Wolves') casually
report in yet more casualties and trundle off to the hospital
where – by the time we come back in off task – a bunch of
them are still sitting on the pavement outside smoking and
waiting for their buddies.

the big debate out here at the moment is whether Iraq is
having a civil war, the simple answer is not quite, but what
is happening is a sort of warm-up bout in the Baghdad-Balil

corridor extending out west into the Al-Anbar province. there's usually about 40 dead a day in the area, the nice recent touch was the vehicle suicide bombing of a school football match where the fucker actually drove right into the middle of the penalty area (and was offside).

the theory over in camp PROSPERITY (you've got to love the Americans, their other bases are LIBERTY, FREE-DOM and VICTORY – i couldn't do 16 months out here without a sense of irony!) is that if we can win the next three months and win Baghdad, we can win full stop, if not then . . . who knows? What effect flooding the streets of a relatively compact and hostile city with 7,000 battle hardened troops who are all seriously pissed off that they just had their tour extended by five months and lost the deposit on their holiday to Miami remains to be seen but we're in a good position to jump in and watch the fireworks.

which leaves me with a question – for the ladies

imagine, if you will, the Liberty Pool. at any one time we reckon there are about 70–100 people chilling there, mostly US Army, then us and then Georgians and Ukrainians, South American contractors and a handful of coalition embassy per-sonnel. The soldiers and contractors, by and large, are natur-ally fit, healthy young men who've been working off the natural frustration of being far from home and loved ones by putting in long hours in the gym waiting for the latest *FHM* to be sent from home. and then place yourself and one other friend in the middle of the pool in bikinis!

enter stage right the two American nurses who sauntered all the way round the pool this afternoon, breathtaking in bikinis with rifles slung over their shoulders and arses that would have converted our interpreter.

it's a strange scenario, especially when the next black hawk thunders in to the hospital next door and the shadow and the big red cross on the side reminds you just as you attempt the back flip with twist that some poor fucker somewhere just lost a leg.

The 0–60 life we lived in Baghdad – Liberty Pool in the morning, patrol at night, mortar attack in the morning, quiz night in the 'Duck and Cover' – was not unpleasant. A soldier is never alone, but we spent an awful lot of time with our thoughts. Looking out over the city from the Tomb of the Unknown Soldier – watching the choppers hovering like flies over the Council of Representatives, the Iraqi parliament building, or walking the lines in BSU, I'd notice the rich plethora of distractions the boys had conjured up. Strenuous in the gym or slightly less so round the pool table and dartboard, the endless DVDs and PSPs and X-boxes which guys would start playing war games on after they came back in off a real patrol. The constantly evolving banter, unique and inane competitions and elaborate gags and wind-ups, plots to shave Gdsm Heavens and the hotly contested 2006 Baghdad Open Underwater Swimming Competition (which was won by Major S. C. E. Wade, beating Lt J. C. Harrison into a poor second whatever his mummy might say). My e-mails home had become an essential part of my routine. We evolved ways of finding privacy in a world which denied it, of processing thoughts during the long hours with nothing else to do but think, perched precariously atop of situations it was far from healthy to think too much about. Surrounded by daily danger,

Messing about in the pool after another 'hard' day – Baghdad, August 2006. Left to right: Harrison, a friend, Sugdini, Wade, Seadog.

daily graphic reminders of arbitrary violence and shocking mortality our skin hardened, our sense of humour grew ever more flippant and tasteless, our coping mechanisms tended to the dark. Our job wasn't exactly suited to introspection, but our pattern of life virtually forced it.

Life in BSU wasn't trigger-happy, but it was spicy because of where we were and what was constantly going on in the back garden. We'd only been in town a couple of weeks when we took Seb out to the Al-Rashid for his leaving meal and barely noticed the sign at the maitre-d's desk asking for weapons to be unloaded please *before* you sit down. Like Gombould, I personally found Baghdad as thorough a holiday from all the ordinary decencies and sanities, all the common emotions and preoccupations, as I ever want to have.

In the car park of FOB Prosperity stood two massive bronze cast Saddam heads, falling apart now and graffitied by each unit coming through, gazing out with what I liked to imagine were scaly eyes on to the pistol range the yanks had built in the back garden of his palace. There was something eloquent in the destruction of all that was grandiose, only the startlingly modernist and strangely beautiful Tomb of the Unknown Soldier unscathed by the violence, perhaps out of a soldier's respect for his enemy but more likely so that the token Georgians had something to do, surly guards making up the numbers in the 'Coalition' to keep the UN happy and Russia off their backs. Down at Crossed-Swords looters had already stolen half of the Iranian helmets that had dangled macabre in nets from the giant fists, gory remnants of the Iran–Iraq war. It was said that the parade ground itself had been paved over the bodies of Iranians, which might or might not have been profound but given what was going on down south didn't unduly bother us.

In July the Surge kicked off, Baghdad Security Plan II, which was privately being talked about in the Brigade Tactical Operations Centre as an all-or-nothing last throw of the dice. 'Like cleaning your room,' one of the guardsmen remarked with dry but accurate wit as Seb explained that things would get worse before they get better. Sure enough, the crumping explosions increased and the morgues got fuller but the boys were more concerned by the rumours from home that the wives back in Aldershot had set up honey-traps to catch the cyber love-rats flirting with other women on internet dating sites.

Those few members of the company not addicted to

myhotfriend.com amused themselves with the endless stream of inaccurate or completely-missing-the-point stories which filtered through from the press back home. The most recent had been the increasing coverage of Snatch and all its glorious inadequacies. Someone had obviously realized that a vehicle designed for the streets of Ulster wasn't at its best in the Arabian desert, and suddenly the papers were up in arms for protection for 'our boys'. Which was gratifying and we knew from the QDGs' bitter experience of being blown up to be true, but which missed the point somewhat. We drove round Baghdad in Snatch while the yanks drove round in Stryker – a vehicle so hard it made our precious Warriors look like prams – but I knew which I'd rather be in.

The IED threat was not the issue. Yes, the IEDs were as blind as landmines and the Snatch was not what you wanted to be in if you got unlucky with one, but by that stage the Iranians had taught the militia how to make ones capable of knocking out armour as well so it was nearly six-to-five and pick 'em. What the campaigning mothers back home weren't taking into account, the shades of grey in which we lived and never saw in the press, was what message your vehicle sent. Drive a Snatch Land Rover, freshly armour-refitted and desert-cammed with two guys on top-cover, down Oxford Street and you'll get a reaction, some stop and stares. Drive a fucking tank past Selfridges and the whole world will stop. Angry kids might come and throw a stone at a Snatch, they might not, but if we'd rolled around outside the Green Zone in tanks it would have been phone for the petrol bombs, Henry, and no school that afternoon.

The problem for us was not our kit, it was that, as the city got hotter, there was less for us to do. We lay by the pool watching the CIA guys hanging out of the doors of the Little Birds sweeping low over the loungers and leering at the nurses. Wankers, we thought, but we'd have loved to be up there ourselves. Having come all that way, longed so much for the excitement of Baghdad, we were coming round to a crushing realization: for all that Baghdad was tense, exotic and top-trump-winning in the post-tour mess-boasting sessions, we weren't going to have a fight.

We watched fights, stood off from them, jumped into the aftermath of them, but still weren't in them and deep down, therefore, couldn't know, couldn't answer *all* the questions we thought might get asked of us at 'war'. Marlow, inevitably, used a sports metaphor. Sat back on our student arses, we'd watched the invasion of Iraq, and it was like watching a big fight on the TV. So something had clicked, and we'd joined the supporters club, learned the jabs and blocks at Sandhurst and watched more fights on TV with a sense of an insider's knowledge. And then we'd got out to Iraq, turned up to the Arena on a big fight night and soaked up the atmosphere, but from the stands. In Baghdad we were ringside, maybe even the trainers, applying the sponge, living each hook and wincing with each hit, but we still hadn't been in the ring.

★★★

The daily Baghdad SITREP cheerfully reported one morning that some 1,855 bodies have been delivered to the city morgues in July – a nice record high, up 300 on last month.

The next slide said that attacks across the city were up 40 per cent, which we knew full well because we'd all been woken that morning by the mother of all eardrum-bursting thuds. The blast had sent the company, and most of the Green Zone, shooting out of bed, sick with adrenalin and heart-pounding, arse-doing the 50p/5p routine. Thorold had come bundling in naked from the shower across the way, diving under his bed as the alarm sirens started, cursing the barbarity of insurgents who launch attacks so early in the morning.

Once the all-clear sounded we took coffee on the banks of the river and watched the blossoming clouds of smoke that were the initial bomb on the market in Karada and the follow-up, timed perfectly to hit the emergency services' response. The sky was alive with angry choppers and even fast air, and we all privately wondered how massive a blast must be to feel so big from what turns out to be a good couple of hundred metres.

With the slides and the bombs and the changes in personnel it felt like the tone started to change. Piers arrived from Afghanistan with tales of zips in the wire and ten-hour engagements, encircled camps of Paras groggily watching the sun rise over heaped piles of Taliban bodies surrounding their perimeter with the machine-guns still hot from the night's festivities, which only heightened the familiar insidious sense of creeping boredom.

The boredom of watching as the yanks go out and hammer the city while we patiently wait for another trip into the Red Zone and kid ourselves that we came here to swim not fight, when we'd all rather do our swimming in Cornwall or Blackpool.

Boredom in comparison to the tales of the medics patching up IED victims, eyes half-hanging out as they're rushed in to the Ibn Shaid CSH (combat support hospital), where we lend a first-aid hand with the battle casualties that come in from the night before and gag and look away while tourniquets are pulled tight and limbs amputated from wide-eyed Marines.

Then again it might just be that the diving board is broken.

★★★

Piers was a senior captain freshly back from a tour with 3 Para in Afghanistan, and his stories round the evening camp fire were really making us feel inadaquate. The media, initially distracted by Lebanon (which it seemed from the papers that made their way out to us was viewed at home as somehow more 'tragic' than what was happening in Baghdad – we could only assume because a few rich hippies had their honeymoons in Beirut) and the *faux* indignant outrage that Iran had a hand in things (as if that was a surprise to any of us after months of intelligence reporting* down south that the Iranians trained, equipped and ordered attacks against us down there; they might as well have had t-shirts made) had just got hold of Christina Lamb's breathless reports of the fighting, and the first returning waves of Toms, wide-eyed from the 'fuck-me' of the whole Herrick experience, were causing people to sit up and take notice.

Baghdad had been exciting, had been many of the things that Shaibah had not and was a tick in the box we were so desperate to get that the mere action of ticking it had been satisfaction enough. But Piers was up there to relax. Piers was taking a break and enjoying the calm after Afghanistan, and something in his eyes as we prised the 'zips in the wire' stories from him betrayed that it hadn't been stuff to boast about in the same way we planned to boast about Baghdad. Piers was there to give his weapon a rest, and for all the hoo-hah and bangs of 'the Surge', the truth of it was that in months none of us had so much as shot a stray dog.

In the spirit of the Reading Club we joked away our days

---

* Much of it diligently gathered by Gabriel, now promoted from the Inkerman Company to battlegroup intelligence officer and who, a fluent Arabist as well as distinguished shin-kicker, spent long hours playing backgammon with dubious locals.

and evenings, playing Fives against the bomb-proof walls in full helmet and body-armour, confusing Harrison with Trivial Pursuit and annoying the CSM's timetable, switching lunch for dinner in the perennial officers vs. sergeants, dinner vs. tea debate (which we finally won by bamboozling him entirely with the concept of 'supper'). Not normally one for superstition, I resolved to give up on *Don Quixote*; in three months I hadn't got past the first hundred pages and I was still in one piece, so maybe it wasn't meant to be. Sunbathing could be done more openly in the chilled atmosphere of Baghdad, although the corrimec roof felt vulnerable to the mortars, and we insisted for decency that Harrison retain at least his pants. With no one left to tease, I resorted to winding up the yanks, leaving my copy of Hunter S. Thompson's *Kingdom of Fear* anywhere they might find it and disapprove of what one incensed major called his 'unpatriotic and insidious rantings'. HST seemed pretty spot-on for Baghdad, although you wouldn't have needed the drugs, and what with the cigars that Piers had brought in all we needed was cowboy hats for our top-cover patrols.

On my last night I sat out on stag to drink the last of it in, my last night with the Inkerman Company, who had proved to my delight that my long-held belief that you *could* treat soldiers like grown-ups was not misguided naivety. X Platoon were my first platoon, 'No Frills Platoon'; no fuss, no bullshit and fuck me if we weren't the go-to platoon for a job that needed doing well. Damn, I didn't want to be leaving. Up in the sangar I wondered if it was unhealthy, this seemingly contagious disease we all had. No sooner had our itch for an operational tour been satisfied than we were looking for the next level. We flicked through Piers' snaps of the rugged mountains of the Hindu Kush and the dusty nothing that flanked the Helmand River and forgot our own carefully crafted montages of convoy ops in Basrah and runs down Irish before we'd even finished them. I was sat in a sangar, cradling a machine-gun in the most dangerous city in the world and already longing for whatever extra Afghanistan would bring.

My ride out hooked north over the slums we had never penetrated on our patrols. Cattle being herded down the concrete streets totally unfazed by the gun battle raging near by in Mansour. In a space which must have been cleared by a bomb it's rubble, not jumpers, for goalposts but at least the kids were playing football and not up at Route Pluto, where the Big Red 1 had just arrived, and it was all kicking off again. Baghdad was everything we wanted it to be, and not quite, and I think part of why I wasn't more frustrated by this was the worrying thought that, if I had been firing my rifle out there, what would it have been for? In Iraq we had seen a

Entrance to Baghdad International Airport – July 2006.

war, been in a war, but perhaps it was for the best that we still hadn't fought in one.

At the entrance to Baghdad International Airport, next to the now infamous Palace of Abu Grahib, is a statue of what looks like an angel – it's a long way from home.

V

All Things Come

At 291605LAPR2007 we got ambushed on the dam.

In retrospect, nothing – between the moment we climbed steeply out of Baghdad, already sweating with homecoming anticipation, and the moment we touched down in Afghanistan – mattered.

At Sandhurst and Brecon we'd fired rifles aplenty, at wooden Hun's-head targets and stencilled likenesses of Wehrmacht storm-troopers. In Bosnia no one had so much as shot a rifle in our vicinity. In Iraq we hadn't properly fired ours. Everything, *everything* for the record-short six-month interval between getting back home and deploying to Helmand had been about the actual fights we were going to have, about the commanding officer's address splashed in bold across the *Sun* to our secret delight: 'Some of you won't come back.'

At 291605LAPR2007 we got ambushed on the dam.

Op Silicon had begun, and the Junior Officers' Reading Club had downed books.

2.v.2007 – Op SILICON

pause for breath, if not for shower or change as twenty minutes in this puny camp will supposedly mark the transition from one Op to the next, not that any of us will notice because we're too encrusted in dust and the bullets being fired at us won't take any notice of the planners' semantic details.

the thing about SILICON is that it's nice and clean, conjures up images of hi-tech industry gleaming in plate-glass offices on some beazley M4 corridor. Op SILICON might have been more appropriately called the Battle for Gereshk, except even that geographical definition would have included the lazy fuckers back in this camp who jumped in their comfy beds when a stray RPG came too close but to whom the names of Deh Adam Khan, Habibollah Kholay, the Dam and the Canal would still mean nothing.

and as things wound down after three weeks parked out on the Dam and the locals started flowing back in on donkeys, whole families teetering on motorbikes or entire villages piled twenty high on the back of ancient tractors, we frolicked in the river, all dog-tags and topless bandanas because fuck it we've all been living, sleeping, eating and killing on top of each other for the past three weeks. Only the little girls smile and wave, flashes of bright green or pink in the incongruous Sunday-school landscape of compounds that would have been comical if we hadn't fought tooth and nail through them days earlier.

ambushed on the canal road before the show had even started as we supposedly snuck into position the night before. RPGs exploding with a boom to kick start the hearts which stopped as the pinging and whizzing overhead we realized were incoming rounds from three directions and there follows a lost hour of charging around as the vehicles get stuck on the skyline and the Afghans, too stupid or brave to move them into cover, just get stuck in with raining hell back in all directions so we're not sure whose bullets are bouncing at our feet as I grab my driver and charge up to the Dam to try and coordinate the fight. As soon as it seems to have started it's stopped and the Afghans have even brewed up chai by a pond as if nothing has been happening and until I drink it I don't realize how thirsty or pumped I am and Christ we haven't even started.

as the others push peacefully and enviously through on D-day it's almost immediately more of the same except this time there's no turning back and so hours which seem minutes become two days in which progress is measured only in compounds and the strangely sweet evening smell of dead bodies or the pit in the stomach that widens every time we charge back for one of our own casualties. But we're lucky in the grand scheme of things and even Bismillah who has his right eye shot-out could have been a centimetre further forward and we'd be scraping his skull out of the back of the wagon. No one is in a worse state than the PoWs we've found where we thought there would be no survivors and so a cliché is played out as I put myself between the Afghans who want to execute them and the trembling Taliban who no longer care whether they're off to Allah economy or business.

sure enough once it had been safe for a few hours the cameras arrive and it's the BBC to sell us down the river with exciting tales of being in the front line in the 'Taliban dominated Sangin Valley' with the plucky team of Brits actually fighting alongside the Afghan National Army. Brave and hilarious and terrifying and mad the ANA who park up overnight next to a mountain of what we later discover is gear but it doesn't seem to affect them as the Taliban kick up again in what will become the regular pulse-quickening night-time pattern of rattle and panic response and bathing the beautiful river valley in the eerie glow of the flares.

through 17 days of pounding the area the i-Pod is unfailingly mischievous, throwing up Dolly Parton '9-to-5' as once again the plaster of the compound behind our heads kicks up as we scurry for helmets and body armour and pound in all directions until whoever it is that was shooting is shooting no more. It all becomes a parody of a pastiche at night when we get the Stones or Hendrix up on the Dam while popping up mortars and picking off 'Terry' as he tries to crawl up to the wire. In the day, the WMIKs bristling with firepower and ploughing through the poppy fields as if they weren't there, we're appreciative of the lift of 2 Many DJs' mash ups or AVH's 'My My My' as we cock pistols or fix bayonets and charge once more into a labyrinth of stone and goats and rabid dogs, as likely to scare an old lady as whoever was firing from the roof the night before and afterwards I'll try and gauge my own response to all this mayhem, maybe staring at the sunset over the valley or luxuriating in the cool water of the river or even steeling myself to loading up more enemy dead, ungainly on to the back of a pick-up to head back to the morgue where sinister messages of congratulations come back to us days later that the most recent batch had 15 rounds of UK ammo in a nice tight group in the chest which means at least we're good shots as well as heartless bastards.

it's all so real that it doesn't seem real at all.

tell that to the Taliban who didn't make it, it's no consolation I guess but everyone's a winner because they're now martyrs enjoying virgins we can only imagine from the cruel FHM scraps sent up with the resupply drops and we're the toast of Helmand – which is a double-edged sword because all I want now is a wash and something real to eat and to lie on a bed and work out what it all meant but it starts again with a vengeance in twenty minutes and it will be no more real than it was last time and all I'll remember is the donkey tethered to a tree which stood there unmoved through the mother of all fire fights as we finally broke through and took the Dam itself and then held the front line which we've now abandoned so it wouldn't really have made any difference if we hadn't done any of it at all and now we'll go and do it all again somewhere else and hope there's more grenade fishing and more lucky escapes and hope that who-ever said adrenalin was finite is wrong because there's no heroin replacement substitute for this shit and for now the show must go on.

Setting out from Shorabak for the start of Silicon had been as vivid as that first Queen's guard. Turning the corner from our side of camp with the commanding officer's and the padre's inappropriate blessing ringing in our ears (but hearing only de Niro and imagining the *six inches in front of our faces*), we were lifted by the insanely glorious sight of the *kandak* ready to roll. A kaleidoscope of headdresses and rugs and blankets and plants and casual RPGs strewn amongst the *naan* breads. Faces we'd never seen before snuck in for the scrap, doubled our numbers and clambered ten to a man over the pecking order of the vehicles, fighting over who gets to man the fearsome-looking dushka heavy machine-gun wagon.

And it was still joyous as we charged in broad daylight, brazen as you like down the A1 towards Gereshk, running taxis with whole families clinging to the roofs off the road, hooting past the bewildered gate sentries in FOB Price. Everyone tensed up the first time we cut through Gereshk proper; the town came closing in on all sides through the

177

The padre 'blesses' the Queen's Company before we head out crusading on Operation Silicon – Shorabak, April 2007.

bustling noise and smell of the *badr** and we were on our own and this was really happening.

Flashes of those hours stay with me, the sight of Qiam – squat and paunchy and ill-shaven like an Afghan Falstaff – roaring up over the dam and into the police sangars, where the ancient guards were cowering behind the Hesco, spraying ineffectual bursts over the top without even looking. Qiam furious, foaming at the mouth and damning us all as cowards as he ran forward on his own screaming, 'I don't need helmets and body armour, I'll kill fucking Taliban with my bare hands,' or as close to that in Dari as the terrified interpreter can manage. *That* was leading by example. Will jogging up his side of the canal with the same ridiculous grin I knew I must be sporting, and Sgt Gillies just behind, crimson-faced and panting good-naturedly that he was too old for all this,

* Market.

but smiling as well now that sixteen years after Granby he'd be able to update his war stories.

But what I couldn't say in an e-mail because maybe at the time I didn't know it or didn't want to believe it in case it ran out or wasn't true, was just how easy it all was, how natural it all felt and how much fun. That night I lay listening to the shots and the ghostly call of the *muezzin* across Deh-Adam Khan, where we knew and they knew we'd be fighting tomorrow. Lying in the hammock, too excited to sleep and too exhausted not to, it felt like everything had built up to that moment, but that everything had also just started. As I reminded the boys, we had only just finished day one of what was supposed to be a week-long op.

Which was still going on a month later.

***

The objective of Op Silicon was to push the Taliban out of the fertile river corridor, the Green Zone, which lay just to the north of Gereshk, Helmand's commercial capital. While Gereshk was vulnerable to marauding attacks from the city limits the government of Afghanistan had no credibility in the province, so we were to clear a 10-kilometre block north of the city.

The teamsheet (the 'order of battle' or ORBAT) was impressive. A Company 1 Royal Anglian to the north-west in the desert itself with the Light Dragoons and their tanks, bristling with firepower and mobility; Big Mick Aston's B Company, also 1 Royal Anglian, on my left flank, supported by the impressive Vikings – lightly armoured, articulated troop carriers driven by mad Royal Marines – bringing the fight to the enemy. To the east, on my right, where I hoped they'd watch where they were shooting, Will and Sgt Gillies and their own ANA. 2Lt Will Harries, one of the junior platoon commanders in the battalion and a good officer despite a predilection for sketching, and Sgt Gillies, possibly a veteran of Waterloo, made an unlikely but good couple, pushing their ANA forward even as they bickered about immigration and whether their boys should be allowed to wear t-shirts.

To their south-east the rest of the ANA, *kandak* HQ, with the pathetic ANA senior officers trying to keep as far from the fighting as possible, and frustrated 'Tac' – our own Company HQ with Major Martin David and CSM Snazle banging Afghan heads together in an attempt to get anything done. Martin had been the Captain of the Queen's Company since back in Iraq, had commanded companies in Northern Ireland and London and knew how to run one like the back of his hand. CSM Snazle was one of the most impressive soldiers in the Army, huge and bald with a head so shiny it risked giving away our position to the enemy. He was exactly the man you wanted charging up from the rear to scoop you up if you got shot and, having already managed to get Martin to drop the C-bomb,★ he'd won his first battle of the tour.

Collocated with them and, inevitably, whichever media attachments were in town, were 2Lt Folarin Kuku and Sgt Davis. Poor old Kuks was a contemporary of Will (which didn't half make me feel grizzly as the 'senior' platoon commander transferred into the Queen's Company for the tour)† and was cursed with being 'the first black officer in the Grenadiers' – a fact which was neither true (Prince Freddie of Uganda apparently, whichever Evelyn Waugh novel he'd

★ Call someone a cunt.
† Which I decided to take as a compliment given that with the passage of time the senior major who we'd teased in Bosnia had now become the commanding officer. No longer to be teased but still, one suspected, with a lingering affection for his old 'Monarch's Mob'.

wandered out of, sometime in the fifties) nor as impressive as Battalion HQ seemed to think. They put him front and centre for every photo shoot and interview going – which he hated because it invariably meant he wasn't in the thick of the scrap – as if people were reading the *Sun* and going *look how progressive they are* when, of course, everyone with half a brain was choking on their Corn Flakes at the realization that it was 2007 and we'd only just got our first black officer.

In the rear in support was 1st Battalion the Worcestershire and Sherwood Foresters (the WFRs), still blinking and hoping they were about to wake up from the bad dream that had seen them crashed out of Hounslow Barracks, where they'd been doing public duties, and suddenly, unpreparedly, dropped in the middle of Helmand. Way to the south-east of this glorious force, distracting the enemy as we crossed the start-line with a dummy assault, were the marauding beards of the Brigade Reconnaissance Force (BRF), the hand-picked recce soldiers whose job throughout the tour was to penetrate deep into enemy territory, have a sniff around and generally cause mischief. It was the pride of the battalion that so many of them were Grenadiers; Sgt Frith and the Seadog, Inkerman Company boys from distant Iraqi days, had already acquitted themselves well, and the Seadog was later Mentioned in Dispatches for his calm and courageous leadership (not, as was scurrilously whispered, for neutralizing a particularly vicious Taliban donkey in the heat of an ambush).

★★★

But after the excitement of being ambushed on the way in, the morning of D-day and all its H-hours and phase lines was an uneventful and boiling-hot slog through empty villages. Uneventful, at least, until Qiam – the mad Tajik major who'd been nicknamed 'Rocky' back in Shorabak because we were pretty sure he was beating the crap out of his boys – decided to do things his way and threw the British Army rule book out of the window.

Not that I could completely blame him as we cleared through compounds complex like our photo imagery and naive planning had utterly failed to understand. Micro-communities behind little tin gates in high mud walls hidden in the fields of thick poppy. Labyrinthine interconnecting passages and mazes of children and cattle and crops spilling out into courtyards and wells with only the broken generator in the corner behind the donkey and the rusting Pepsi cans hinting that it was the third and not the first millennium. Every time we glimpsed the Anglians I winced for their slow progress, weighed down by the full issue of regulation kit and bewildered by the alien worlds through which they were clearing at a pace which made our ANA seem like whippets. I might have gloated until a wailing prompted me to run round the corner to find Qiam holding a pistol to the head of a boy on his knees and the old mother screaming in the corner and the ANA grinning and pointing at the boy and shouting 'Talib', with which the widow increases her wailing and Shirzai, our consistently unreliable 'terp, shifting uncomfortably on the fringes.

When Qiam's repeated demands to be shown the weapons elicited no answer he fetched a stinging back-hander across the boy's face, and as I started forward to stop him I suddenly realized that I was on my own with only LCpl Price watching at the gate and the ANA looking at me, not hostile but curious, like why should my rules and regulations get in the way of their job?

Desperate, I grabbed Shirzai and got him to accuse Qiam of cowardice. It was the last thing I suspected he was guilty of, but surely the high and mighty Englishman act, some crap about never striking someone unarmed, was worth a shot. For a second Qiam looked like he was going to rise to my bait but instead roared his Brian Blessed laugh and cocked his pistol, at which point the mother rolled her eyes, sighed and gave in with a little shrug and calmly led him to a haystack and pulled out a bundle of about eight AKs, magazines, ammunition and even tacky little assault vests.

High-fives all round on the way out indicated there were no hard feelings, and I sounded like a fool explaining the 'hearts and minds' theory and why we should have searched for the weapons instead of intimidating the people while the 'terp translated Qiam's response, patient as if explaining to a child: 'Force is the only way to deal with liars and anyway, how on earth will we have time to search all the houses in Helmand?'

How indeed, once the sun got up, and the ANA, satisfied with their morning's work, sat down for their usual mid-afternoon snooze, which wasn't exactly on the agenda in planning but which everyone's so astonished by that they don't even bother to bollock us. Which was just as well because B Company found the enemy or vice versa, and there wasn't time for worrying about the little things like waking up the ANA so, much to LSgt Rowe's annoyance, we left them behind and pushed up alone to where Big Mick was taking pretty uncomfortable mortar and RPG fire.

★★★

I'd worried that the second time would be a letdown. That some of the thrill of the contact was its novelty, something so long anticipated, finally fulfilled, and that next time round the adrenalin-burst response would be less. Instead it felt even better. The emotional baggage of the previous day had gone, replaced by a calm focus which got serious as we realized that this was a different type of fight – not an opportunistic ambush on the start-line but a coordinated defence, with the bastards moving through prepared positions, fighting from trenches and trying to lure us into their killing areas.

I'm amazed that time is not an issue. That clattering into one of the compounds to find Marouf sweating heavily and bleeding from the foot, man enough to admit that he shot himself climbing through the window, I looked at my watch to call back the casualty and found that hours have passed since we started scrapping forward. Sure there's amusement on the net when we call out the IRT – the awesome Chinook-borne Incident Response Team who never failed to make it out to a casualty and get them back to the hospital in Bastion within the crucial 'golden hour'* – for a self-inflicted gunshot wound to the foot, but it didn't last, as Bismillah, one of the only reliable Afghan NCOs, was shot through the eye, and the casualties started to mount.

A kilometre forward I can see our target, the limit of exploitation that the original plan had us clearing towards, trying to winkle out Taliban, except that now it is just a mad dash for the line because the Taliban need no winkling, determined to hold their ground. Silhouetted as the sun starts to set, the sluice-gates, the convenient point on the map and now strategic ground, not because anyone wants to divert the canal but because that's where we've decided we want to camp tonight and that's where the enemy has decided to stand and fight. The evening becomes a slow but steady pincer, relentless as the Royal Anglians' firepower forces the Taliban

* Casualties who made it back to a field hospital within an hour had a substantially increased chance of survival. We all knew that in most circumstances, if you were alive when chucked on the back of the IRT, you'd be alive the next morning – a comforting thought which made a hell of a difference.

The heavy dushka machine-gun and RPG team providing support to the final assault to take sluice-gates – Upper Gereshk Valley, D-day, Operation Silicon, 30 April 2007.

into our skirmishing vanguard and the hard shoulder of the wide canal. Strange how detached I feel from what's happening, how I seem to be watching myself as we manoeuvre the vehicles up for a point-of-fire and let loose all three GPMGs and the deadly GMG at the same time. Even in all this we didn't forget the photos, the cameras in easy reach for the perfect comedy timing of the lucky unobservant Afghan who gets his beret blown off by the RPG back-blast or the magnificent muzzle flash of the roaring dushka.

Although the closer we get, the longer things take, and the last click has been hours; as we approach the final hundred metres the momentum suddenly increases and, caught up in it, we fix bayonets to push forward to the ditch which the last of the Taliban were trying to flee down. I'm about to charge off when CSgt Yates grabs me with an experienced paw, suggesting that there's no need to risk it at this stage, so we lie exhausted in the dirt, shooting at the occasional head that pops up like a game at a circus.

★★★

'A fucking good scrap and a fucking good day' was Mick's Aussie assessment when we meet up with the Anglians that night for orders and congratulations, a tough day that could have been a lot worse. My boys – Amber 63 – have been the first to the finish-line, and our reward is to hold the sluice-gates we took, and, although Sgt Thornborrow is freaked out by the dead man's sandal that dropped off as we loaded the bodies on to the police trucks to take back to the morgue, still lying in the middle of our admin area, there's something amazing about the feeling of holding ground that we physically took, of sitting back, propped up against the wall we were shooting at hours earlier, enjoying a brew on our hard-won territory.

It was *jamsai*★ all round when the posture slipped and we could hold back the inevitable no longer, we posted sentries and, with no enemy for a few hours, stripped off and jumped into the cool, fresh water of the Noor-I-Bugrah. All the fatigue and sweat and excitement of the last few days flowed away downstream with the giggling of the ANA, who, I suddenly realize, without their weapons look very young. I suppose that without our weapons so do we.

Our instructions for the next day, and all successive ones, were brilliant in their simplicity: HOLD, which is to say, do nothing but of course, just as we're stripping down for another cooling dip, mortars start dropping on our heads.

★ Well done!

The donkey, unmoved by the previous few days' bedlam, started braying as the ANA dashed for non-existent cover and we remembered with a surge of excitement that with CSgt Edgell and his fire support group, we've got a £70,000 solution to this problem. It was a curious counterpoint, firing the Javelin missile compared to the close fighting we'd been getting used to. The enemy mortar was over a mile away, and watching them load and fire through the fifteen-times magnification of the command launch unit, the whole thing is stand-off computer game and, instead of the hours which run like minutes in contact, the minutes seemed to last for hours as we set everything up and then wondered how to proceed.

The mid-morning sun is so bright it is difficult to make anything out through the binos. Squinting at the hill the other side of the river, I want to make absolutely sure that the trio scurrying around with what looked like a motorbike were definitely the *dushman*★ the ANA insist. We're the only unit in position, so the commander on the net insists it's my call and I'm about to bottle it when the next incoming round lands a little bit closer and the whole thing gathers its own momentum.

The ANA have gathered round in a spectacularly untactical huddle to watch the firing of the magic rocket and are clamouring for action. Even our recently acquired hardened-warrior posture slips as we take things to the next level and I am just praying for the little puff of smoke, the little sign, the little anything which would remove any doubt that we're not about to drop a missile on someone for no reason. To increase the pressure, CSgt Edgell announces blithely that the rocket is now armed, so either we fire it or we have to throw it

★ Enemy.

away. Either way the tax-payer is out of pocket, and we might as well have an explosion to show for it. To my relief, there's a little puff of smoke on the hill just before the next round lands, dangerously close, and so it's all systems go for the picture-book launch. The rocket obliges, popping out of the tube with a ferocious whoosh and hanging in the air for just that split second before the boosters kick in, and Sgt T shouts an encouraging 'Go on, my son!' as it speeds off and smashes the hill with an orange thump and whoops from our Afghans and a follow-up from all nine barrels of Worthers' mortars. And the incoming stops.

Firing the first Javelin of the op was the icing on the cake. Our patrol harbour was a cluster of euphoric cheers and people comparing footage, and I was still staring with relief at the blackening pillar of smoke to the front, sweating and wondering exactly who it was on the receiving end. CSgt Edgell caught my eye and diffused the situation perfectly with a shake of his head and a chuckle: 'Don't worry, sir, they won't be trying that again, whoever they were.' I guess not.

The reality of our actions was brought home that afternoon. The Anglians dragged in more of the dead bodies from yesterday's clearance patrol, and after all the high-fiving of the deadly Javelin firing there was a release in the macabre task of loading the trailer with the ghoulish and stiffening corpses, and it wasn't the cloying smell but the swilling in the body bags, reserved for the unlucky bastard turned inside out by the Apache 30mm cannon.

And still there was time to rest. Being by the water was like being on the beach, just without the ice-creams. No one stays down for long when all you have to do to cool off is haul yourself to your feet and take a running jump in, lie back and allow the current to float you downstream to the footbridge where the ANA have centralized all their stores next to the marijuana fields. Which was a mystery until I swam past and, catching a whiff of something different in the air, paddled to the bank and rounded the bushes to see a section of Pashtuns squatting over an enormous mound of freshly harvested weed. We knew that they smoked and had simply hoped they wouldn't do it out on patrol, but it seemed that the reports of drug runners owning a lot of the land were not wrong and the stash was so enormous that it was hard to be anything other than amused, and before we ordered them to get rid of it all we took running jumps on to the heap and lay on our backs, making 'hemp angels'.

As the Engineers arrived to build the patrol base, the Hesco-bastion fortress which will mark in edifice our new front line and the achievements of our op, the air was thick with the unmistakable smell, and a crowd of ANA gathered dancing around the pile which the wise-arse sergeants had just set on fire. For the rest of the week a fug of rich hemp

Hemp Angel – Upper Gereshk Valley, May 2007.

Hide and seek in the ganja fields – Upper Gereshk Valley, May 2007.
Left to right: *LCpl Price, Gdsm Lloyd, Gdsm 'Sherlock' Holmes.*

smoke hung over the canal, which made for a very chilled couple of days guarding the Engineers and their tractors while they built like ants. To our rear, Will and Sgt Gillies play hide and seek in the ganja fields and must be getting the worst of the paranoia and the munchies from our little bonfire because every time we meet up with them they're exhausted and shooting at shadows.

We get our first bit of media ops when the Anglians drop off their embedded reporter at our location. 'Fat Al' has communications gadgetry that should have made whoever procured our own crap kit blush, and within minutes of flopping down behind the still-smouldering ganja he's online, checking the football scores for the boys, while I try to smile, thinking of all the times in the last few days I've had to dash all over the place for a 'face-to-face' as our own comms routinely let us down. I'm sceptical of the press, always what we call the 'Goldilocks' distance behind the fighting (not too hot, not too cold, just right), but for all that he's a bit ill-informed and full of gushing praise for the REMFs he's just travelled up with – two days late to the front line and where does he think we've been all that time? – it's hard not to feel a frisson as he chats back live to the UK (in the half-time break in the Liverpool vs. Chelsea game, so Sgt T is almost creaming).

It's not just my e-mails any more, it's stomach-churningly, fist-pumpingly real, and the news reporter in his blue flak jacket is actually talking about us: '. . . under a full moon, strangely beautiful up on the front line in the Taliban-dominated Lower Sangin Valley with the Queen's Company and their partnered ANA on the site of the last few days' fierce fighting . . .'

Patrol Base South

The structure that rises out of nowhere in the next thirty-six hours as the Engineers work away is incredible and cements Hesco in my mind as one of the genius ideas of recent times. So staggeringly simple all I can feel gazing at the signature blue logo is envy and admiration for the lucky vision of Heselden, who had seen the direction the world was going. Where once the grunts would have toiled for weeks to build sandbag structures, the Engineers fill lightweight steel-cage boxes with rubble and hardcore for instant blast-proof protection – the Lego-brick building block of every camp and war of the last twenty years. In one night the Sappers flattened what had been the mound at the sluice-gates and ate chunks out of the bank to fill the Hesco walls, which went up 2 metres high in a neat and impregnable triangle, barely 20 metres by 10 at its widest but a hell of a lot better than sleeping under the WMIKs in the dirt, which had been our bed up till then.

A young ANA soldier celebrates the completion of our new home by performing circuits round the mortar tubes – Patrol Base South, May 2007.

The nice touches are added last: the sangar positions at each apex hotly contested for the cool shade of the tin roof, the twin desert-roses – our own drainpipe urinals – defiant in the middle of the base and the luxury of a double wooden throne above the burning shitters at the back. All the pains-taking Sandhurst harbour lessons came to mind – pacing out the perimeter, unfurling twine from the fishing rod reels we bought just for the purpose and digging in our little shell-scrapes, wondering what was the point because we knew as soon as we were attacked the CSgt would make us bug out anyway. We wouldn't be bugging out of Patrol Base South.

Patrol Base South was ours to defend – one of three forts

192

on the new 'front line', a hard shoulder providing elusive 'security' for Gereshk back down the valley. Commanding awesome views over the Green Zone straight up the river valley, arcs linking in to the WFRs' firepower up on the high ground to the flank in Patrol Base North and a cheery kilometre away from Will and Amber 61 down in Patrol Base Centre – so relieved no longer to be on the constant move that they gratefully occupied the vulnerable middle position without a murmur. Maybe because we were so excited to be settling into somewhere we could actually defend – somewhere we could more than half-sleep through the nights, jumpy at the slightest grunt from the donkey, convinced that the Taliban were slipping back into the positions – it took us by surprise when the *toolay zabit*,* Aziz, came forward with young Nasrullah, who had tears streaming down his cheeks.

We'd taken bets back in Shorabak on how young Nasrullah actually was. He claimed eighteen, which there was no way was true and was too on the nose to be believed by us who'd learned the hard way to lie big if you didn't want to get ID-ed heading into the Crown on a Friday night. His blue eyes gleaming with defiance, he had waited until now to admit that he'd been shot two days previously, half his thumb blown away and now a rancid pulp in a bandage, so we just stood round in awe of the calm look on his face, barely wincing as LSgt Rowe applied some sort of proper dressing to the mess and realizing with guilty relief that he needed further treatment and we finally had a legitimate excuse for a run back into camp.

★★★

* The ANA equivalent of a company sergeant major.

It seemed weeks not days since we had fought up the towpath for hours we mockingly drove back down in minutes with the wind in our hair and the taste of NAAFI stock already in our hungry mouths. It seemed like we were older and wiser driving past the dam, where we had fired our first rounds a week before, but we weren't, just hungry and tired and bearded and dirty.

It was amazing coming in and staring down the comfy-in-the-rear G4 types who didn't like our dirty combats but could hardly stop us from getting our first fresh lunch in a week and amazing hearing the subtle intonation of the officer in the ops room who turned round as I was signing us in and said, 'So *you're* Amber 63.'

Amazing phoning home with shaky hands and clicking 'send' on e-mails we'd waited days and years and lifetimes to send. Amazing after all the hyped-up faint contacts and unapologetically and honestly typed-up tense patrols and warning shots, finally downloading the never-look-back glorious melee on the dam and the rapture of a real fight.

Amazing cramming junk food in the NAAFI, coming back up on the sugar high with the sickening combo of blue Gatorade, ice-cream and toffee popcorn. Staring open-mouthed at Nelly Furtado on the TV, fit in a fringe beyond our wildest fantasies with Timbaland yelping away in her ear, and everything else meant nothing at all to me.

It was amazing, but it was a holiday, and for all the creature comforts even after the first hour we knew we were enjoying it because we weren't staying. Stocked up with Pringles and cookies and fresh newspapers, we felt as good pushing back out through Gereshk to our new castle on the river as we had done coming in.

Back at Patrol Base South I realized we could relax in a way we never could back in FOB Price. FOB Price was cool and comfortable and well fed and safe, but we always knew it was only a matter of time before the vehicles would be mended or the batteries charged or the errand run and we'd have to punch back out to the line. Vulnerable on the front with a tin pan for a loo and hammocks strung up between the Hesco walls, we knew we weren't getting back to the air-con and laptops and camp-cots back in Shorabak any time soon, but at least there was nowhere else anyone could send us, at least it was home.

★★★

At least it was sufficiently far forward not to be bothered too much by the press and the politics which swarmed around the rear as silly season started at home and all the news was apparently Afghanistan. Fingers had been wagging and blame had been apportioned in the Brigade HQ in Lashkar Gah ever since the *Today* programme had run a story about soldiers on the front line *complaining about communications and vehicles*.

Journalists were a fact of life, but it didn't stop them being a pain in the arse. The best-case scenario would be a formal embed, a reporter with you for a week, maybe two, ideally with his own protection team so that he wouldn't need babysitting. The documentary crews out for the long haul gained the most respect, came closest to becoming 'part of the team' and would then get accused of losing their impartiality once they got home and their programmes were made. The junior commanders bore the brunt of the extra work the reporters generated – subjected to not only the scrutiny of whoever or whatever it was reporting on your particular job but also the extra interest of the more senior officers who invariably swarmed like flies whenever cameras were near, and all the while we kept half an ear open just in case one of the lads in a moment of artless naivety should stray too far 'off message'. Which must have been what had happened during Silicon, as angry messages from HQ demanded to know from whom the BBC could possibly have got the idea that there weren't enough vehicles.

Well there must have been more than 500 troops on the start-line, and that would have narrowed it down to about any one of them they had spoken to. We'd fought our way forward in a WMIK we'd borrowed from the mechanics back in Bastion and which turned out not to have a spare tyre. Then again at least we had wheels, which must have made the Anglians slogging through on foot pretty jealous. We had two WMIKs for each team, six in total without counting Tac, which was just as well because on more than one occasion we limped back to the workshop in FOB Price in a sorry convoy, the last three that worked towing the three broken down; iconic or not, they were vulnerable – metaphorically and, potentially, literally a pain in the arse. And we were the lucky ones. The WFRs were probably whingeing loudest as they deployed all the way up to the line in Snatch and even plain old Land Rovers. The line was that we had enough vehicles to go round, and if you counted the ones the RAF were using for shuttle runs to Timmy Horton's Coffee Shop in Kandahar we probably did, but try telling that to the miserable private bouncing over minefields in a glorified car.

I didn't doubt that someone somewhere, tired on stag, had whinged to a reporter. There were enough of them around and they knew what they were doing; giving a wide berth to the officers, who at least had rudimentary media training, chumming up to the boys with satellite phones and fresh rations and then waiting for something controversial to slip out. I suppose what riled us about the media, especially the journalists who flitted in and out like butterflies, got snaps of themselves looking stubbly in the desert and then back up to Kabul to flirt with the NGO girls, was that they hadn't earned the right to broadcast our whingeing. Soldiers whinge and purge and moan, that's what kept us going, and, as the old saying went, the top brass should only really start worrying when the guys on the ground *stop* complaining. The well-intentioned journalists might even have been bemused at our resentment, thought they were doing us a favour, fighting our corner in public in a way we weren't allowed to – but that was the point. We were like a family, allowed to slag each other off and curse and damn each other for all we were worth, but someone who wasn't related didn't have that right.

Of course there weren't enough vehicles and of course communications were rubbish, of course we needed more helicopters and of course the boys were tired, but it had ever been and would ever be thus. No army in the world ever had all it needed, no commander ever suffered from too many resources, and the funny thing was we resented the presumptuous journalism more than the shortages.

Which was probably why we had a fight with the gobby Territorial captain in charge of the camera crew who came with us for the next phase and started trying to tell us how to do our job instead of shutting up and taking photos of it like he was supposed to. It was frankly a relief when the B Company patrol forward kicked up such a scrap that we crashed out to join the fighting, and the urgent requests for ammunition resupply that night were a most eloquent reminder to all the gossips and commentators that we had more important things to be worrying about.

Making our way back from the forward patrol, the sun setting silhouettes the hulking patrol base and shimmers on the water at the sluice-gates. The Hesco sentry positions look like towers in the lengthening shadows, the uneven loading of the top row forms the battlements, and it's every inch a castle. Tac visited and left the mail and some cans of pop, and

Home, sweet home, downtime in Patrol Base South – Upper Gereshk Valley, May 2007.

the ANA cooked up some fresh rice from somewhere, the smell of which wafts up deliciously from the riverbank.

Down by the river was home, sweet home.

***

What ensued was a nine-day odyssey when hours and days blurred indistinguishably into being on stag or not being on stag, driving into Gereshk for resupply or pushing out forward on clearance patrols. Moving up north for briefings or into the JDCC, where the ANA had set up the *kandak* HQ in the middle of Gereshk, for orders, down to the river for swims and washes and grenade fishing and push-ups and bar curls using the six-foot pickets that are the makeshift gym. The slow-burn madness of drifting off to sleep in the gently swinging hammock as nothing changes.

Progressively clearing the ground around the new front line, we found treasure troves of Taliban goodies: mobile telephones, computer software, radios and even the kit left behind by the Marines who got ambushed not far away six months ago. There were improvised infra-red and remote-controlled devices and even English phrasebooks and crudely doodled exercise books, ORBATs alongside with childish drawings of imagined Taliban tanks and burning infidel stick men.

We grew accustomed to the haphazard, side-by-side Afghan living, the unfamiliar compounds; donkeys in the courtyards and primitive tools hanging from the walls, brick kilns and stacks of dry opium and fearsome-looking scythes. We pushed through doors marked with good-luck-charm cat's eyes into rooms decorated with garish digital posters; luridly coloured mock-ups of Islamo-utopia, dreamlike estate-agent brochure pictures which seemed to depict Palm Beach but with more mosques. Chickens strutted through passages strewn with discarded medicine bottles and cassettes and plastic sandals, looking for the fallen *toot-toot* berries, which looked like a cross between a gooseberry and a maggot but tasted deliciously of light kiwi-fruit.

Once the fighting had calmed, normal life seemed to resume on the sluice-gates, the main upstream crossing of the river for everyone making their way down into Gereshk. A daily bustle of life and colour through the ANA checkpoint; venerable white-bearded *haji-sahibs* and young boys with close-cropped hair like Spartans driving forward impassive cattle, donkeys impossibly laden with poppy and cloth and ever-comical herds of skittish, wobbling fat-tailed sheep, the invisible women a ghostly procession of powder blue and green burkhas and teenagers whizzing back and forth on scooters, beaded skull-caps glistening in the sun in the steady flow of families, those from downstream moving back home, those from upstream running away.

Down on the river, it was all Major Qiam. He was almost

certainly a bully and maybe a thief, and I knew that without me watching him like a hawk he'd be pounding the crap out of the latest guy he was interrogating; the problem was that, for all that, he was a one-man army. Qiam's father was executed – he explained to me over lunch in his lean-to, getting fat on greasy *pilau* and *ghosht* while the boys preferred the MREs we'd robbed from the yanks – in front of his very eyes when he was fourteen. His brother one year later, that time in public. The man lives for one thing and one thing only, killing Taliban. He's good at it as well, smells things out, knows the area and the locals. He'd take one look at suspicious men being questioned at the checkpoint and wave them off, apologizing profusely that they had been inconvenienced by his idiot soldiers, maybe cuffing the corporal in question for good measure, and minutes later he'd pounce on some young guy about to be waved through, whisper something menacing in his ear, and we'd gather in amazement as the bloke would hand over explosives, ammo, radios and meekly offer himself up for detention.

Perhaps more importantly, he was more effective at motivating ANA soldiers than anyone or anything else I saw. Between him and the quietly meticulous Lt Majhid, the ANA planned and executed patrols beyond the wildest expectations we'd dared to harbour back in Shorabak. Never correctly dressed and always reliant on us for supplies and support but with a nose for the enemy, they'd clear through sectors in hours it would have taken a company of Brits days. But it went both ways, as we discovered one afternoon when the officers had all disappeared and we were woken from a siesta by the general commotion to discover a couple of clowns had got high on the last of the weed and driven their truck straight into the canal to see if it could swim. We stood on the bank, unsure at first whether to laugh or cry as the 4-ton

Major Qiam, typically relaxed, during a lull in the fighting later on in the tour. In between us is LBdr Greenwood of the Royal Artillery, a member of our excellent Fire Support Team who was awarded the Military Cross for his actions on the tour.

Ford Ranger wagon bobbed downstream with the dopey idiots babbling incoherently, perched on the roof.

In the end we laughed.

Qiam came back the next day to beat the guilty pair and explained apologetically that he'd been off looking for a wife. I was pretty sure this was a joke, but you could never be certain. His soldiers giggled and the 'terp blushed as he explained that he took a wife from every place where he had fought and defeated the Taliban, each one younger and prettier than his first wife, who was, so he said, famously ugly. It was hard to reconcile the jovial character sharing out sweets he'd picked up from wherever he'd been with the cruel bully cracking gags at the expense of some poor woman somewhere

Lt Majhid (left) despairs as the ANA try to recover their non-amphibious truck from the canal – Noor-i-Bugrah, May 2007.

('So ugly, Toran Padi,* that when she asked me when she has to stay covered up I tell her I don't care as long as she stays covered up in front of me!'). He was fearless, tactically astute and obviously cared for his men far more than any other Afghan commander (more than plenty of British officers for that matter) but, when he flew into one of his rages over something trivial and I saw the look in his eyes I'd seen in the first ambush, I knew he was slightly unhinged.

★★★

* As he always referred to me. *Toran* was the Dari for 'captain'; I was still a lieutenant at the time, but the ANA always promote their mentors one rank up to make themselves feel more important, a habit that proved catching.

Resupply runs back into FOB Price were the treats of roughly once a week, the opportunity to ogle music vids and check out beard growth in the mirrors and gorge on NAAFI stock before snatching time on the internet and phones and, best of all, a trip to the real flushing loos. In retrospect these days seemed an eternity of i-Pod nostalgia and nights not quite yet warm, but too tense for blankets, endless excitedly scribbled blueys and an overwhelming sense, even through the occasional IED bangs, of security. The ANA were happy, the hierarchy were happy, Silicon had been a success, and the token triumphal gesture was to rename the Lower Sangin Valley the Upper Gereshk Valley, and the only unsettling question, initially unspoken but sensed among the guys, was how and when would we ever be pulled out of the line we had created for ourselves.

It was perfect. I don't mean perfect in any sense of ideal, perfect in any sense that living rough on the front line of a hot and bitter fight could be, but perfect in that it was all so clichéd. The dead man's sandals on the first night, the patrols through thick, head-high fields, the days in the firebase under the sweltering sun, all bandanas and dog-tags and cooling off with dips in the river, the cowboy ANA element still stubbornly toking away and the drone of choppers overhead, the nightly boom and pop and eerie glow of the mortar illum and thud of distant air-strikes and rattle of nervous ANA defensive fire as the perimeters were tested.

The noisy cicada, the occasional braying of the donkey, the trickle of water through the sluice-gates, the long night hours gazing at the sky, picking out the satellites through the NVGs, the Nimrods from the shooting stars and the thrill of a comet or the majesty of the Milky Way, these became our canvas. A sense of balance sprung from the enforced reduction to nature, the meaningless taste of the same ORPs, the fading smell of unwashed bodies and the banter sat round watching the shitters slowly burn at dusk. The casual professionalism, the fluency of radio chatter and sudden easy familiarity with weapon after weapon after weapon – Afghanistan felt more like being on set than real life.

It seemed that, finally able to write the letters home I'd spent the last three years apologizing for not writing, I couldn't, because no one would believe them.

'All Along the Watchtower' played out into the night as the projected five days of Op Silicon rolled into their third week and we were still on the ground we'd taken and held, abandoned first by the Anglians, off to prepare for something else, and then by the WFRs, off back to the comfort of Price, until it was just us, the three Queen's Company teams and the three ANA companies spread thin along the patrol base line. We were Silicon, we were the valley, and there was no way out of there, there was too much confusion and we couldn't get no relief.

A Short Walk in the Hindu Kush

What should have been a routine move back down the tow-path for more toffee popcorn and fresh batteries and into week four of our long camping trip in the valley somehow became the mother of all road-trips. At the JDCC everyone was a flurry of excitement, announcing that we're being attached to the monster company group that B Company Royal Anglians and the Viking Troop have put together, to fight through the desert up to Sangin.

Sangin itself held all the romance and mystique of where the fighting was as fierce as you like, but the drive up to Sangin was the stuff of legend. The BRF, with all their fighting punch and specially trained hardness, had only got as far as Zumberlay before turning back in a hail of rounds and early casualties. The Canadians only did the journey in Leopard tanks and LAVs, rumbling armour formations through the heavily mined desert passes where the French SF had ignored entreaties to wait for an escort and had paid a heavy price, ambushed and tortured to death in the desert that was definitely Terry's. You only flew into Sangin, holding your breath as the enemy mortar teams ranged in on the landing site at FOB Robinson, the ever-growing base just south of the town, and if for some suicidal reason you had to go by road you went in heavy armour and as fast as you could through the night down to the relative safety of the A1 – the only road in the whole country.

The plan of Op Lashtay Kulang was to roll our massive group, slow as you like in broad daylight, up the valley from Gereshk to Sangin, picking fights all the way. The concept was to create a mobile operations group, a MOG, which sounded nice and clinical, but we might as well have put loud-hailers on the vehicles shouting 'come and have a go' as we rolled into Zumberlay and Pasab and Hyderabad and Mirmindab, a-MOGing in the month of May all the way up to what the guys had charmingly named the *Kessel* after the trap in which the German 6th Army found itself, hence 'Sangingrad'.

You couldn't not be impressed, though, awed by the gargantuan statement of fighting intent. The Fire Support Group WMIKs in the van, Javelin and I-Law hanging from every available strap, .50 cal and GMG nimbly proving the route for the twelve articulated Vikings rumbling behind, sweeping top-cover GPMGs eating up every possible gradient and terrain, countless Pinzgauers and Vectors in the rear with all the comms teams and logistic support you could eat and even the drops and the hulking fuel tanker in the middle, vulnerable like painted targets but still screaming 'we're off to war' and to hell with the Taliban dickers, frantically waving laundry from rooftop to rooftop across Gereshk to signal that something was up

On the day we moved out I only realized how serious it was when we were roused by the sentries at four and took in the majestic steel-blue dawn over the dunes and the massive company group, the only thing for miles and miles the lead wagons already kicking up sand columns on the horizon.

Trying to follow the armoured Vikings through the dust as we charge north towards the mountains – Pasab, May 2007.

There are no crossing points for vehicles between Gereshk and Sangin on the Helmand River, so we followed the south side, popping into the villages which occupy the little bends and fingers, snaking upstream as villagers poured out of each hamlet we came across, full of assurances that there were no Taliban then feigning confused surprise when the inevitable ambushes kicked off. Being in a fully kitted-out UK company group was a mixed blessing. We drew confidence from our awesome fighting presence but suffered the reports from the attached electronic warfare team employing their black magic and listening in to the Taliban. Radio updates built the suspense as we moved in from the outskirts of a village to be told that the enemy had spotted us, that the nervous forward sentries wanted to open fire but are being told to wait until we get closer and then that the *big things* were being brought forward – which usually meant the RPGs.

Even out on the cut-offs the enemy were slick, and mortars landed nerve-rackingly in and around the vehicles, which was enough to send the ANA scuttling but not to distract the B Company ground troops who were caught up in the main ambush in whichever village it was that day. Ominously our obvious task was always to secure a landing site for the IRT to come in and pick up the casualties the forward platoons had already taken.

We regrouped in huge desert leaguers, where I would produce my trump-card from the back of the WMIK, a bright green frisbee, and pretty soon in the afternoon stand-down the tension of the morning's fight would ease into a riotous game of frisbee-rugby with even the Anglians, who had been suspicious of the trigger-happy ANA stoners at the back of their company group, joining in with giggles and gusto.

During the day we charged pretty quickly across the desert, billowing dust clouds marking us out to the spotters on the hills, but because we're looking for a scrap why not let them know we're coming? At night, movement became almost impossible, with vehicles lost in the monstrous dust, the NVGs useless and the ANA with no kit flashing on and off headlamps like an infuriating disco at the rear of the column. We lost depth perception through the goggles and were constantly rolling and slipping through uneven *wadis*,★ left waiting for the recovery vehicle in the sudden patches of impossible fine sand. We would arrive at the FUP the next morning ill-tempered, dusty and tired, an inauspicious start to the day which the ANA superstitiously and accurately suggested would get no better.

Afghan camping, catching some sleep in a leaguer on the way up to Sangin – May 2007.

Bruised after another intense fight and more B Company casualties and the release of the massive 2,000lb bombs and the Apaches spitting angry 30mm rounds to cover the withdrawal, we push on for Sangin itself. Past the nomadic herds-

★ Ditch or stream.

men and under the shadows of the Kush, more formidable with every mile we get closer to its foothills, the natural spectacle of the drive sustains us until the maps become a colourful, dangerous blur of minefields, and everything is edgy silence on the limited approaches to Sangin. The final bend of the *wadi* which leads to FOB Robinson, our destination, is the notorious 'fish-hook', and we inch through it past the haunting carcasses of trucks and previous military vehicles which lie rusting in the desert like dinosaur skeletons, and jarring Stravinsky would be about right on the radio at this stage.

And sure enough a mighty thump from the front of the column and the billowing horrific smoke of a Viking ablaze from an IED strike, poor bastards running on fire from the inferno, and we grind to a halt on the vulnerable valley floor, waiting for a follow-up ambush and the arrival of the Apaches to deliver cathartic hell-fire vengeance and cover our limping progress into the base, where we collapse in an exhausted heap in the middle of the dust bowl and sleep.

It took us four days to fight from Gereshk up to Sangin, and then we sat in FOB Robinson for another four doing nothing, which we would have enjoyed if we hadn't been choking on the swirling brown-out clouds of fine dust which caked the place and whipped up every time the choppers came in to pick up another casualty or resupply the busy gun line. We mooched around trying to play with gnarly-looking yank SF guys and pissed off a visiting delegation of generals with our uncleanness and unshavenness (and the inappropriate t-shirt I'd got from Finchy and lent to one of the Afghans: *My brother went on jihad and all I got was this lousy t-shirt!*). And after all that we got back down in four hours, tootling along peacefully behind a column of Canadian tanks and ready to start again.

26. v. 2007 – How Patrick's boys were briefly the toast of
Afghanistan and nearly won $10 million (and lost an eye)

i'm slightly nonplussed when the random Major from
Regional Command South HQ in Kandahar rocks up to my
O-group to attach to a routine patrol we're putting forward
but the plan is just to make nice with some of the villagers
on the front line, so if he wants to tag along and take some
cheesy pictures for the REMFs back in KAF, a last hurrah
in the twilight of his twenty-two, then fine by me, an extra
pair of legs to carry water. And up until about half-way
through the patrol it's all going according to plan and we're
sweating buckets through the midday sun carrying everything
because we've decided to go 'soft posture' and maybe the
vehicles are a bit aggressive. And Kuks' boys are forward
because they're fed up with my lot getting all the action and
want some for themselves and we're all posing for fun snaps
in the shade of a vineyard when the unmistakable wumph of
an RPG comes in from the flank and our cowardly pathetic
excuse for a 'terp has jumped into the nearest ditch which is
a sure-fire sign that things are about to kick-off as a steady
burst of machine-gun fire rattles off the building next to us
and a 107mm rocket hurtles overhead to remove any doubt.

and there's a look in the Major's eyes like maybe he hasn't
done this for a while, or maybe even at all and I want to sit
with him in the ditch and try and explain, try and piece
together what it is about the contact battle that ramps the
heartbeat up so high and pumps adrenalin and euphoria
through the veins in such a heady rapid mix. I want to sit
with him in this beautiful field, apart from the well-trained

mayhem that has now begun and wonder what compares; the winning goal scoring punch, the first kiss, the triumphant knicker-peeling moment? Nowhere else sells bliss like this, surely? not in freefall jumps or crisp blue waves, not on dance floors in pills or white lines – I want to discuss with him whether it's sexually charged because it's the ultimate affirmation of being alive . . .

but first we've got to win the fight.

first we've got to be the gloating fuckers who are alive, not the crumpled forms barely recognizable in the bomb crater who the Afghans smile and point at – *ne mushkill* – no more problem from them commander sir.

so on the contact we whip round to face our full flank towards the buildings we're being fired upon from and your brain is at once in a thousand places and I start screaming instructions at Sgt T and the 'terp at the same time while shouting on the net what's happening and scrambling the air support. We've turned east so poor old Kuks is now at the back cursing his luck again and bleating to be called forward but we've got it in hand and move up under a terrific weight of fire to a ditch about 100m short of the compound. I turn to the random Major whose CIMIC fact-finding jaunt has just taken an unexpected turn and apologize that regardless of rank I'm about to order him around for the next few hours before throwing him forward with some heavy weapons to try and suppress whatever the fuck it is that's going on up there. The Afghans with better eyes than us have spotted 7 or 8 Taliban moving around the compounds to the front and there's too much open ground for us to roll straight up at them so we pop up and down from the ditch trying to keep them penned in with RPGs and UGLs. Meanwhile I'm tying myself in knots on two radios with every fucker in Helmand suddenly wanting to know what's going on and the only people I want to speak to are the jet pilots bearing down on our location to buy us some breathing space. Confident there's no civilians around and regretfully remembering the commanding officer's instruction that platoon commanders take risk first, I run forward – no longer feeling the ridiculous weight on my shoulders and sweat mingled now with the ditch water so it doesn't matter – and use the cover of a donkey who is serenely walking up and down the track, oblivious to all the firing – to crawl into a position to pop the smoke grenades. Red and white billows up from the green poppy fields and it's a high-risk strategy because now the enemy know exactly where we are, but so do the pilots who swoop in from 1,000ft to a mere 200 and thunder overhead, first pounding the compounds with cannon fire before I'm screaming down the net that fuck the safety distance they need to bomb the compound so we can get out of the ditch.

it's testament to the calming effect of so much going on at once that not only do we cease to feel the physical burn but also the mental drag. I know somewhere in the recesses of my training that troops should be 250m from a bomb and I know from my eyes that we're only 100m tops but I'm happy that the ditch is deep enough and the boys are all for it and screaming fit to burst that we can't exactly stroll back a safe distance anyway so I assure the WIDOW callsign (not so much hearts and minds from the RAF then ...) that it's my call and before we can draw breath time seems to stop and all the air is sucked out from around and there's no noise or motion until the wumph which is part shockwave and part ear-splitting thud, cannons out and there's a few seconds of insane whooping from the Afghans who do love a good bombing before the cloud engulfs us and it's raining mud and crap and bits of wall and goat.

but we use the debris for cover and before the air has cleared we're into the compound with bursts round every corner and a grenade for good measure through every door and window, and it's sheer exhilaration, leaping over every wall and barely feeling the impact of thudding down into the dirt as another burst comes in from the now retreating Taliban. It is chaos and only very loosely managed, the bomb and grenades have deafened us all so I've no idea if anyone can hear me screaming, trying to coordinate our move through the buildings so we don't blow each other up, keep myself at the front so I can keep a handle on it but somehow the Afghans sweep round the flank with the PKM and the Bravo team (try saying that in Dari at 100 decibels over the constant rattle of gunfire). The air's thick with the smell of sewage and meat where a nasty mix of gore and crap is forming in the bottom of the 20ft deep crater that was once the dining room of this compound and on the far wall a cow and person have been flung forty feet across the space and slammed into the bank so that it's hard to tell where cow ends and Talib begins but the Afghans still let loose a triumphant burst of fire into the corpse for good measure.

as quickly as everything starts, it stops.

there's nothing but the trees swaying in the breeze and the open fields to the front and the odd rattle of machine-gun fire as the forward line watches for any movement but the overwhelming sense as bits of rubble still fall, is of stillness and only the drone of the Harriers monitoring overhead and just as the exhaustion kicks in (and the searing pain in my eye) so do the endorphins so it's all good and everyone's faces read the same high, the lights back on at the end of a massive night in some hardcore warehouse and everybody drenched and no longer as beautiful and cool as they were under the strobe lights but still deeply satisfied.

Kuks still muttering on the radio and I can't resist calling him forward now that action's finished to help us mop up and the best is yet to come because we fish a mobile out of the pockets of one of the dead Taliban and it turns out he was none other than Mullah Omar's driver; big MO is the 2nd most wanted man in the world with a fat reward from Uncle Sam on his head and dammit if we didn't nearly get him, maybe. But it's all good because it cuts me enough slack afterwards that no one is in the mood to question the somewhat loose interpretation of the danger safety distance of an air-strike and, after all, if I'm the only one who suffers (more from the pirate jokes from a couple of days of walking around with an eyepatch than anything else and hell a shrapnel wound is cool as long as it doesn't actually do any damage) well then it's all worked out rather nicely.

i really can't explain the buzz except that looking back at the radio logs when we're all back in and swilling grateful Gatorades and already exaggerating the kill count (the seven I counted becomes ten, so I think by now it's twenty and climbing . . .) I see that I called first contact at 1130 a.m. and we finally closed at 1500. Christ, nearly 4 hours and I swear it all feels like minutes, every time you're transported to somewhere else where you watch your own actions through a lens (or the headcam or shaky snappy snaps of the random

Major who had the trip of a lifetime) and none of the ordinary feelings apply until afterwards trying to conjure up pity which is somehow more easily done by regarding the unfortunate goats than the unfortunate Talibs (so English). I guess like anything this could get boring but every time it starts again and there's the crack or wumph or the overhead fizz it just kicks in and off we go. The Random Major didn't exactly get to talk to the locals but he got to shoot the bad-guys which is much more fun.

Something was needed to shake us out of the dangerous enjoyment we were getting from it all, the growing swagger and knowing graffiti in the sangar, a tribute to BFBS's dedication to Amy Winehouse with a wry *They tried to make me go to Sangin, I said no, no, no.* For all our heroics in the Green Zone and the favourable reports of the breathless major from Kandahar, our run of parklife in FOB Price came to the inevitable halt, and we were back out on the line coming back in only to help HQ redraw the maps because we *were* the Upper Gereshk Valley.

Whole days were spent sweating under the makeshift shade out in the patrol bases, balancing the impossibility of moving in a heat we couldn't ever have imagined against the cool invitation of the canal, which remained the essence of the front line. Long evenings of token tanning and half-hearted sit-ups from the guys counting down the days not weeks till R&R because we already knew by heart the tattered magazines lying around the base and there was literally nothing to do.

The two weeks we first spent in the base and which seemed to stretch like an addled eternity were laughable by comparison,

Passing time, home-made chess set – Patrol Base South, June 2007.

a distant and fleeting memory in the slow-motion, dying-battery afternoons spent watching the fish attempt to jump the sluice-gates upstream, feeling slightly that there's an unfair, unBritish advantage to tossing grenades in the broiling water, swirling with enormous freshwater carp and *mahi*, which we thought was a local specialty until we realized it's just the word for 'fish'. Then again the new 'terp was pretty handy frying it up with rice and chilli powder from the MREs and no one wants Lancashire hotpot for lunch on another hundred plus day, so we would sit back and let the ANA play and add the expended UGLs to the next ammo request.

On quiet days the entire valley spread out below our castle, hazily beautiful and deceptively calm, and with each patrol forward and scrap the Taliban were less and less up for it until our nights were back-to-back calm and the locals started to emerge. In groups they came, tentative at first but with increasing confidence and numbers, to the easy *shurahs*★ we held under the ANA lean-to with suspiciously good-looking and made-up young soldiers serving *chai* and sweet yoghurt. The requests of the grey-bearded elders never changed. We offered blankets and medical supplies and maybe petrol for the decrepit generators rusting in a garden up in Habibolah Kholay, legacy of some long-gone, obliging but clueless NGO. The Americans offered us millions of dollars for QUIPs (Quick Impact Projects) and all they wanted was the one thing we couldn't provide, the one thing which all our guns and armour proved was in short supply: *security*.

The basis of all my hope and optimism for Afghanistan lies in the fact that the more specific requests we occasionally got were always for schools and teachers, never clinics and doctors. Even for these timeless men with craggy, biblical faces who could be fifty or 150 – and either would be a good innings out here – the violence is temporary but learning is permanent. Our new neighbours had come down from Oruzgan province, awarded the land we took in the last op by a ballot conducted by that mythical entity we're fighting for, the government of Afghanistan, which they kept repeating, GoA GoA GoA, like it's the password. They are so chuffed with the fertile fields that are suddenly theirs in this lotto – as long as we stick around so the Taliban don't come back in (which of course we won't). They offer to continue building the 'school' which is currently only a brick lavatory block (which of course they won't). All was going well but relationships deteriorated slightly after they were accidentally terrorized by the Czech Special Operations Group.

The SOG are awesome, bigger men (if it were possible) than the yanks we'd met up in Sangin and certainly with

★ Meetings, councils.

217

bigger beards and more defiantly non-military heavy-metal t-shirts. You could almost hear the WFRs' warrant officers grinding down their teeth in barely concealed frustration every time the guy with a plait and beads *in his beard* came in to lunch with one of the two *enormous* Alsatians they never went anywhere without. Two female 'medics' spent eight hours a day in the gym, the most noteworthy girls in town working out on the cross-trainers, waiting for their Visigoth warriors to come back in off patrol. The whole British camp could only watch on with awed jealousy and wonder if the SAS get this sort of thing.

We were shaken uncomfortably when the owner of one of the compounds we hammered a week before turned up

Shurah *with a couple of local elders. The Afghan officer at bottom right was supposedly the company commander, but we rarely saw him except on occasions like these, when the Pashtunwali rules of* malmastia *(hospitality) meant we wouldn't be attacked – June 2007.*

for an afternoon chat like a neighbour with a broken window and unmistakably your football. In the heat everyone was sleeping on the roofs, and it wasn't to complain about the fact that we've destroyed his home but to ask that we stop firing illum, the sharp metal cases of which spiral alarmingly down to earth once it's burned out, because it's scaring his kids. This man who now has no home is actually thanking us for destroying it, for having the courtesy to get close enough to make sure his wife and kids had fled down the ditch before calling in the air-strike, and is now politely and calmly asking us to keep the noise down after lights out.

I can't imagine how it must seem to him as I trot out the usual blithe and meaningless assurances and my own heartfelt and sincere apologies and hopes. Shaking hands as they leave, so utterly foreign we might as well be from different worlds, me so *jawan** and the old boys unblinkingly calm and only the cosmopolitan young nephew who knows how to work the village mobile slightly distrustful of this young pup who gives with one hand and blows up with the other.

Our ANA were much less respectful of the old Helmandis. Apologizing to us for their backward kinsmen and despising them as yokels, liars and Taliban sympathizers. Up north at home, they assured us, every house had a VCR, and the women walked uncovered. Of course, it's a two-way thing: we calculate the reparations for another destroyed home and accept the slightly exaggerated livestock figures but are suspicious of the claim for three million Pakistani rupees that the family apparently kept in a chest which also got destroyed in the bombing. Stiff with pins and needles from long hours sitting cross-legged, strolling past the river I noticed that the guys had built a diving-board down by the sluice-gates and

* Young.

219

was overcome with a mixture of shame and pride that the stinking young infidel is master of all he surveys.

Dark Days in the Valley

Surprisingly Tac and the units back in Price didn't come up to visit us so much with each fresh IED ambush or mine-strike, which left us more and more vulnerable on the front. With increasing regularity the ANA resupply patrols got hit, and arms were lost, and then legs, and then whole company commanders vaporized and Ranger vehicles ripped in two.

Up in Sangin the Grenadiers were taking casualties of our own – Guardsman Downes had been a great favourite in the Ribs, and the mood in camp was sour. We patrolled all the way back to Shorabak with a compassionate case of our own – Sgt Cooper's mother had died, which was somehow worse because you prepared yourself for the possibility of losing mates out here, but not for losing family while you were away. The flags were still at half-mast and tempers short and we were barred entry to dinner until we'd shaved. We put the pettiness down to the misplaced frustration of the proud soldiers stuck in the rear watching their young guys take the hits and unable to help. We wore our beards as proud badges of how long we'd spent away from the comforts of a camp, the running water and the safety, but it all seemed so petty in light of the casualties, so we showered and shaved and left defiant horrible moustaches and scoffed seconds and thirds of the rich puddings we'd earned.

We pushed back out to the line, freshly shaven and thinking ourselves lucky to be escaping camp bullshit until we got back to the patrol base and the temperature nudged up to unbearable. As we sprawled through the hellish midday hour

Amber 63 (before shaving) back in Shorabak over a month after we set off for the 'week-long' Operation Silicon; we only stayed one night. Left to right: Sgt Thornborrow, me, LCpl Price (on bonnet), Gdsm Lloyd, LSgt Rowe (kneeling), CSgt Yates.

like sweaty lizards, unable to move for the oppressive heat, we'd have gladly shaved our whole bodies to be back under the air-con. An ominous storm blew in from Pakistan, a welcome drop in temperature and the ANA sheltering in the sangars like old ladies at the bus stop watched bemused as we greeted the downpour like primitive revellers and danced naked in the cool rain. But the dust storms that followed had us waking up blind and deaf, choking on the crap that hung in the air so thick you couldn't see your rifle in your hands and pointless stag.

For days everything was either annoying or depressing; either too hot or too wet or too dusty. The Taliban started using human shields, ambushing the patrols from buildings which they wouldn't let the families leave, which the poor old WFRs didn't realize till it was too late and the air-strikes had already been called in. Of course, the next morning they were back in FOB Price, licking their own wounds. We pushed out with our ANA to reassure and help, and collateral damage was no longer a trite phrase but the bloodstains on our trousers and the heartbreaking kids we patched up as best we could before sending them back down the towpath to the hospital.

The moments of lightness were fewer and further between. We caught one of the 'terps shagging a donkey through the night-vision goggles, but when you thought about it, it wasn't actually that funny. A desperate plea came forward from the planning cell in Gereshk for help with their mapping. Back at HQ they're trying to reassess the valley, so I'm called in with my 'expert local knowledge' to tell them which cluster of houses is actually a village, and which still exist, and what the hell do the people who live there call them. I'm wondering how these monkeys can have been monitoring our battles if they don't even know where we are on the very maps that they're making for us when I'm suddenly struck in my weariness by a marvellous and mischievous sense of opportunity and decide to make my own contribution to this quasi-colonial nonsense that's going on. So having given them all the real and valid info I have I pick an innocuous and unnamed village which we pass through from time to time, full of friendly hash farmers and cool kids racing donkeys in the fields, and leave a little mark of my own on the map.

I imagine they might not be that impressed up at Kandahar with the antics, but it's the least tribute I can think of to the girlfriend I miss more than I've the time or the balls to tell her, and the boys all thinks it's hilarious that next time the sun breaks out the ISAF patrols will be rolling through the village of Jen-i-Deen.

But the days stayed dark, shrouded in stifling dust-cloud, and it might be memory playing tricks, but now it seemed like everything was building up to the inevitable. We'd endured Afghan casualties, friendly casualties, Grenadier casualties and now civilian casualties, and with the weather unrelenting dark and oppressive it was only a matter of time before the company itself, according to one commanding officer 'the luckiest call sign in Helmand', took its first casualty.

★★★

In retrospect, it was always going to be Kuks.

It was always going to be Kuks because he was a friend. Like Will and Worthers, like Marlow and Harrison had been before and Fergus and Mark before them, forged in something elusive out on the long patrols, greater than the sum of shared banter and time passing in-jokes and professional jargon and our own narrowed tour perspective – Kuks was a friend. He was too obvious, too young and dashing and hot-headed in the heat of the scrap. Too determined to do everything as well as he could and too devoted to his boys and his Afghans to accept my offer of a lazy lift half a click down the road where we were all meeting up with Tac for a quick orders session before the next patrol.

We were getting the brews on outside Patrol Base Centre when a massive thud rocked the track and all heads turned back in the direction of the billowing black smoke, unmistakably an IED, and while the fresh R&R replacements began crawling around on the floor in the vehicles there's just a flash, and we knew instinctively and began to charge back to the scene with the nervous call of 'casualty T2' echoing on the net and the faces of the boys around white with the shock against the mud and dust of the blast.

In the immediate aftermath the image was strangely unaffecting because it's such a cliché and we've seen it all before, the posture and the gore and the burned and ripped combats is such a perfect replica set of Robert Capa stills that I'm unmoved as we whack Kuks full of morphine and I clutch his hand as we wait for it to kick in with the smell of cordite thick in the air with the sweat and the piss.

It wasn't the sight of an injured friend, but his voice, that hit me. So instantly recognizable as the voice I'd exchanged daily pleasant abuse with for the last three months, but only under unfamiliar layers of fear and pain, in need of a reassurance that we give without knowing. He's a big fucker, but light as a feather between three of us pumping panicked adrenalin and we try and keep him awake as we hump him back by getting him to recite the alphabet and repeating meaninglessly, 'You'll be OK, you'll be OK.'

The Chinook which comes thundering into the hastily prepared landing site turns out not to be the air ambulance but a diverted R&R flight, and I'll never forget the look of horror on the face of the young, possibly pretty, journalist who's sitting in the back in gimpy blue helmet, unsure why her flight home has just dropped into the Green Zone, where the air is still a-rattle with fire from the ANA on the cordon, when suddenly the reality of Helmand charges on to her lap as four sweating, swearing, emotional soldiers drop a bleeding, naked, morphine-babbling black man on her brand new hiking boots.

I scream his vitals over the roar of the rotors and point the medic towards the info card we've stuck on his chest. The on-board medic gives me the thumbs-up, and I freeze, unsure of what comes next because there's nothing more to do.

The medics have obviously seen it before and give me a well-meaning shove off the back of the tailgate as the chopper takes off again and I'm left sat in a heap in the grass, wondering what the hell just happened. Afterwards, like squaddies, we dissolve into laughter at the memory of the sight of his cock, flapping in the downdraught as we load him up, but the merriment is forced and Elastoplast-thin over the emptiness.

We got word the following day that Kuks was fine, already up in Selly Oak and wouldn't lose his leg, but there was no looking back. The mortar shell, dug into the side of our track under cover of the dust storms, had destroyed the last sense of innocent adventure in the project which had already been systematically dented with each ANA soldier we had lost and each casualty taken elsewhere by someone else. It was impossible in those hours and days afterwards to rationalize the sight and sound and smell of losing a friend. Anger and questioning and also relief that he was fine and guilty relief that it wasn't you and even for fleeting sick-making inexplicable but unavoidable seconds envy that he was back home with the cool story and the cool scar and perhaps if you worked out the odds we were more vulnerable the longer we spent out there and the married men trying to stop themselves wondering if things hadn't got sufficiently silly that a 'blighty' wasn't the way forward.

We lost our first friend.

***

As they must, things start again. A camera crew arrive from Shorabak, Ben and Robin from BBC's *Panorama*, in for the long haul, a proper documentary not some in-out get the juicy quote and stitch up the boys job, so we decide to give them the benefit of the doubt. Of course, they were expecting Kuks, had been assigned to Amber 62 and promised the glorious multicultural Army so it's not clear who's more bemused, them or CSM Edgell – the old-school Bristolian who's stepped up to command 62 now that Kuks has gone.

Edgell would have made priceless TV if you could have understood his west-country drawl. In the muted muddle after Kuks had been hit we'd tried to keep an eye on the guys who'd been first on scene, make sure they weren't more shaken up than they appeared. Young Barnes was smiling, but his hand, the hand that had held Kuks' tight as we loaded him up, was still shaking. I'd asked him if he was OK and he nodded, but said he felt a bit numb . . .

'Do some press-ups then, you fucking HOMO!' had been Edgell's reassuring contribution. He'd meant it compassionately.

Ben and Robin had arrived in time for the shaping ops for the next big push. If the recent casualties we'd taken told us anything it was that we'd been resting after the success of Op Silicon and that the Taliban were getting stronger, bolder. Op Tufaan was to be the response. The next big thrust up the valley, Op Silicon, Phase 2. It would have been nice to have some of the assets that supported Phase 1, but someone in their infinite wisdom had decided we could do the same again with half the men.

Against twice the enemy.

The BBC's first patrol out with us was a little prelude to the op itself to sniff around the FLOT – the forward line of own troops. Some of the credit the *Panorama* guys have is instantly used up when we step off and Ben is wearing a bright-red daysack, in the *Green Zone*. 'Is it usually this quiet?' they ask seconds before the contact flares up and RPGs boom overhead.

The ANA officers who've only come on patrol because they saw the cameras charge to the back of the column before we've even started laying down return fire. The lead Afghan scout is shot in the neck, and as his head flips out like a Pez dispenser Robin wonders aloud and urgently if we might not pull back. The grizzly moustachioed Marine visiting from Kabul is itching to get up front and has unsheathed an enormous knife from somewhere in sharp contrast to the young Intelligence Corps officer who's accidentally found herself attached to the wrong unit and couldn't have been more at the bottom of the ditch if she tried. I want to tell them to get the camera ready, sit back and enjoy what's about to follow, but the cracking of rounds overhead and excited buzzing in our ears would drown it out, so I just laugh and point upwards.

The *DUDE* callsigns are out today and sure enough within minutes of our call F18 Super Hornets off the USS *Eisenhower* way back in the Persian Gulf roar into view, jaw-droppingly low, almost touchable, deafening overhead, and even with the ground spitting around us we smile and wave – the angels on our backs.

As I ran back up the track to save time and was sent sprawling by a last-minute dive underneath an oncoming RPG I suddenly and with crystal clarity remembered watching *Blood Diamond* in the Coronet on one of my last nights in the country. Not the best film to take a nervous girlfriend to, but it was out of genuine conviction, not to calm her down, that I had scoffed then at the fighting scenes and the Hollywood notion that Leonardo DiCaprio could look down the street and dodge the oncoming RPGs. The CSM's last-minute scream warned me off, but I could distinctly see the fucker as I hurled myself down and then bounced back up off the incredible adrenalin surge with a roar of *fuck me!* and what the CSM told me, half-despairingly half-thankfully, was a beaming grin of manic proportions.

It was three days later that I woke in a cold sweat, crippled by fear and the memory of the RPG round. Field Marshal Slim had reckoned that courage was like a bank account and, commanding the 14th Army against the Japanese in Burma, he should have known. Everyone is born with a certain amount of credit, hopefully never having to make a withdrawal. The things was that you couldn't check your balance, didn't know when you might be about to bounce a cheque, when yesterday's bravest man was about to go overdrawn and think 'fuck this'. The idea that everything that had passed to that point had been luck, that all the tall tales and well-earned envious REMF glances were nothing more than an accident of us having been in the right places at the right times (or the wrong places at the wrong times depending on how you looked at it) and none of us yet having run out of courage we hadn't earned or built up, but had simply been born with.

Which made me wonder the next day whether suicide bombers counted as brave.

★★★

You didn't need any experience or training or instinct to know that 1 July was going to be different when freshly promoted CSM Edgell burst in screaming and covered in blood to shatter the morning peace of the tent. Like the shake in Sgt Dragon's voice that told me somehow that Kuks was the casualty when they'd been blown up the week before, you knew even through the mumbled shouts of 'suicide bomb' and chaos of the crash-out that the worst had occurred. Barely conscious outside, half of Amber 62 were blackened and pumping arterial bleeds all over the med tent but there was barely time to stare in horror as we flew out towards the ominous column of smoke on the road outside the camp.

Then there was too much time to stare in horror at the crumpled shell of the WMIK and dead Sgt Wilkinson and the scattered piecemeal remains of the bomber, and even Martin's emotions were up to rage-spitting point as he demanded of the uncomprehending 'terp whether the bastard would be going to paradise. The finer points of Islam were not for debating on the nervous cordon through the hot afternoon and the sickly sweet smell amid the remains and the tentative work of the evidence-gathering team who come and scoop up legs and bits of head which are all that remain of the bomber, and the ANA, almost as though they're trying to compensate for the violation of hospitality, shooting wildly at anything that moves.

Peeping out from shops and round the corners of curtains that hang in front of doorways, Gereshk knew that the happy few months of ANA soldiers shopping in the *badr* and British patrols strolling down to the river were over, that it was warning shots and nervous over-reaction from here on in. Even as we'd been pushing the security bubble out, someone had pricked it from inside. There's no precedent for how to feel, no convention for this except surely it's inappropriate to feel as hungry as both the CSM and I guiltily admit to each other we later felt, fighting the unwholesome barbeque cravings. Kuks was joined in hospital by his entire callsign, and with days to go before Tufaan began, Amber 62 had simply disappeared.

The Longest Day

D-day of Tufaan was to be 7 July, which would become for all of us who were there the longest day, but for me it started before that, perhaps on 1 July, when Gereshk lost its magic

The last thumbs-up. Cheery scenes like this, common for the first couple of months we operated around Gereshk, ceased after the first suicide attack – Gereshk, June 2007.

and innocence once and for all in the ball of fire and death of the first but not last suicide bomber, perhaps even back in the last days of June, long, endless summer evenings back home and festivals and parties and weddings while we were scrapping forward yet again and not only noticing but filming the new intensity of the fight.

We could have been distracted by the hasty reshuffling of personnel, by the sense that something was wrong in Orders that we couldn't quite put our finger on until we remembered that we didn't have three platoons any more, just two, and LCpl Mizon, the lone survivor of his team. Could have been distracted by the cameras rolling in the background as Martin talked us through the impossible scale of the task ahead, but for once the firm set of Mizon's jaw was not a pose but determination, shared by everyone in the room, that after the events and casualties of the last few days, however hard the op was going to be we would take it.

We could have been distracted by the pure Shakespeare of the massive reparations *shurah* that some idiot timetabled for just before the op kicked off – genuine high politics and millions of dollars changing hands between aggrieved parties and big-cheese GoA and ANA officials, and us snoozing at the back of the hot room while the rude mechanicals prepared the feast next door and our own ANA ran around on the cordon giggling like schoolchildren because there's a note from Karzai, and Afghan media are in town.

We could have been distracted by the arrival of the Number Two Company forward elements, new rising-star company commander in the seat and Mark in town and suddenly in the middle of a shit-storm, having promised his fiancée he'd be flying a desk in Bastion for three months. Could have been distracted by the insult of our 'relief' arriving just in time to hunker down in our comfy cot beds and secure patrol bases and wave us off on the mother of all deliberate ops, but we weren't. We were too focused on the absences, the names scrubbed off the zap-cards; no Kuks, no Shad, no Mac, recovering back in Selly Oak. Of course, no Sgt Wilkinson. No CSgt Yates, back in Shorabak with a knock he picked up on what should have been Amber 63's last casy patrol forward before a rest spell in camp. No LCpl Price, grinning as we dropped him off for R&R.

We could have been distracted sleeping on the dirt outside the patrol base, unceremoniously kicked out of our castle while we snatched our last rest before the big push. Could have been distracted by the ominous and familiar open-ended nature of the op, the 'what-next?' of reaching the new LoE, pushing the front line another 10 miles up through the thick

Green Zone, and then what, with only the agonizingly week-close promise of my own R&R to sustain an easy 'let's-cross-that-bridge-when-we-come-to-it' mentality.

And then Fuck Me!

Groggy in the three a.m. dark, stepping off at the rear of the swelled and now unwieldy *kandak*, Amber 61 in the lead boosted by Rob's return and all the new attachments which had beefed us up almost enough to cover for the missing Amber 62. Us moping at the back with the instantly useless quad-bike, stuck in the ditch on the line of departure so the casevac plan had gone to shit before we've even started. Kakaran was familiar as the light came up, painfully anticipating a slow and heavy day but maybe too calm as the BBC remember *is it always this quiet?* Thirsty and aching before morning with the stop-start, up-down at the back of the snake and we almost might have been back on the long Sandhurst insertion tabs, willing the mind to wander in time-chasing daydreams to bring the leave weekend a step closer.

Then there was a surreal pause, just after we'd switched the lead rolls and we'd echeloned through Will and Rob and taken up the forward positions, just after the ANA had become jumpy and the i-com was chattering ominously and a few sporadic shots which might or might not be ours rang out. A fifteen-minute calm as the camera pushed up greedily and Azim and I stood tight to the wall in earnest discussion about the next move which was probably neither the time nor place but there's unmistakable movement in the ditch, so he slams a speculative RPG into the treeline.

And off we go.

Tight in on the wall with fire coming in from the front and side and the BBC looking unhappy but the ANA whooping with the release of all the morning's built-up tension and boredom and I'm laughing with Sgt Davis and Sgt T that the call on the net is once again *Amber 63, CONTACT WAIT OUT*. We decided to push straight into the compounds 80 metres forward. The Taliban obvious now, popping up and down in the ditch in front with obligingly beaded skull-caps sparkling in the rising sun and setting such a pattern that I was conscious even as I watched one through my sights get up, adjust his position with the RPG and then fall back in the ditch. So immediately after I twitch the trigger that the two events are no longer distinct but part of one chain in which to think it and will it is for it to happen and I know in that instant, even while noting how unlikely it should have been for a captain to find himself popping away like this, we'll be all right today.

Perhaps it's this feeling, as certain as if some fairy godmother had assured it, that keeps the mind clear from the nagging thought that we're doing all the things I'd scoffed at in training, all the full-frontal, lung-bursting assaults of yesteryear which I'd never signed up to in my peacekeeper daydreams, and that the enemy are right there. Perhaps it's just the kick of fixing bayonets and then waiting for the point of fire to start up from our left and the 51s before breaking cover and charging with the shouts and screams we always thought were token but turn out to be primordial, but suddenly we're out in the open and there are bullets flying everywhere.

Out in the open, but completely alone and with no time to stop or think or wonder as Lloydy tripped under the I-Law and went sprawling and we've still 40 metres to get to the next wall and cover. The ANA, after all their brilliant and match-winning performances of the last few months, finally lived down to expectations and calmly sat back to watch their idiot mentors – foreigners with comfy beds and beautiful girlfriends and lives back home so what the fuck are we doing out here anyway? – charge through the enemy positions.

Maybe they just decided to stay with the cameras, but there was no time for contemplation or recrimination as the Taliban further back had just withdrawn to the next compound along and so, while catching our breath, we called in the Apaches and let someone sitting down do a bit of the hard work.

Except, of course, that the blue smoke we threw and the grid references we gave in the midst of the confusion weren't enough for the pilot who started ramming 30mm cannon fire right across our toes, and with energy I didn't realize I had I'm screaming 'CHECK FIRE!' down the net to a suitably nervous and apologetic-sounding Tac. The callsign had regrouped, and at least a handful of the ANA had joined us behind the outer wall of the compound, and there was a wonderful slapstick moment as the next round of blue-on-blue cannon fire from the Apache came in even closer with everyone lined up behind me charging into my back to push round the corner of the wall, except I wasn't budging because round the corner there was fire coming in the opposite direction from the enemy so we really had nowhere to go and concertinaed like the Keystone Cops. The Taliban in the depth positions had us pinned down and unable to consolidate our current one, and it was only after recommending a Hellfire strike that Lloydy observed with bleak humour that if the last two efforts have been wrong, how did we know the pilot was not going to drop the missile on us as well. I shrugged; we won't be in any position to complain if he does.

The roar and crack-thud of the missile coming in, sure enough, on top of our position, was felt rather than heard. My first thought was that we're all dead as the thick stone wall started to collapse on top of us, and then the ANA were running around screaming like madmen and there was dust and tingling everywhere and mouthed and silent shouted *FUUUUUUUUCKS!* At least one of the guys reacted pretty

234

Calling for air support from the cover of the ditch before assaulting a compound. The ANA soldiers on the road were high as kites by this stage, which was probably why they were more interested in playing with a donkey than the fire that had the rest of us pressed down – Kakaran, July 2007.

badly and started ripping off his kit, screaming up at the Apache pilot and anyone within range between firing off massive bursts towards the enemy positions, still untouched 100 metres further forward which, once we've calmed him down, seemed to have had the effect that the choppers couldn't. It was the shockwave and the deafness and the winded gasping for air which slowed down time and what I couldn't believe is that, despite the rantings of the ANA and a few burst eardrums and cuts and bruises, we were all in one piece. From within the compound we could hear voices and movement, and everything sped up again as we primed grenades to finish off the remaining enemy, who were presumably waiting for us to clear the rooms, and at the last minute the same feeling I had just before the contact kicked in and we opted for a green instead of red clearance and burst through the door.

I'll always be more haunted by the sight of what *could* have been round the corner than the actual screaming and terrorized family huddled in the rubble of the missile strike. Streaked with tears and covered in dust like shattered ghosts they were so alive that I was gasping with relief that the fifty-fifty calls were good. The thick walls which somehow saved our backs somehow saved their fronts, and I'm thanking I don't know what for the 500-pounder we *didn't* drop which would have killed us all, for the 10 metres north the missile *didn't* land, which would have killed the section, the 10 metres west it *didn't* come in, which would have killed the family, or the red clearance drills we *didn't* use, which would have had me even now staring down the point of my bayonet at a mess of women and children and horrific narrowly avoided carnage of my own doing, so for all the tears and screams I can only stand there wildly and giddily thankful.

It had been the classic Taliban gambit of occupying the compound and forcing the family to stay in as insurance and then, if we'd killed one of them by mistake, propaganda. Darkly, in nights and daydreams long after the battle, the haunting image of what might have been is far more difficult to dispel than the otherwise perfectly ghastly reality we're still slap in the middle of.

Tac came galloping in with the cameras and the rest of the ANA. Suitably keen to make up for things, the Apaches didn't make the same mistake four times, and the USAF and mortars joined the party so the Taliban in the forward positions got a healthy dose while we consolidated and tried to calm down the family who've been caught in the middle of a really, really bad day, which was easier said than done with an entire ANA *kandak* pinned down in their compound. The fierce battle ebbed and flowed for the next few hours, with each attempt we made to break out and forward drawing a terrific weight of fire from the positions to the front even while we hammered the Taliban and watched and listened to them taking casualty after casualty. Martin set up in the cool shade of the vines and the guys starting to go down in the heat were stacking up worryingly near the well as we tripped uncomfortably over each other's toes, and I was keen to try another break-out when we realized we'd used all the water for the injured guys and they weren't getting any better.

So we broke out to the rear instead to find somewhere safe enough in the bedlam for the IRT to land. It's a thankless mission in the heat, whoever carries the casualties almost bound to go down themselves with heat exhaustion, and even the medic, having spent a heroic few hours charging from man to man, had collapsed with the horrible pallor on his face, and the thermometer said 106, which means *hurry the fuck up!* The CSM pulled his casevac party out, and the promise of water being brought in on the chopper kept us going, but when the guys returned with the water, there were only three of them, and we were suddenly so down on numbers, having lost a couple more to the heat on the extraction, that, heartbreaking though it was, our only realistic option was to pull back and regroup.

Pull back from the building we'd fought into and held for four torrid hours, pull back past the positions we'd charged through that morning and, with the over-watch of the British units on the high ground in the north who had done next to nothing all day, pull wearily all the way back to the start-line. Pull back over ground we'd lost a third of the Company group taking, pull back over ground we'd been shot and blown up by both enemy and our own side alike on, pull back in one steady, demoralized trudging hour over what it had taken us twelve to take. The faces of the Welsh Guards mortar lads in the first patrol base we stumble back into told us how bad we looked, like the moment when a veteran of LSgt Alexander's years and grit stumbled only 500 metres short of the harbour and, looking around hopelessly, dropped the ammunition he'd been carrying, and I'd never understood 'command legs' as much as when I wordlessly picked it up and carried on even while every fibre in me was too exhausted to move. Approaching the vehicles we'd left behind that same morning, Martin summed pretty much everything up in his hilariously angry response to the repeated buzzing questions of the Number Two Company sentries.

'Amber 21 this is Amber 60A. I've just had the hardest day of my life. Fuck off and leave us alone. OUT!'

Despatches from the Battle of Adin Zai

Before Sandhurst the joke was that they gave you the Bible and *Stalingrad* to read and told you that only the latter was important. All they should have given anyone was Michael Herr's *Despatches*, which, quite apart from being the best writing on war, period, was probably as culturally influential as anything written in the second half of the twentieth century. This guy *was* the Vietnam War; in fact, this guy was war.

I think what thrilled the sensitive souls was not the gory hellishness of it all – the crazy-eyed LURPs (Long Range Unsupported Reconnaissance Patrols) guys who thought collecting ears was for girls and constructed entire Vietcong mannequins out of body parts – but the way the further you got into the war, into the jungle, into the heart of darkness, the more the scales of normality fell away.

Normal parameters were meaningless, rules didn't exist, time bent, and only the heat and exhaustion were real enough to remind you that this wasn't a dream sequence. The lost philosophers of the twentieth century missed a trick. Their world wasn't Parisian cafés but out here in the Green Zone, where signifier and signified had become so detached that we didn't know what was going on any more. As Lloydy intoned with Bill Murray comic deadpan brilliance into his own video diary (the actual journos long since scuttled back to camp to assess how much they actually wanted the footage we were madly scrapping for) – *Day 86 in the Big Brother House and no fucker will give us a break.*

Everything after 7 July became a blurred trip, the days and hours and minutes just interludes of snatched sleep and fire fights and the odd few pages of Ayn Rand to grasp vainly at a recognizable world of books and leisure, counting down to R&R, which seemed like something that would never come, could never come. The next day we pushed up on a different axis and occupied the quiet compounds in Rahim Kholay, eyebrows raised in silent amazement at the complex defences abandoned by the Taliban, defences that no way in hell would we have ever been able to fight through. Just to be sure, the Engineers blasted mouse-holes in the walls of whichever compound was to be *chez nous* that night, and, too tired to take in our surroundings, we flopped in the cool, dark rooms during the day and like lizards on the warm stone roof at night, the stag rota meaningless, with no one really asleep and the defensive battle the WFRs were finally fighting forward all the night-time entertainment the insomniacs needed.

We pushed forward on a reckless ambush, picking a fight just to see what was out there. The doctrine called this 'recce by force', and it took to a new extreme the sense that we were actually doing things we'd laughed at in training. The Taliban recce screen was a series of dogs chained in the compounds, somewhere out in the dark human sentries

Strain and fatigue beginning to show on the faces of Gdsm Lloyd (left) *and LCpl Mizon – Adin Zai, July 2007.*

monitoring our progress by the progression of barking. So we gave in completely to the jungle 'Nam fantasies and advanced noiselessly up the waist-deep irrigation ditches. Nearing the objective, we occupied a long-deserted hut, and suddenly I was face to snout with a nightmare vision of a grizzled mongrel Saint Bernard, a huge snarling Beethoven with myxomatosis who smelled of rabies and bit me in the arse as I turned to warn the others, but we were too close to the enemy to risk the clear report of a gunshot, so I smacked him in the face with my rifle butt, and he's the luckiest dog in Helmand to be spared the pistol execution that's almost routine for these Taliban scouts.

And it was a good thing we saved the ammo when the forward ANA stumbled on the inevitable and, as was the plan all along, our tiny cowboy patrol fired everything we'd got and charged back down the river like naughty schoolboys as all the fire support that had been sitting silent and invisible all the while up on the ridge opened up and over our retreating and laughing heads, pours UGL and .50 cal and GMG, and it will be another night of no sleep, slow fags and coming down feeling like the World War Two mayhem-raising vagabonds we all wished we were and hoped we look like.

Unfortunately it was all merely putting off the inexorable next big push, 7 July Mark II, which we knew would be like Mark I, only worse. Martin returned from Orders with HQ up on the hill and announced that we were to clear eighty-odd compounds in forty-eight hours while the better-equipped, better-manned units up on the hill would take on a dozen. If we hadn't already, it was about this time that we all began thinking of ourselves and the ANA as one unit, together and distinct from the other 'British' units, who always seemed to be on the flank or just behind.

We were ambushed on the line of departure, but there's absolutely nothing to do but charge on, roll through compound after compound, through the bodies, with no time to work out whether they're the guys who seconds before were firing at us or the guys from last night's raid or the night before or maybe even stiffs from last week.

Propriety went out of the window at about the same time we barely stopped to listen to Will call in his own casualty status on the radio: 'Amber 60 this is Amber 61B, I've been shot in the leg, applying tourniquet now, OVER.' The boys wolfing down the Taliban breakfast we'd discovered in the courtyard of the next compound we took, ignoring the blood trails and corpses of the guys we'd disturbed. We were too hungry and it was only nine o'clock and we'd another forty-six hours at least of this. The air-strikes which were our oxygen, the only thing which bought us the time and breathing space to bounce from compound to compound, coming in so close that we could actually see the 1,000lb bombs come smacking in. From somewhere, one of the ANA sergeants found a rainbow umbrella, an enormous, bright Joseph's-Technicolor-Dreamcoat of a thing with which, noticing the sweat I've got on, he follows me around for the rest of the day, a walking parasol man attracting fire from all directions. But the gesture was too kind and we'd gone past the point where that sort of thing was going to make a difference, and there's no point in wondering why Will got shot correctly crawling up the bun-line and I was fine walking around all day under a multi-coloured target. Our entire lives, our entire world, had filtered down to crossing off compound after compound in our progression through the objectives, and when night drew in we literally stopped where we are, put sentries out and collapsed in the dirt.

Somewhat unorthodox parasol – Operation Tufaan, July 2007.

The next morning it was gone. The valley was quiet and, although the ANA do their best to gnarl things up, initially refusing to fight and then accidentally shooting each other in a farcical replay of yesterday's start, we moved forward relentlessly. Morning turned to afternoon and then, as certain as the tide and without a shot being fired for hours, we were at the end-line, job done, half the company gone and two days till R&R and nothing, nothing left to give. Nothing left to do except leave Rob on the hard shoulder by the river and push north to link up with the WFRs for congratulations and tea and medals, except that half-way up the road the Taliban, quiet all day, suddenly revealed why.

Martin and Tac had led off and made it to the northern link-up, about 400 metres further up the track, Rob and Amber 61 were about a kilometre down behind us in the hard shoulder, and just as we were passing a couple of huts the ambush opened up on us with a ferocity unprecedented even after the last few days. And I don't know why we climbed, like the stupid but cheerleader-fit girls in the horror movies who back up and up to the attic even though we know they're going to get stabbed, but there's something instinctive about scrabbling on to the roofs of the two huts to get a better position to fire back into the treeline which had suddenly erupted 50 metres away on the flank. Once we were there, of course, we were stuck there and nothing for it but to fight from our precarious roofs through hour after hour after hour. Eight British soldiers and thirty Afghans as day turns to night and the mortars and the artillery and the tank-busters and the 500-pounders and the 1,000-pounders pounded and pounded and pounded the treeline with even the French Mirages joining in, and every time an attack was repulsed and we were firing alarmingly down off the roof into the oncoming Taliban, every time there was a pause and the i-com registered more Taliban casualties, and this time surely they were broken, every time they started up again.

You couldn't hate an adversary like this. A slugger in an old-school boxing match, Queensberry rules out of the window, and we curse the rules that mean we can't just burn the bastards out, fire up the treeline with shake'n'bake and catch the carnage. Hit after brain-damaging hit and he won't go down, and we're reduced to individual heroics, LCpl Mizon running without a weapon the mad-dash ammo-resupply gauntlet up to where Tac were having the time of their lives, joined by the Czech SOG with the quad-bike-mounted AGS-17, *und you vant some help, ja*. It was strange to chat to Martin on the radio, an amazing calm and reassuring presence throughout the night, knowing that I could see him off to the flank but that with us stuck up on the roof we might as well be worlds apart.

Ten foot by ten, perched eight foot up, the creaking stone roof was our twelve-hour heaven and hell. We bombed and blasted and burned and shot the enemy and it wasn't until four in the morning and the first hints of a perfect mid-summer purple dawn that things were finally, finally quiet. The roof was ankle-deep in brass like some warlord's paddling pool, fag butts everywhere, and, sticky with the all-nighter and the numb sense of not really being in our bodies, we tentatively climbed down and had a sniff around.

And nothing but quiet and dawn and Martin on the radio saying he's coming down to link up with us, and the BBC are back and the CSM is grinning on his quad-bike that Sherlock and I were being sent back for R&R and to let the commanding officer know we're running on empty. Nothing but smiling like a loon, sprawled on the back of the quad like Martin Sheen flying out on the Huey, drinking in the sense that we've bust the icons and made our own, have taken and held the spray-painted, blasted walls of Adin Zai.

What was home after this?

16. vii. 2007 – Intermission
there are moments when the tone changes.

standing in the middle of the road for five baking hours surrounded by the spread carnage of the suicide bomber who ran into the rear vehicle and detonated 1.5kg of PE packed with 600 ball bearings. Not so much the pumping blood from Shadders' neck or the hollow feeling in the pit of the stomach which emptied instantly when we finally found the driver's body, thrown from the WMIK into a nearby sewer, and could only think of the blood and the charring and the fucking mortality. Sgt Dave Wilkinson had volunteered to come and give a hand at the sharp end because he was that kind of guy and a damn good soldier and in unimaginable seconds after being hit and the flaming WMIK careering into the shitty ditch which would probably be his ignominious corner of a foreign field, I can't imagine the thoughts of the rest of the boys in his wagon. I keep trying to get my head around this as we secure the scene and control the incident but you can't ignore the incongruous legs, thirty metres apart on either side of the road, the only tangible evidence of what remains of the cunt bomber except the sickening sweet smell of barbeque and faeces which he's martyred over the dual-carriageway. It's with almost detached curiosity that another hundred yards away I find what I assume to be a bit of head but which turns out to be jaw and beard – unshaved so it's a rushed and opportunist job and all the boys know that it's just a game of luck – front wagon vs. back wagon, morning vs. afternoon, chomping down junk food during the strange hunger, trying to shut out the image and smell when we finally get it all cleared up vs. already on the plane back to Birmingham.

so that's when the numbness kicks in and the streets of Gereshk are no longer strewn with biros and sweets tossed to the waving kids but filled with soldiers gripping white-knuckle tight on cocked and ready pistols, blasting warning shots at any fool stupid enough to come close, now that word has got around that the luckiest team in Afghanistan's luck finally ran out.

but it's such a bastard way of fighting that we're glad to push on with a big surge, there's a grim sense of determination, something uncomfortable but understandable in the thirst to get back out into the valley. Until it kicks off again and epic contact follows epic contact through grizzing hours of wilting heat, half days drenched in sweat as the company loses casualty after casualty, surrounded by Taliban, fighting break-out and carrying the poor bastard heat injuries over our backs as we cover our withdrawal with massive bombs and angry spitting Apaches and I'm thinking the whole time that surely this sort of thing went out with our grandfathers.

it's the moment when we launch an assault on the next compound, bayonets-fixed and old-school rules but our Afghan comrades have had enough so half-way across the murderous open ground I glance left and right and there's six of us alone to do the job.

or the moment when some idiot cowboy airman doesn't check his bearings and drops his missile on us, actually fucking ON US, and I'm screaming 'FUCKING CHECK FIRE'

246

down the net as he starts strafing us with 30mm cannon and someone has had enough and in the middle of the fight throws down his kit and stands up firing everywhere and nowhere and screaming 'fuck this shit, fuck it, fuck it fuck it' till one of the boys has to rugby tackle him down from the bullets whizzing round our heads and we calm him down again with Haribo and the soothing sight of the life-saving thank-fucking-God-for-those-boys yank F15 Strike Eagles zooming low overhead and pounding the enemy firing point.

and even then there's an exhilaration, so we all just laugh when *Panorama* decide we're too mad for them and they're not going to follow us any more and now ashen-faced, Ben and Robin who had casually name-dropped their 8 war zones and Sierra Leone and ambushes etc back in Price, look decidedly less keen to continue the interviews as the RPGs come hammering in again.

but when Will gets hit, shot in the leg in another bloody assault on another bloody push forward as the British regiments continue to take forever in the north and we curse them for bastard cowards on a shameless game of Operation 'Get behind the Afghans', that's the moment when I'm the last platoon commander left standing and all Will's stoic English brilliance – 'Am I going to lose my leg? Only, it's so much better having two' – can't quite compensate for the fact that the company is now down to less than half of what it was two months ago and there's no end in sight.

and i think that's when we start to lose it, when the message comes through on the radio that I'm being pulled out for R&R the next morning so get my kit ready – and we all roll around in hysterics because I have no kit and haven't had for the last 72 hours.

but when the CSM appears like St Christopher through the dawn still hazy with cordite and phos smoke I only feel hollow as I flop down into the trailer on the back of the quad-bike and watch the guys on the roof wave and slowly disappear as we pull away, unable to square the exhausting relief that I'm finally getting a break with the feeling that I should still be up there with them. And the *Panorama* boys reappear as we pass and joke that if I'm gone then there'll probably be no more trouble which I hope is true for the sake of the boys but which worries me as well because it's hardly the professional reputation you want to have.

but the showers are too good back at camp to continue giving a shit and the news comes through that we've dropped more bombs than anyone else in this bone country since the Paras rocked up in Helmand last year and given that we've now got a Pietersen-respectable cricket score in dead Taliban chalked up against our callsign it's probably time to give some other fuckers a couple of weeks to try and catch up.

so the tone has changed again, and finally not for the worse as my breathless reports to the commanding officer are heard and the boys get pulled out for a break only a few hours after I'm back in the now creepy camp full of clean and curious idiots who treat us like we need to be wrapped in cotton wool. It seems like for the moment the Taliban have at last had enough and meetings are arranged and new plans are in place and and and . . .

and I couldn't give a damn because I'm coming home and R and R are the two sweetest letters in the fucking alphabet.

Whiplash

Finally back in the UK on R&R, I was saved by the smoking ban.

CSgt Yates had been so affronted by the very idea of it, ashamed that his beloved, native Scotland had taken the lead, that he'd negotiated with the ANA for an extra brick of local snouts and out in the Green Zone we'd held a 'First of July Smokeathon'; Lloydy cruising through the last of his Lambert and Butler from home and the Afghans laughing at my pipe.

Back in the UK I couldn't have been more grateful to slip away from the suffocating noise and colour and smell of the dance floor downstairs at whichever predictably cool venue we were celebrating Newton and Brinnie's birthdays. If any-one was watching, worried – which they weren't except for the random, half-pretty American that Adcock was flirting with – thankfully they must only have thought I was smoking a bit more than usual.

The fact that Adcock was flirting with the American was really the only reason to engage her at all, politely making eye contact every now and again but really staring across the dark, red bar at people I'd rather be telling the gritty stories to, or wondering why I didn't really want to tell them at all to the few people who actually mattered. It was only when she picked me up for fiddling with the prayer beads that Marouf had given me when he came back from the hospital with his toe patched up and an apologetic smile which made me wonder if perhaps he hadn't shot his foot off on purpose after all, that I was completely back in the throbbing room.

I had to get out because the room seemed so incredibly hot and close and red and then blue and the music was so loud except that it shouldn't have been hot because it was hotter back out there and it shouldn't have been loud because the .50 cal was a damn sight louder and why was everyone so good-looking as I pushed up the stairs almost gasping for breath?

I couldn't do it because seventy-two hours earlier I'd been smoking from the same packet with Sherlock as we fired down from the roof on to the Taliban, who just wouldn't die through twelve hours of the ambush, which I just couldn't process. The cheers which go up as Max drops a favourite tune and everyone is dancing and merrily Friday-night-fucked in that carefree London summer way were to my ears the same cheers which the ANA whopped up as we dropped mission after mission long into the night.

We nearly got a taste of our own medicine when the pilot dropped a bomb on the compound we'd left minutes before. We just laughed, not that there was anything funny about it, but the release had to come from somewhere, and we were still rolling about on the roof when rounds started chipping off the stone again and Sherlock sighed like it was his turn to get the brews on and with a deafening burst, because I'm not expecting it, fired off most of a magazine at the cheeky buggers who've crawled back up to within 100 metres.

So I'm smoking out on the street somewhere inevitably in Shoreditch because I can't engage with these people. My people, the people I've been writing blueys to and whose throats I've been forcing myself down with each shrill e-mail like a Simple Minds ring-tone, 'Don't You Forget About Me'. I had even weighed up on the plane back from Kandahar the relative merits of appearing to be a little zapped by the whole homecoming thing, tried to work out whether the most effective ploy would be to sit a bit more quietly than usual in the corner and let the curious and surely by now respectfully impressed hordes come sympathetically to me. Hadn't bargained for not being able to control it at all, for simply not having the mental strength to deal with how quickly everything had changed, how quickly I was gratefully back in Jen's arms, exhausted on clean sheets, infamously sipping champagne in a Chelsea bath.

For three years I'd imagined the occasion when I could sit, garrulous and over-confident with booze, and spin real tales to the girls I wanted to fancy me even if I'd stopped fancying them and the boys I wanted to be jealous of me, just to get even. For three months I'd plugged into my headphones and jogged around Shorabak or lain swinging in the hammock staring up at the stars above the Helmand Valley, salivating for a cold drink and the familiar pattern of a night out that I'd really really earned. The hardest thing about getting what you want is knowing what to do with it.

I bolted from the bars. We'd been lonely and isolated out on the line but we were just as lonely and isolated surrounded by our nearest and dearest, stiff to the welcome-home hugs and honest wide-eyed questions, the shoulder-patting teasing of the guys, distant from those I'd missed being close to. Two nights ago we'd gone straight through on our roof, our entire world the muzzle of our rifles and the vast expanse of night around us with the A-10s snorting majestically in the dark and the violent orange flare of each fresh strike momentarily sparking up the open valley. There had been nothing all night but to get through to morning, no thought of sleep or hunger or anything but who was going on the next ammo run and Martin's calm reassurance on the net. Had we slept, I'd have dreamed of all my beautiful friends, open-ended nights of limitless possibility, a glorious lie-in and weekend papers with cold fresh juice and iced finger buns and sex for breakfast and the four a.m. music still ringing in my ears.

Now I had it, was in the middle of it, and all I could see was Sherlock, stood over me as time slowed with the deafening surprise of his latest burst in a picture of a Brecon nightmare; no helmet, no body-armour, stood upright on the roof silhouetted against the 'lum still popping up with his rifle jammed into his hip with one hand loosing huge bursts of automatic while lighting a fag with the other:

'Fucking hell, Sherlock!'

Even I had interjected, as much for the deafening as the wanton affront to all that the British Army held dear, and he'd looked down at me apologetically and dropped to the floor as if only just realizing his slackness. And then fished out another fag.

'Sorry, sir, I should have offered.'

★★★

Later, somewhere in a field in Cambridgeshire, Echo and the Bunnymen are playing, and I'm still imagining the D'n'B tent on fire from the schmoolie incident, which the revellers might or might not notice but probably wouldn't be good either way, but the rocket had sailed safely into a distant field and, panting, I survey the two a.m. weirdness around the lake. According to the song, nothing ever lasts for ever, but this weekend seems to be the exception as R&R, which I had thought would run by in terrifying fleeting seconds and spit me back out on to the line, has dragged.

Two weeks in and sure it all tasted good and smelled good and felt good, stumbling around with Adcock surrounded by the beautiful summer girls in shorts and wellies, but you still wanted to check the BBC website every few seconds to see what was going on, still hoped in every quiet moment that

Lloydy and LCpl Price and LCpl Mizon were kicking their heels back in Shorabak because, after all the build-up, it turned out that the thought of missing a scrap was worse than the three summers reality of missing the party.

I'd driven up to Selly Oak to visit Kuks and Will on the ward, thinking the guys would be jealous of my two weeks of R&R hedonism, but they were more gutted to be missing the scraps, and deep down I knew why.

Two weeks of R&R had taken on a mythical importance out on tour: the agonizingly closer we'd got to them, even as the intensity seemed to ramp up on purpose with their approach, the more we'd wanted them. The bitterest fights I'd seen were over who was going when and if you missed your flight out or fucked up your hire car or the RAF inevitably screwed the precious hours of your fourteen-day oasis because of their unionized tea-break system. R&R had been everything, and for two weeks of sensory overload you could see why but it was too much 0–60 or maybe 60–0, but either way the body couldn't take it, and you couldn't have relaxed anyway because you knew as soon as you did you'd be back in Brize and the flight which would drop you back into the alternative universe which was somehow where you felt you belonged.

And Echo and the Bunnymen played as I looked out over the giant party and could think only of the valley and wanted the fireworks to be air-strikes and the huge euphoric-trance drops to be the lift and surge of a scrap and I *had* walked there through rings of fire and *had* lived in dreams today but it was always wanting more than we could get and R&R had to come to an end because they were right, nothing ever lasts for ever.

★★★

253

Sat in Brize waiting for the flight didn't feel as bad as I thought it might have done, the two weeks didn't seem to have raced past as quickly as I had feared they would, and mostly I was too busy enjoying the double-takes my battered and faded helmet cover was drawing from the crowishly clean combated guys who were deploying out for the first time. Almost exactly a year earlier I had sat in the terminal at Basrah waiting to fly out of Iraq for the last time, sneaking envious glances at the similarly gnarled helmets of the big PWRR Fijians, whose boots and battered Warriors told of a slightly more exciting Telic than ours. By the time we were loading up I was almost looking forward to getting back into things.

It was at Kandahar with its hideous 200-man RSOI tents and lack of purpose in the air that the post-R&R depression kicked in. KAF a purgatory where we neither come nor go but where no effort is made to separate the latent joy of the outgoing bods from the hang-dog expressions of those going back in.

And when I arrive there's an amazing sense of calm in Shorabak, familiarity in the mosi-nets and, perhaps danger-ously given that there's two months of this to go, a sense that an anxious wait is at an end. The very temporary nature of R&R prevents us from completely giving in to it; hanging over the fortnight, stopping you from letting go, is the know-ledge that in fourteen days, then seven, then three, then two, then one, you've got to go back out again. Sitting in the briefing room receiving orders for the RiP with the Inkerman Company up in Sangin, gorging on buffalo wings in the American D-Fac for movie night, there was nothing to worry about any more.

I was back in.

Back In

Disaster struck as I was looking for the pay bloke in one of the huge huts at the back of the camp, peering gingerly through the improvised curtains and four-month intricate screens, delicately constructed between the established bed spaces of the real camp rats. I found LCpl Maskell, couldn't help but notice that he was watching *24* – and the next few days were a write-off.

It's a testament to how professionally chilled we had become in such a short time that no one seemed to notice as I disappeared into the DVD box-set, emerging only for meals and Black Forest gateaux and grateful that my return from R&R has coincided with a spell in camp to wean me off the rich culinary excesses of leave with the chef's incredible scoff rather than going cold-turkey out on the ground on rations. The reality is that we've nothing to do, and now that we've proved that, when there is something to do, we can do it, no one hassles us when there isn't.

Lying in bed, resisting the urge to send expensive text messages home because apparently someone's installed a mobile-phone detector and we're all supposed to have handed them in to be locked away, I tried to remember previous days lost to *24*, Jack-filled hours of my life I'll never get back, bored of the beeping and the inevitable next double-cross but somehow not able to stop watching.

In Baghdad it had been during the handover, an antidote to Piers' awesome stories of Helmand, which just took even more shine off our finishing Iraq tour. Glum because I was going home before everyone else, kicking heels in the transit bunk and watching prep for the patrols which I knew the second I left would flare up excitingly in a way they hadn't while I had been around.

Before that it had been on guard, nothing else to do but lounge on the sofas in t-shirts and shorts pretending we'd just been on or were just going on a run, seeing if it was possible to squeeze an entire series into a forty-eight-hour guard. (It was as long as no one bothered to do the rounds, check on the sentries or any of that crap so patently less important than finding the triggering device.) The trick was to skip the updates, the *previously*s and the obvious ad-break moments, letting them run through only to dash to the night-tray and grab another round of scampi fries, which by the end of our public duties stint we instinctively knew contained an average of sixteen per packet.

The first time had been in Brecon, as if we didn't already have little enough spare time on that course. Foolishly thinking I could pass the long evenings with an episode a night from Si Greenman's box-set and then getting sucked so far in I missed a whole week of lectures in a sleepless zombie trance, watching slides of the Assault on Longdon or Routine in Defence and pretending to nod while wondering what the hell Tony was up to and where Kim was. The beat-up exercises unbearably between seasons two and three, and I had to make up for lost time when we got back in, propping my laptop up on a chair and watching while soaking off the Salisbury Plain grime in the bath, which should have demonstrated a brilliant infantry officer understanding of the value of concurrent activity but which just wound-up the DSM and health and safety.

Everything in the world had happened since then, and nothing had changed. There I was lying between two empty bed spaces, Will and Kuks' stuff stripped down and sent to join them in Selly Oak, and I should have been wondering who would have called that play but instead was marvelling at Jack's resistance to torture.

It wasn't until the Captain flew in from his recce of the FOBs we'd be occupying in Sangin and our chat after orders over brews and more gateaux in the mess that I realized I'd been lonely. What little Junior Officers' Reading Club we had had been blown up, literally, and I realized how much I wanted to be sitting around throwing stones with the guys. R&R had been like the Korean version of the afterlife in which heaven and hell are both identical, lavish banquets, only everyone has 3-foot-long chopsticks; in hell everyone is starving because they can't feed themselves, in heaven it's a party because they've realized they have to feed each other. Surrounded by everyone I wanted to see and utterly unable to engage with any of them, and as another nuclear disaster is averted in LA, I realize that the most real and honest conversations I've had in months are with Sgt T or CSgt Yates and the boys.

The thought hit me: what if I'll only ever be able to have real and honest conversations with the boys in future? What if an invisible curtain has come down between me and all the people and things I thought I held close, what if the numbness of R&R was not temporary but permanent and after putting bleeding Kuks on the back of the IRT, the batting order of the marriage XI will never seem important again?

I load up the i-Pod and jog it off round the perimeter. But, I'm almost pulled up, gasping for breath with the sudden counterpoint *déjà fait* shock of jumping the ditches along the back fence. Barely four months ago and in the same clothes listening to the same tunes our afternoon routine was to acclimatize with a jog along this same route – keeping fit with earnest sincerity, conditioning ourselves for the scrap we hoped and knew was coming. The tunes had been per-fect then for the bloodthirsty daydreams, what we would encounter and how well we would react through the slow build-up of 'My My My' to the bridge and the action and the imagined bloody fire fight.

Waiting to go up to Sangin after R&R, I'd done it. All the things I'd imagined doing, all the questions I'd wanted answered had been answered. We'd even engineered the fucking tunes so that we'd pounded the ambush routes behind Gereshk with the right beats in the background. There should have been no more to imagine, nowhere else to go, there should have been peace.

But the daydreams are all too troubling, as bloodthirsty as they had ever been.

I put the violent jogging fantasies down to the frustration at having missed Op Chakush. I'd been spared the guilt of leaving for R&R because I'd had a mission – get the boys pulled out – and it had been successful, and I had known that, as I was flying out of the country, they were spending their first night back in Shorabak in a long time. I could deal with being missed out of the end of op photos, dirty poses of the crew who captured Adin Zai, because we'd always know who'd taken it and held it in the first place.

But weeks later, while I'd been prancing around a field, the boys had been crashed out on Chakush and scrapping hard all over again. The close-up videos of US Apache run after run pouring down fire into positions only yards to the front, and the strained smiles of the ragtag bunch thrown together to crash out in Chinooks, told me that it had been a decent fight. As much as it meant for Sgt T and Sgt Gillies to say that they wished I'd been there, it didn't make it any better to have missed the party.

In the week before we deployed out for the two months that would see us through to the end of tour, packing up bed spaces we'd never see again and trying hard to remind ourselves that two months was still a hell of a long time to go, every daily SITREP was full of Sangin and in particular a patrol base called Inkerman. Isolated, eight clicks up the valley and taking hammering after hammering after hammering. Even though it was pencilled in for another unit, with every fresh report from the beleaguered outstation, I knew where we'd be spending the rest of our tour.

Because deep down I knew we had some fight still in us. Sgt T agreed, it was too soon to be thinking of home, but not late enough to be thinking of hanging up our arms – while there were WMIKs in theatre and a ruckus up the valley we had a few runs left in us on our barbed steeds. Qiam would have agreed if he hadn't been fuming at his demotion, an extraordinary reward for the man who more than anyone else pulled the 1st *Kandak* through Tufaan and who I wanted more than anyone else to get a Military Cross (if only for the brilliant PR as much as the balls of a company commander who charges the enemy alone with a spanner).

A different type of bullshit from our own patented British Army stuff, but not less infuriating, as I later learn that, after Qiam's demotion, Lalaam, his utterly cowardly and completely useless counterpart, was promoted. I think I knew at that moment that we couldn't win. The ANA, no matter how much we mentored and enabled, were ludicrous and, watching the videos from Chakush, as utterly dependent upon us for our booming air power as we were on them for the veneer of credibility and slender exit strategy which sustained the whole mission.

And, as I had sensed all along, just before we fly off the last-minute change of plan is confirmed.

That night is a final bustle of activity, taking our last showers for months, greedily soaking in hot water before it becomes another aspiration on the end-of-tour tick list. Even though it must be ten years since I've actually played more of a computer game than a quick FIFA after lunch with the Stanley Road boys, I borrowed *Civilization* from one of the signals corporals. Passed some of the idle last few hours in a nostalgic run-out, knocking up wonders of the world and churning out battleships as if I was fourteen all over again and I can't help smiling when he's not in his bed space so I have to leave it for him with a note.

Because we'd finished for the time being, and were leaving Civilization behind.

Amber 63 are off up to Patrol Base Inkerman.

Sangingrad

There would be no e-mails from FOB Inkerman. No NAAFI runs, no weekly snatched bites of fresh food, no running water, no respite.

Nothing.

Except, of course, dust.

And a diary.

In the relief of 'wheels down' after the hard Chinook ride, during which I felt more apprehension than I think I have done at any point so far on this tour, finally able to shift position under the ridiculous and crippling weight of the bergen I couldn't remove, we charged out to head for the base and could see nothing, nothing but dust.

It is safe to say Inkerman is not how I had tried to imagine it from the comfort of Shorabak, a larger, more accommodating PB South with maybe a couple of tents and a friendly Anglian ops room. The Anglians lost a guy this morning and are sprawled around in exhaustion and grief, naked in the heat. An arrow drawn on a sleeping man's back in permi-pen, 'insert dick here', is the only brave stab at morale in a camp so low we can feel it. The compound is vast and bare, walls enclosing nothing but a token compound building, cool enough but punctured through with bullet holes and SPG-9 craters and forlorn posters of Pinder and Keeley. All around are Taliban and the most appropriate Inkerman graffiti for us reads in black marker on the white wall 'Welcome to Bandit Country'. A cross sticking out of the mound in the middle marks the previous Anglian to die here, and on another pillar a memorial to Gdsm Downes is poignantly fresh.

As if to hammer the point home, the evening brief is interrupted by the enormous crack of two SPG9 rounds overhead, and a short, sharp battle is joined on all sides with the mad dash from our CP to the Afghan compound involving a terrifying sprint down an exposed forward slope with the rounds pinging at our feet before clambering up the frail skeleton of a ladder on to the front roof. Here it's a toss-up in the chaos of ANA RPG rounds and good forward arcs as 'stone-cold' Sgt Ross gets stuck in with his sniper rifle, dropping the enemy from the trees with practised ease and 'Gilly' – nineteen-year-old Gdsm Gillespie who only arrived in Afghanistan two weeks ago and is the newest member of the team – looks around in wide-eyed ginger bewilderment that betrays his age, reeling that his first contact has come within hours, not days, of deploying. The paper-thin wall on top of the compound which separates us from the rounds whizzing in causes me to glance enviously up at the Hesco on top but it's the conspicuous if protected Anglian sangars being aimed for rather than our flimsy, front garden position, and everything seems to be whistling mercifully over our heads.

I'm guilty, if that's the word, of an astonishing relief. I knew we had a scrap in us and we're clearly going to get it.

LSgt Price and the ANA defend the paper-thin wall which was the front line at Patrol Base Inkerman – Sangin, August 2007.

I was pleasantly surprised by the way we relaxed into the contact and realize with a jolt that I had been partly crushed back in Shorabak by the thought that I might have already done my last fighting. The tired looks in the eyes of Vince and the Inkerman Company boys we're taking over from would have calmed our anxieties on that front even if we hadn't just had what is apparently the normal tea-time shoot-off in this OK Corral of a base which makes PB South and its much-missed river look like a sleepy backwater.

Being hit like this will become tiresome. It's a different type of strain on the nerves to rolling forward to a contact, but it will certainly pass the time in what is a bare-arse limbo of nothingness. Everywhere filth and dusty beards and emptyish ration boxes and a feeling of isolation permeate the sweat and sand. Trying to sleep in the meagre shade of the

mosi-nets on rocks and rolls in the uneven ground and looking at the hunger in the eyes of the guys leaving, a hunger to
get the hell out of here, I realize it's going to be a long, hard
final few months.

Quite how hard we realized after lunch when another
attack thundered in ferociously and the RPGs came uncomfortably close overhead down on the ANA roof but smashed
into the back of the compound and took the legs of an ANA
sergeant. In a lull in the battle I legged it back up to the little
command post and at first I thought it was him bloodied and
rasping on the stretcher but once the fighting died down I
realized it was Captain Dave Hicks, the acting company
commander, who'd taken the brunt of an RPG airburst up
on the roof. The casualties were more numerous and more
serious than we had first thought, and even as the contact
died down we poured such fire into the treeline that it was
obvious everyone was shaken up.

Back in the little OMLT room we'd thought to chill in with
old papers and whatever we could tune into on Sgt T's radio,
fresh bullet and shrapnel scars pockmarked the walls, and a
frenzy of defensive activity had begun, partly out of necessity
but partly I think as the pleasing physical monotony of
filling sandbags took people's minds off the casualties of the
last few days.

Gdsm Gillespie, who is now my thermometer for this last
push, certainly has the look of a man whose baptism of fire
has been too hot, one of the first on the scene to treat the
early casualties, so we keep an eye on him, having fired his
first rounds and dealt with his first casualties in far too quick
a succession for a fresh teenager now out with a bunch of
seemingly hardened strangers in the arsehole of the world.

When the news that Dave hadn't made it came through

there was something that snapped in everyone. It was partly the unnerving knowledge that the bloodied and bandaged figure you were trying to reassure actually knew better than you did and was on his way out and the realization that no one's last moments should be in fear, covered in the fucking Sangin dust while chaos rages around. Dave had been with the battalion in Bosnia, and over quick snatched fags since we arrived we'd swapped the usual Army stories and compared mutual acquaintances. He'd obviously been holding the company together well while the OC was on leave and then, boom. It felt like everything was crumbling. There was a flashback to seeing Kuks, the same shock of the familiar juxtaposed with the bloody and iconic, the same touching morphine bravado and it's just one unlucky guy who chose the wrong moment to go up to the roof, or was stood one foot too much to the left.*

On the front wall, feeling the thuds of the rounds striking lower down, we are fine while Sergeant Abdullah, re-supplying the ammo from the back, loses his legs. Kuks will be fine and Dave is dead. I felt a prick of that same fear that I felt in Shorabak. We haven't been here twenty-four hours, and there's already two dead and six or seven back in hospital.

Poor old Vince and his ANA, keen as only we can imagine after six weeks up here and smell of home in their nostrils, are pissed off that they'll be stuck here another two days.

---

* Not, as was ridiculously reported in the less-responsible newspapers, plugging imaginary gaps in the wall. One of the most upsetting aspects of the inaccurate press coverage was the way it detracted from nonetheless exceptional stories and feats. Many times on the tour the balance between good copy – thinly veiled in the journalists' gossamer 'we just wanted to show X or Y in the best light' – and accurate reporting was misjudged.

In high dudgeon the ANA down tools and storm off to a neighbouring compound to sit out the next forty-eight hours in protest, an action which, mildly laudable for its comedy value, adds to the sense of madness that everyone is starting to foster as the big joke around camp is to pretend that we're only on exercise, and we radio back to brigade that we'd like to sit out the next serial because we're not getting that much training value any more.

Major Calder, who I last saw only months but lifetimes ago round the planning table in Camp Bastion before Silicon, has now been flown in to steady things up and assume command. To the general hellishness of the base is added the tedium of more defensive works and the nause of stand-tos and similar measures which, though entirely sensible and correct and which we should have been doing anyway, we still resent. People are probably right that the ANA have slackened us as much as we've sharpened them, but I'm still vainly hoping that the *inshallah*★ method of shrugging, sleeping and scrapping will see us through and help us more pleasantly pass the days.

Days which at this rate will be interminable. Days which will be hateful in sweaty, dusty grime as all decency goes out of the rocket holes in the wall which pass for windows and we're more cut off than I can ever imagine.

But there is again that funny sense of pride when the ops room back at Shorabak accuses us of having brought the trouble with us. It proves that nothing welds a team like adversity. We're all smiles and laughs at the thought that the last few days have been the Queen's Company welcoming committee, and I realize that, even though this is the very substance of nightmares, as the dusty ground crumbles like

★ God willing.

quicksand beneath our feet and the threat warnings become more and more diabolical – I would rather be here than in PB Tangiers or PB Blenheim or certainly back in Shorabak, idly reading about the action in between games of solitaire on the AFT terminals. It seems that everything up here is tinged with the dust to give it a grey, more hostile feel than Gereshk where we trusted and ate with the locals and the Green Zone was a lush Eden. An Eden crawling with Taliban, yes, but an Eden with a lovely cool river. Crouching under the once-a-week shower, a bucket pricked with bayonet holes, I'm struck by how much we will miss that river, how much we already do.

The Line of Beauty

Of all the books to find in this most improbable of libraries, amidst the stinking grunts and crumbling lads mags, I would not have expected a copy of *The Line of Beauty*. But here it is, less worn, admittedly, than Beharry's 'autobiography' or the various Sharpes which seem to be kicking around. With tonight's threat warning still ringing in our ears (apparently 300 Taliban preparing to overrun the base tomorrow morning, which after the last few days we're just about tired enough to vaguely believe) and, knowing that I shouldn't, I take it to bed instead of getting much-needed sleep.

I think it shows how much has happened since Kush Dragon, our pre-deployment exercise six months ago on Salisbury Plain, when we all snickered like repressed school-boys in the huts in New Zealand Farm when I read out the rude bits. Then I'd been struck by the depressingly brilliant accuracy of the parties and the people and the places and, worst, my nostalgia for it all. Then, I had felt a saddened anger that those days and things had already been taken away, not ridiculously and dramatically, as they are in the book, but by the simple evolution of things and the passage of time. Now, as I try and join the dots, lying out here in the half-dark, listening to the occasional pot-shots and waiting, like everyone here, for the next big hit, I realize I couldn't give a fuck.

Out here I'm already simultaneously nostalgic for the hard-fought patrols out of Gereshk and the contrasting hedonistic release of R&R and I wonder whether this habit of looking back is a generic thing or whether only certain points get fixed and remain special. Will these bloody days seem a golden age from whatever perspective five years' time has to offer?

Because it should all seem ridiculous from out here. I should be meticulously planning tomorrow's patrol, considering anything and everything in detail to make sure we all get home to have the memories at all. I shouldn't even be reading *The Line of Beauty* whether or not I read it and feel moved. Instead I look at the boys and wonder to which worlds they retreat with cordite-grey, stubbly faces and long stares and burned fingers nursing stale fags, while retreating to my own and composing hyperbolic letters home to all the girls. When we make it back from here I'm sure I'll sit staring out of train windows yearning for Sangin and all the things we learned about ourselves under siege in Inkerman. It seems strange that part of that will be the indulgence of sitting in the lull between attacks and yearning for the things before.

These thoughts of past fripperies are so out of place here that perhaps it is a triumph that I am thinking them at all, that my mind is capable in the whirl of bullets and rockets and the bleeding and dying of recalling somewhere beyond the black-and-white, life-and-death of the fire fight that it's

Claudia's birthday today and I fondly remember her twenty-first, appropriately themed 'The Last Days of the Raj', sigh and pick up a Dragunov and, with Sgt T spotting on my shoulder, register my first sniper kill. Watching the tumble of foliage, the man-shape which changed only just perceptibly but so fundamentally even as I was still focusing on exhaling and releasing the trigger, I should be moved, or appalled, or at least worried that Sgt T is now filming LSgt Price instead of watching for the enemy response, but instead I'm back at school recalling Graham Greene.

'This is hell, nor are we out of it.'

***

If these weeks are going to pass at all every stolen midday hour's nap and cigarette or unread magazine and discovered curry and rice in a box of Menu E will have to be lingered over like a treasure.

I escape the C Company daily business to share *chai* with the ANA, which has the advantage of being my job. It allows me to sit, calm in the eye of their chaotic storm, amid the soothing philosophy of *inshallah* and the happily familiar endless Dari squabbling. I realize with a pang that what we have lost which we had in PB South is our own empire: we are no longer kings of our own Hesco castle, we're joint tenants with the real English soldiers, who implicitly disapprove of these idle hours. I'm torn between how much more chilled life would be out here if it *was* just us and the ANA, and how hopelessly vulnerable that would leave us.

With nothing better to do on the long night shift I find the photos and old files on my laptop (the perk of watch-keeper duty being access to the precious generator) and marvel at how far we've come. Harrison, chunky-thighed in his shorts non-commissioned, desperately tanning and reading

The Game as if it would be of any use to him out in Iraq. Marlow grinning with his USMC buzzcut and something pretentious, me writing flippantly away about how we'd never win the war if all we had to read was Jeffrey bloody Archer.

Where were we now? Harrison's boys bruised back in Shorabak, the memorial to Downes more touching in its scruffy immediacy on the wall next to me. Marlow's gritty months down in Garmsir already immortalized on the first of the video montages, the benchmark set maudlin high and for all the *Baywatch* skits and smoke grenade tomfoolery you only had to listen to the poignant 'Set Fire to the Third Bar' to know that none of them would ever fully get over losing Gdsm Probyn ,who'd been killed a month before.

Me?

As Well Ask Man What He Thinks of Stone

Eight dead Taliban today so we celebrate with a precious tin of hot dog sausages.

I'm more amused than worried that this seems now to be a perfectly natural reaction to things. More than anything, I'm jealous of the Mastiff troop and their giant air-conditioned rolling fortresses. The patrol today was a good shake-out, and being cabbied in the back of the heavily armoured trucks is certainly the way to do business, especially at the final position, when the Taliban decided that the i-com chatter traffic was becoming too boring a way of teasing us and had a few pops with RPGs, which bounced harmlessly off the monster trucks, which had already brushed off a mine-strike on the way in, and then we swivelled turrets and hammered .50 cal and GMG into the position while the C Company platoon jumped in the back, fixed bayonets and simply drove on to the position to assault it. Slightly off to the flank we had a brave old time up on the hill, sharp-shooting in fire support with the troop's guns thundering away beside us and watching the fires started in the dry poppy stacks by the tracer and thinking that from 600 metres watching someone else do the work for a change was a good way to fight the rest of the war.

Not that I didn't notice again that flicker of apprehension, which I think will only be more regular as the tour draws to an end, as we clambered into the back of the Mastiffs and rolled off. Countless journeys we must have done around the country in paper-thin WMIKs with not a thought for the IED and mine-threat beyond the annoying vulnerable point checks. Yet here we are in the most heavily armoured truck in theatre, and the reluctant thought flashes through my mind – I don't want to die in the back of one of these. I can't help myself casting a nervous look around the cabin at the nonplussed ANA transfixed by the fresh stack of *Nuts* and *FHM* and Cpl Gus fiddling with the sick-making monitors that show you any angle of the journey except the natural one from where you're sitting, and imagining the burst of overpressure or the agony of burning, scrambling in vain at the rear doors.

Of course, once we're out and rolling into the familiar compound-clearing drills and objectively, rationally, far far more vulnerable, everything is OK. Chatting up an ancient *haji* and scanning the horizon for the enemy, who we can hear are out there and waiting for the rounds to come in, it's all fine, and there's not a thought of caution except for the rabid dog in one of the target compounds which has me reaching for my pistol but proves the greater coward, and at the end of the lengthy contact which drags the patrol into hungry hours we're all grateful for the cool and easy lift home and chilled bottles of water from the air-con units, rolling back to Inkerman, which in our absence hasn't been attacked. We're well fed on sausages, and spirits are high everywhere as we collapse into deep, exhausted sleep.

And there's that glimmer of euphoria which we used to feel rolling along the desert from Price out into Gereshk and the unknown. It's pretty random, barely containing the frustration of failing comms strolling back from the Snatch to the admin area, and it's the stifling bullshit of a company in defence, the ringing warning that we're not in PB South any more, Toto, and contact booms and flares up for Blenheim on the darkening horizon, but from nowhere I can't suppress a smile.

The boys are sat around the pot and reading aloud as the *Telegraph* and other papers eulogize about Dave Hicks and realizing that, for all the hyperbole and exaggerated reports, no one who hasn't been in this mess can understand what it is to go through.

I suddenly know that I hate this and love it at the same time because I can already feel both how glad I will be when it is over and how much I will miss it. How difficult to convey to anyone that matters something which they will never understand, and how little anything else will ever matter.

I guess this is partly resignation as the intensity of today's clockwork lunchtime contact had us thundering away perilous RPGs with back blasts shaking the roof fit to decapitate whichever unfortunate came up the 'ladder of death' at the wrong time. Over the top and on to the flimsy positions which the UK guys up in arms about their own defences haven't even looked at. Sgt Ross makes the wry observation that now the Anglians have lost a few guys, Inkerman is the number one Helmand priority, and everyone's concerned, and even the deputy commander comes in for a quick

Queen's Company love-in complete with brown shirts and side-hats and plans and defensive schemes aplenty, but never mind that no one even noticed when LCpl Perry's head was nearly taken off by the one SPG-9 which actually *did* penetrate the ops room, let alone the ANA and OMLT casualties that went before.

Now everyone in theatre is arguing about the SPG9 threat and the RPG airburst threat like experts without bothering to ask the only guys who actually use the things apart from the enemy, the Afghans themselves. Suddenly everyone's talking protection and one-in-thirty-six chances of dying. Defensive resources are on the way and not a moment too soon as another 107 shell pounds into the ANA sleeping areas, and miraculously no one is hit, but the guys taking a cheeky siesta will be deaf for a couple of days. Frustratingly, when the Hesco does arrive, it's prioritized to the 'Brits', which doesn't seem to include the OMLT – as if Sgt T wasn't a scouser and Sgt Roper didn't grow up in Grantham with Isaac Newton and Thatcher.

The one-in-thirty-six thing, some paper's dubious calculation of becoming a casualty in Helmand, was bollocks anyway. It raised eyebrows, but not nearly as much as the infuriating government response. The panicked bastards read the World War Two comparison headlines and quickly calculated our casualty statistics as a percentage of the whole ISAF mission – as if they were getting shot at in the cappuccino bars in Kabul. You couldn't compare what 7,000 Brits in Helmand were doing with the Germans loafing up in Herat who weren't even allowed out at night. We didn't blame them; in quiet moments on patrol at three a.m. we could even be envious, but nothing rankled more than having friends and colleagues spun by clueless, career-politician dickheads.

*

This hit claimed Sgt Abdullah's leg and shows the sort of damage the base was sustaining on an almost daily basis during the height of the defence – Patrol Base Inkerman, August 2007.

There's something vaguely familiar in the daily game of cat-and-mouse with whichever tasking seems like it might be most strenuous and, as so often seems to be the way, the day which promises so much (or rather, so little) is the one which delivers so little (or so much). Tired after the inevitable lengthening of whichever the latest patrol is that we're on, we eventually launch on a bemused petrol station (the wrong one), which yields nothing until some idiot local gives away his concealed dicking position and we switch the rummage to his house and unearth a sack of Taliban goodies. I can't quite be pissed off that we're out again at four in the morning, rolling down IED alley to picket a route for a convoy that won't go out.

Looking out at the tanker driver preparing his cot bed

beneath his cab, the work parties from the platoons making their way to the burning pit with the day's accumulated piss bottles, we're all drawing strength from how far removed we are here from anyone's understanding.

Anyone at home, obviously, but even back in Bastion, and I understand how 3 Company felt for the first half of the tour, what forged their incredibly strong but quite us-against-the-world mentality. I can't decide why this is something to draw strength from, but I do and even enjoy the lumbering suspense of the night-vision patrol, back behind the windscreen of a bullet-ridden Snatch. The last time I was night patrolling with a monocle in a Snatch like this, tense and helpless against the explosive roadside, was down in Iraq, and the fact that my current view is obscured by the bullet hole in the windscreen says everything about the difference between the two tours.

★★★

Then.

FUCK FUCK FUCK.

The pent-up emotion which I think at one stage is going to see me cry instead has me smashing my fists in inarticulate rage against the Snatch. The 107mm shell that sent me tumbling down the dash of death hill like Humpty Dumpty with the tingling of shrapnel and scorch of cordite on the back of my neck blew Gilly sideways in a cloud of dust and frag' and must have missed both our heads by inches.

It doesn't do to dwell on the inches and split seconds involved in the *one, two, three, GO!* that I shouted seconds before we broke cover and began the run which saw me blown forward and Cpl Gus back and even Zabi at the back bleeding from his eardrums and covered in rubble. Apparently Gilly initially sat up in bewilderment and looked incredu-

274

lously at the enormous twisted shell just feet away from him before collapsing back T2 with a shattered arm and shrapnel and blast damage to his right-hand side.

My first response was to jump to my feet, dry, so I obviously haven't been shot, and whooping insanely with the thrill of it, I may have even screamed 'That fucker was CLOSE!' to the bemused Afghans, and LSgt Price at the bottom, perhaps imagining Gilly was still just feet behind me but charging on regardless, up the ladder and on to the GPMG giddy with the high and no idea how close 'CLOSE' actually was. It was only after blazing away madly for minutes which I genuinely think I lost, pouring rounds into the firing points forward sat up like a target on the roof, that the worried ANA pulled me down off the perch and pointed down to Zabi, who was shouting up about the 'casualty'.

Perhaps I knew the moment the blast came in. Perhaps to have turned round and acknowledged what part of me must have known instinctively would have been to acknowledge how close I was to the same and to break down on the spot. Nothing makes sense to me until I realize that I'm pretty much deaf and, without knowing why or how, I've run back up the hill and the doc is trying to talk to me but even through the ringing in my ears his words mean nothing because at that exact moment I spot Gilly bloody on the floor.

The impact of this is immediate in a way I just can't understand let alone explain and I feel what I imagine must be the utter helplessness of a parent at a sick bed as the doc and his team crack on sorting him out, and Gilly himself is impressive as he waits for the morphine to kick in, demanding only the odd sip of water. Once the pain starts to go like a true soldier he's gasping for a fag and wondering if this isn't one of the few moments it wouldn't be rude to beg one off the platoon commander, which almost has me in tears as I light it for him and he chuffs his way through three reds before the IRT make it in. On the back of the quad-bike down to the HLS he's already joshing about beating us all to the first cold beer and make sure we save the shell and photos for him as souvenirs. I've rarely been more sincere when I drop off the stretcher and tell him how proud I am of him and then trudge back to the ops room, empty.

This is now getting ridiculous. It's fairly evident that the aiming markers for these attacks lie unchanged and unchallenged. We haven't dropped a bomb in the weeks we've been here, and it will go on daily like this with misses so near I don't know which way to turn to hide from the thoughts which assail me.

It's the most versatile word in the language which finds it as I catch myself repeating *sotto voce* at nothing and no one in particular.

Fuck fuck fuck.

I would probably rather be anywhere in the world right now than here, but if I was anywhere else in the world I would just want to be back here.

It's best not to try too hard to understand why such a feeling of completeness can be drawn amidst more dire threat warnings and the hateful chaos of deadly rounds and shrapnel and I can't pass the gaping bite taken out of the wall where split seconds and inches separated Gilly from worse, and me from Gilly and me from God only knows what, without another *piano* fuck.

It's not actually a supreme mental effort not to dwell on it, it's just the way the hours and days roll on, and we're more determined to make it all the way and hammer more Taliban as we go and let events and luck take their course. Just as the Liverpool vs. Chelsea game kicks off, and some angelic signaller appears out of nowhere with hot dogs, and it seems life is as good as it gets, the message comes through about more casualties, which leaves the football forgotten, and even the bad luck Liverpool apparently suffer doesn't matter a shit against the good luck that it's not any of our boys, and so the point-counterpoint goes on, just caked in dust.

Tac confirm that we won't be heading back to Shorabak to end the tour, won't be heading back in on Main Body 1 but will be stuck out here till the bitter end and will meet up with bags and kit again in Cyprus on decompression.

So it's square-heads down for the next thirty-four days, and no respite from the patrolling and mortars.

Less Than Zero

Time passes in taskings and moments of introspection. Orders, briefs, the patrols themselves, the roller-coaster attacks all come and go, and then we notice over a day, with all the clarity of a meal or meeting at home, how we felt about something.

Two things struck me during that time with a violent, physical pang of recollection. The first, which drags me back nearly seven years, is the familiar double-click left-down pause double-click left-up of classic Nokia snake on the Roshan mobile. Instantly I'm back in college, idly clicking away, trying to beat Ewan's high score and even at the time registering the wasted hours being spent in the most pointless of activities. It's a slow day, and I've shot-gunned the only unbroken chair and sit comfortably as memories flood in of St Mary's girls and bops and Toploader's 'Dancing in the Moonlight', and I hate that it will probably never be recreated, and that where once that buzz was achieved by an innocent student experience, I now find myself in the hell of Inkerman, pursuing the buzz into the next fire fight, and doesn't that just show how right old Waugh was *et in arcadia ego*.

The second, in the far more recent past, is the hooligan boyish thrill of pissing in a bottle. And it's not just the strangely pleasing monitoring of the prodigious amount that we actually seem to piss every day or the lazy sink-pissing relief of only having to stagger a few yards each night to the ammo-bunker and its emergency empty bottle collection, but the memory of how heaven-sent seemed that wonderful piss the morning after the night before, and how far removed is it possible for pisses to be only a matter of weeks apart, from the bursting hedonistic excesses of a desperate and groggy lunge for some normality of bodily function to the post-contact dehydration. It strengthens the resolve to get through these bottle-pissing months of dust and danger and make it back to a world of earthly pleasures, and proper loos.

I'm still thinking of earthly pleasures when the next fuss kicks off, and pissing in bottles is, again, a world away.

★★★

Sitting cosy in the ANA HQ room in a peaceful evening, I'm told that Kandahar pomegranates are the best in the world. We are a few weeks short of the best time of year, and the fruit not quite yet fully ripe, but the Afghan tongue is far sweeter than mine, and casually picking out the refreshing little seeds while we discuss bringing up the heavy weapons is one of the most pleasant eating discoveries since we tried the *toot-toot* berries for the first time on Silicon.

Flip-flopping back up the dash of death, I find the angle from which you can look out over the valley without anything military in your line of sight, the silhouettes of the barrels poking out of the sangar positions too far left and just behind above. Somewhere out in the gathering dark the Mastiff Squadron are refreshing themselves after another day of scattering the Taliban, who are increasingly terrified of the invulnerability of the 'trucks'* and spend the evenings whining to commanders back up in Musa Qala. Further north the Estonians and BRF are making mischief and then Kajaki and its minefields and contact northings and iconic dam, but from where I'm currently stood it's peace itself, only the quiet talk of the ANA, still munching pomegranates and sharing out grenades.

I barely notice my birthday with Inkerman heavy with the sense of anticipation of the big op which starts tomorrow, nerves and minds steeled more against the inevitable fatigue and discomfort of the next few days than the possible and probable danger. My present is the way all four mortar rounds that flop lazily in at some quiet point in the afternoon miss us by metres during our siesta and land in the Engineers' accommodation while they're all out working on the defences.

I've bored the medic so much with my whingeing about feeling unwell that instead of worrying about the forthcoming op I spend the day as high as a kite on the wonderful co-codomal she's given me to shut me up and vegetate my way through thoughts of an early-life crisis and the gentle ribbing of the boys that I might be the youngest captain in the army, but I'm no longer 'young'. It is odd to reflect on a birthday not only as just another day, which is I suppose a natural feature of getting older, but as a complete non-day, a day which we're all willing over to tick off another day till

* The Taliban had pretty logical nicknames for most of our kit – Apaches were 'wasps', WMIKs 'porcupines' and the squat Vikings 'frogs' – but they were sufficiently rattled by the awesome Mastiffs that they were just 'big trucks'.

the end and everyone else in camp is willing over so they can push out and get on with the extended patrol, which, best present of all, we're not on.

And then morale.

LSgt Roper had arrived in the small hours of last night with the Inkerman Company Tac and the welcome sarcastic presence of CSM Scully and C-B, but with the chaos of the deployment had just been sent to get his head down. Dawn reveals not only the peace of a camp finally ours in more than just name, but the bulging mail sacks and welfare boxes so long awaited from Shorabak. For me the sheer twelve-year-old joy of birthday parcels and cards and goodies galore and for the rest of the boys, the simplicity of Coke and crisps and Haribo, which seem to make the next three weeks seem much shorter and more bearable. There is the quiet contented hum of the fan and the rumble of the outside generator as the only disturbing noise to the happy reading of letters from home and a tantalizing sense of what is not too far away now.

On the ground, things seem to be going more quietly and to plan than any of us might have dared hope for at this late stage in the tour. Apaches hum overhead, and our own mortars pop from time to time, and later in the night with the company groups nervously harboured up 4 kilometres north we hear the thump and then eerie whine of shells whistling overhead as the valley bathes in illum, but there's been little actual fighting and no friendly casualties. The crows are cursing the quietness, filled with the fear of not getting to fire, but for the rest of us they're months too late, and the only thing they can learn from our weary and smug expressions is a warning to be careful what they wish for and our earnest desire that we all get through the next three weeks as peacefully as today has gone.

Inevitably with over 100 stinking soldiers and over 100 even stinkinger ANA living in half a football pitch of dust with a big fire for a lavatory, sickness is rife. I'd gloated back in Gereshk as Kuks had been bedded all the way back to Shorabak with crippling DnV after drinking from a well and I had still managed to avoid going man-down, largely I think because I ate so often with the ANA. However, 'Inkerman Aids' finally gets me, and I haven't felt this sick since I got food poisoning two years ago and spent excruciating hours thinking I was dying, hugging the Wellington Barracks porcelain and somehow making it out on to the Mall for another farcical two a.m. early-morning rehearsal. I tried to concentrate on the ghostly dummy-carriages, the extraordinary sight of us dotted down the Mall with no troops, wondering who the hell jogs in St James's Park at three in the morning, but couldn't hold it in and was bent over double vomiting at the salute as the Major General trotted past.

I wouldn't have felt the injustice of the occasion as much if I hadn't been the only sober man on the parade, the Micks all still rolling around from the flaming Ferraris they'd got in minutes before jumping in cabs and rolling straight out on to the square.

It was unfair being ill then because everyone else was drunk; it's unfair now because everyone else is shooting at us.

★★★

The funny thing about the dirt is how much more you notice it when you try and wash.

Everywhere the dust which clogs and floats and swishes between toes and sheets, hangs in the air and in the lungs and cakes us so that I've never been so dirty in my life. My feet are the unrecognizable things of Third World beggars, hard-chip-caked in grime and loose dust, my hands stained beyond washing in brown with endlessly black nails, and we've almost strayed into OCD territory as I catch myself in each bored moment trying to vainly scrape out the crap from beneath them with a makeshift nail file.

A vague attempt to maintain tidiness – Patrol Base Inkerman, August 2007.

Trudging through the dust for a twice-weekly crouch under the closest Inkerman comes to a shower, standing on a shattered palette underneath a watering-can head affixed on a canvas bag, for a heavenly approximation of a wash. For three hours afterwards we can actually run our fingers through our hair and for at least the first half-hour we actually smell unfamiliar, because we don't smell.

Walking past the Snatch today, I came as close as I ever have done to 'not recognizing the face in the mirror'. I knew the face, but bearded and grizzled and massive-haired and streaked with grime in the wing-mirror, it was very unfamiliar.

★★★

For my thirteenth birthday I remember my father taking me and two friends flying for a treat. From Halton up in the little four-seater to Duxford, where, having stubbornly and nervously refused so much as a wobble on the joystick, we all begged him to let us ride the 'flight simulator'. I wonder if there's something similar playing out here as things seem to have finally settled down a bit in the Upper Sangin Valley, and so we spend our free time watching *Band of Brothers*. *Grey's Anatomy* I could understand, *Grey's* was escapist and wilfully incongruous, and those of us with imagination fancied Addison and those without Issy (and the medic McDreamy, of course), and I knew we were still human when the chat on PRR in the middle of yet another attack was all frustration because the mortars had started landing just as Meredith was about to kiss Derek, or not.

Band of Brothers was something else, and with it the creeping and unpleasant sense which I thought had finally dispersed of an itchiness of feet. I'd been happy through Palk to sit back and interpreted that happiness for a mature realization that enough was enough. Listening to the inspirational old boys at the start of each episode, realizing anew just *how* good it was as we watched the shelling of Bastogne episode in helmets after another mortaring, we couldn't help but feel a little shiver of excitement.

Maybe, maybe there's a couple more patrols to be done, but the time still drags between them, and we watch whole films and then can't remember what they were two hours later. We couldn't be further, physically, mentally, from the troops that began in Shorabak months ago, but it occurs to

283

me that this tour might be ending not dissimilarly to how it started: in boredom, counting down the minutes, hours and days.

★★★

After a sleepless night on sentry duty we haul ourselves out of bed at 0430 for a long patrol out on to the 611. Still groggy after breakfast, shorts and flip-flops give way to the reassuring sturdiness of boots, trousers and belt, and our wake-up is the comforting routine of preparation. The bulge of morphine in the left pocket and then the strapping-on of pistol right leg and magazine-holders left. The final checking of straps, pouches and radio switches, forcing down sickening litres of pre-patrol water and then the final action of black sweatband on the right wrist and the Wimbledon one under the watch on the left, the slow, deliberate tying up of bandanas, and then we're ready to go mentally as well as physically.

Once we're out there's one of those extraordinary moments that sometimes happens on exercise when there's an incongruous calm in the middle of what should be tense or hectic or nightmarish, and we debus from the Mastiffs, and the whole valley is as quiet as a mouse, so with the ANA chewing the fat with locals at the bottom of the hill I lie down flat in the sand, gulping grateful lungfuls of fresh air after the cramped and bumpy ride and feel the day already warming in the harsh sun and fall into a deep and dreamy sleep.

I'm troubled by faint memories of Sandhurst bollockings, being woken up from snoozing in the FUP with helmets propped craftily against the foresight and being screamed at that we weren't taking it seriously and that we wouldn't fall asleep if we were doing it for real.

Little did they know.

Every so often I wake up and groggily sit up to check that the ANA are still happily in position, wondering idly what would happen if next time I wake up the Mastiffs have somehow driven off or the ANA have disappeared or there's an AK in my face and some improbable Taliban snatch-squad have snuck up on us. But I know it won't happen and feel the reassuring weight of the 9mm against my thigh and flop back into the wonderful sleep that can only be snatched out somewhere, illicitly in the sand.

★★★

It's amazing how crisply the dawn thump of a nearby explosion wakes me from a pretty deep sleep and has blood charging and all stations ready to go for the inevitable stand-to. It's funny to see which mosi-nets stir, which commanders balefully stick a head out of sleeping bags now cuddled against the coming autumn coolness of the mornings, and we wait for a second thud and the scurry of frantic activity, or hope for nothing.

And we think we got nothing until the ANA wake me with slightly more difficulty two hours later to come and see the old guy they've brought to the gate, he who triggered the earlier mine blast in the desert. A bundle of rags is pushed in on a wheelbarrow, and the doc laconically observes that 'this could be interesting'. An elderly man lies unconscious on the rags, flaps of skin and grotesque long vessels dangling from beneath the gap where his lower left leg should be, a 'perfect' traumatic amputation, according to the doc, and as we stretcher him up the hill I can't believe he's still alive, he should by all logic have bled out hours ago, but with horrific blast injuries – his bell-end blown clean off as the boys can't refrain from remarking – he's a typically stubborn Afghan bastard and simply won't die. There's an uncomfortable few minutes after I call in the 9-liner and request IRT while Bastion all too obviously probe to find out if ISAF are at all responsible, and we can almost hear them over the net, squirming at trying to get out of casevacing the guy, and we're already mentally coming up with pitiful excuses as to why his family should just wheelbarrow him further on to a local hospital when we finally get wheels up. Someone, I suppose, remembered just in the nick of time what the fuck we're supposed to be doing here in the first place.

And it turns out to have been appropriate to ask as we get the second-hand news that there's been a big hit on the WFRs in Lash. We get the news in the form of an instruction to stop all non-essential patrolling and movement and *minimize risk* (a wonderfully bland and meaningless phrase out here).

'Why?' asks Sgt T fairly enough, and when the doc looks up as if surprised that we hadn't worked it out and points out that all the beds in the hospital are now currently full, we know for sure it's time to go home.

★★★

The rapid fire which wakes me from my post-stag slumber around midday (a sign of the cooling days that it is now possible to still be snoozing as late into the day as lunchtime) and has C Company stifling the cries of 'Stand to!' in their throats, is not the enemy but the ANA giving an exuberant 'Beirut-Salute' to a passing wedding. Everyone shakes their heads in disgust, and I'm secretly delighted at the eccentricity of our little brigands.

Later, the Vikings push out on patrol with Sherlock and me escorting a squad. All quite token as we're tasked with 'Rear Security', but even from the comfy vantage point of the front of the Viking, even enjoying the ride, as the driver throws the little cab over improbable drops of the *wadis* and up the rollercoaster-steep sides all the way back to base (and laughing at the guys crammed in the back like sardines, groaning on the net), I can't quite dispel the images of the burning Viking hulks back on Lashtay and find myself pining for a Mastiff.

It's one of those patrols where, without unnecessary fuss and bother and nerves, we have known throughout that someone was going to shoot at us. So much so that, when the contact finally comes as we're pushing back after an uneventful clearance, during which all we've done is shoot a local through the leg with a 'warning shot', it's almost a relief.

What isn't a relief is the initial ferocity and accuracy of the ambush which has us cabbying around frantically in the Vikings and my mind a whirl of whether I'm happier inside the armour but stuck in the commander's seat looking out through a decidedly flimsy-seeming windscreen or whether I'd rather be free and in the prone position and getting rounds back down but out there where tracer and RPGs are flying back and forth in the furious chatter of the exchange. The Vikings are actually magnificent, with rounds pinging off without a bother, and we push the doors ajar enough to wedge out rifles and AKs and spray out bursts of automatic, setting the treeline aflame across the whole 300 metres of the ambush. Overhead the .50 cal from the Mastiffs cracks and the GMG thumps and Sherlock pounds down a reassuring quantity of UGL while the 81s come on task and, for the finale, spectacularly low F15 strafing runs, by which stage we're all just having great fun with extensive watch and shoot as i-com reveals the Taliban taking casualties and so the ANA jump out with glee and pink flowers behind their ears, unleashing RPGs and round after round of PKM to dust it all up in time for tea.

As the contact dies down we dismount and push neckily forward, pure infantry porn now with bayonets fixed, but it's difficult to see anything beyond the apocalyptically scarred earth where the mortars came in and the smoke from the poppy-stack inferno is making the dusk light even harder than it should be. Just beyond in the ditch lie the shattered bodies, and the vivid redness of blood against the dull earth is mesmerizing. It's the closest we've come to what my vision of the aftermath of a battlefield should look like, and it's most certainly the best way to view it, from the comfy and armoured vantage point of the Vikings, which then thunder wonderfully back, cutting swathes through the head-high poppy and maize, bouncing like the first terrifying tanks of World War One over ditches and streams as we push back for Inkerman, pretending that we won't be haunted that night by the flashbacks of our gory voyeurism.

More importantly, when we get back in, Issy slept with George.

I'm not sure how a phone conversation can go so quickly from sexy whisperings and longing for clean sheets and sturdy double beds to tearful recriminations and complete lack of understanding, but somehow that's the trajectory of my call to Jen, and I'm cursing the waste of precious sat-phone time. I'm not sure if this disjoint is a symptom of what we will all have to deal with when we finally get back, the wall that's been quietly built between those of us who are here and have lived these things and everybody else, no matter how close to us they previously were.

Deep down we all know there's something incredibly selfish in what we do, something self-indulgent that makes it far easier for those of us who have left and are dealing every day with new and previously unimaginable challenges than for those we've left behind, for whom each day is the same as the one before, simply without their loved ones. Part of me, part of everyone I suspect, wants to shout down the phone that we're sorry, that we love you and the only reason we pretend we don't know what you're going through is that to acknowledge it would be to acknowledge our own crippling longings. How do you say good night to the person you miss more than anything else in the world as if it's that last tender whisper in the ear of the warm body next to yours, when in fact you're thousands of miles away, and the only body close to yours is Sherlock's because he's next on stag.

We have to keep a maddening separation, don't want in the space of a quick phone call to remember who we were at home, because we hope that's not the person pushing out on patrol tomorrow to kill or be killed. So it's easy to dismiss these things as the inevitable frictions of seven-month separation, to ignore them and crack jokes with the lads about 'the trouble and strife', but in quiet moments when we miss you the most, we're scared by the question posed cheekily in the next episode of *Grey's Anatomy*: 'how would you spend your last day?' None of us out here could answer that question with the certainty I suspect those at home would want and expect.

Maybe it's just not a question we want to ask ourselves while a possible answer remains 'scrapping with the boys in the Green Zone'.

★★★

We're horribly, disgustingly, unbearably close to the end when LSgt Ball loses a leg in an attack on Amber 64. There are certain things I realize as I try and get my head down that, when we are back home and the dust has settled, I'll always associate with this country and this tour. The taste of *chai* and hard, stale *naan*. The incessant barking of dogs long into the night. Dust. The raw smell of unwashed sweat.

And the emptiness of learning of another casualty. The mind games and mental images and subconscious reckonings, the shock, helpless grief, debilitating anger and the whole cocktail of barely identifiable emotions which we go through when a guy in his early twenties, fastest runner in the company, has his leg blown off.

Ramadan

On the *Laylat-ul-Qadr*★ the ANA commander is patiently explaining to me, Muhammad received the first revelation of the Quran. This, among other reasons, is why Ramadan is such an important celebration and why I'm handing out laminated cards to the Anglians telling them not to get cross when the Afghans seem to be lazy (six months too late) because it's just the effect of the *roza*.†

I've fought alongside these guys for six months now and know that most of them are pragmatic about their religion at best. We've had the odd soldier who puts down his weapon in the middle of a fight and bangs out a quick prayer, but I'm not surprised by the confusion of the Anglians as we ask them to refrain from eating, drinking, chewing, even smoking in front of the boys for the next month, and they wonder where they'll get their supply of cheap fags and Miranda from.

The atmosphere down in the ANA compound is, however, electric, and everyone and everything seems different.

★ The night of power.
† Fasting.

Even for our most agnostic of soldiers, it seems, Ramadan is huge, which I guess is appropriate because, for even the OMLT ourselves, the most non-Muslim of soldiers, Ramadan is huge.

During the build-up to Eid, we're going home.

The start of Ramadan is, for us, the beginning of the end, the justification of no more patrolling with the ANA, of preparing things for the handover/takeover with 2nd Battalion The Yorkshire Regiment, the unit who drew 52 Brigade's 'short straw' and have come to take over as OMLT Battlegroup. The tracker annoyingly reveals that Worthers and Sgt Davis and God knows how many others have already gone back. Chatting with a handful of punters around Inkerman, I realize it's not only us infected with the end-of-tour fever. Each department is jealously regarding the other and calculating who will be home first, and the CSM good-naturedly threatens to cancel our helicopters because the OMLT are supposed to be the first out. I laugh along but check the FLYPRO once he's gone to bed.

Hazrat bets me I can't last a day observing the fast, to which I reply that I didn't spend long Lent weeks when I was younger giving up chocolate for nothing (even though we only counted actual chocolate bars, so ice-cream or cookies were OK, obviously) and I'll see his day and run a mile. We're idle, and all I have to do is carry on writing handover notes, but by afternoon it's starting to kick in and I have to stop.

And fantasize about proper food.

Subsisting on exactly the same rations for more than a month has taken its toll, and I can barely look at meals which were perfectly acceptable a few weeks ago. Only the chilled sugar rush of the tooth-rotting orange Miranda hasn't quite got boring, and I force down biscuits or Haribo with which to take anti-malarials and multi-vitamins and slip into reveries of ordering real food from a menu or cooking up improvised deliciousness from a well-stocked fridge, deciding what I want and then being able to feed that hunger on crisp, fresh salad leaves or with heavy, biteable pasta or potatoes with fresh butter and anything, anything for the slightly salty and warm succulent bite of meat.

Later in the day, having a wonderful cigarette stroll across the dark of the base with the stars still bright in the moonless sky listening to 'Chasing Cars', I'm massively amused that *Grey's* fever has spread to the Anglians, that now this whole base of dusty, cool sand trapped between my feet and flip-flops, a base of beleaguered and six-month veteran fighters, has become addicted to a hospital soap. My stag hours pass in blissful abandon to the latest episodes. Pte Emmitt collates his int-brief for tomorrow with half an eye on the newest series while the rest of the ops room try and look away from spoilers; the doc heads to the fridge for saline and pauses to reflect on the hotness of Addison Sheppard; while Dave strolls around like a caged lion cursing the cruel fates that took Sgt Evans and his hard-drive away when he's the only man with the first half of season two.

★★★

I make my way back up the dash of death after a hearty Ramadan supper with the Afghans, a veritable feast of not just the usual *pilau* and *naan* and *ghosht* but tomatoes and onions and aubergine and courgette and sweet milk and watermelon and pomegranate. It's easily the best meal I have had in months on the back of yesterday's food fantasies and the earlier and equally delicious scoff I wolfed down with Sgt T and the boys as we finally succumbed to our western palates and fried up sausages and bacon slices in tins of their own delicious and woefully bad lard and finished off the cheap Army tomato ketchup. So wrong and so right.

Hearty Ramadan feast in the ANA Compound. Major Hazrat (left), who commanded our ANA Company in Sangin was, along with Major Qiam, the only strong officer and real leader our ANA had – Patrol Base Inkerman, September 2007.

The day has been an incredibly peaceful one at Inkerman – strange given the contact that has been raging slightly to the north – but from the dawn call to prayer which sounded up the valley with a volume and intensity I've never heard before to the warming dusk sight of the ANA all crammed on to the small hill with mobile reception, phoning home their Ramadan greetings with the free minutes the networks give them as presents, I'm filled again with a sense of just how enormous this festival is. Even the British soldiers, whingeing about the jubilant evening gunfire that announces into the gathering dusk the end of the day's fasting, can't shake me from being deeply moved.

The Ramadan afterglow wears off pretty quickly, however, as I awake somehow instinctively from my sleep, immediately aware that it's earlier than I would like it to be, and see Hazrat and Zabi hovering apologetically, blurry through my mosi-net. A civilian has come in to the front gate to report the Taliban laying an IED down the road; my first reaction is damn these Afghans and their four a.m. starts.

It's followed by a sudden and unfamiliar resolution. I'm not going to get caught up in this. There is an unusual stubbornness in my subconscious, which is to do with the recent, bitterly-close-to-the-end-of-tour injury to LSgt Ball, and to do with the bad dreams I can only hazily recall having just woken up from, and is to do with the fact that as of today we officially have only a week to go, but presents itself with black-and-white clarity to my thoughts. *I am not getting caught up in this*. The ANA can go and get themselves blown up, the UK callsigns can flap around and wait and sweat for IED disposal team. I am absolutely not going to get myself blown up today.

My hope that it's nothing fades as the Roshan mobile chirps up the wonderful old-school tones of 'Groovy Blue'. I let it run for a few bars too long and am briefly transported back to idle suppers at university and the days when we all had it as our ring-tone, before picking up and learning an anonymous caller is giving the same tip-off. I can't damn the success of our earlier psyops patrols as heartily as I'd like to, recalling that patrol that went into a village where the Taliban had chopped off someone's hand simply for having the slip of paper we'd been handing out with our mobile helpline number on: dial for quick assistance to the ISAF hotline (thirty seconds' guaranteed HOT AIR-STRIKE ACTION). As magnanimously and responsibly as I possibly can I explain to the commander that my priority remains the security of the landing site for the Chinook which is coming in this morning to extract my guys (and his guys) back to Shorabak. If he remains concerned, I suggest, he should send out a squad. He nods in assent and doesn't seem bothered by the unspoken implication: the OMLT can't deploy with him today, reduced as we are to the final three. And anyway, I am not getting blown up today.

Events take their usual course, and once the pair of crows have been extracted for the long march to 3 Company and a bonus month on tour (with LSgt Roper cock-a-hoop at his late call-up to run the RSOI back in Shorabak for the next week, which will see him even this evening, while we're still sweating out the IEDs, chowing down on fresh food and gateaux). The Anglians push out a cordon, and we wait for the arrival of the IEDD team and all their precious little habits. I can tell I feel slightly guilty, like deep down I know that with an ANA squad out there in the cordon, even though it's now logistically impossible, I should have made more of an effort to be out there myself, because without hesitation I volunteer the OMLT (or more accurately myself, Sgt T and a broken Sherlock, who has been subbed off for LSgt Roper and faces an extra five days of this crap with the final trio) to oversee the VCP which will freeze movement on the 611. The ANA are being predictably 'Afghan', and the company commander gets more and more wound up on the net until we decide it would be best to pull them in. Hazrat, who has actually been out on the ground himself, can't see what all the fuss is about and wants to know why we spend hours out in the baking sun, waiting for the idiots with cartoons on their sleeves to blow up devices we could blow up ourselves within minutes. His boys have been fairly scatty but they've also been out for eight hours during Ramadan without food and water. Next time, he tells me, only half-joking, he won't inform us about the bomb until afterwards and will just blow it up himself.

As the Chinook drops the fifteen-man IEDD team down and the whole company is pushed out in various moving parts for the deliberate clearance op and I'm sitting down on the 611 with a pistol lazily enforcing the no-road-movement and fucking up everyone's Ramadan in the process while the stoner squad of whingeing Pashtuns who've been left behind listen to endless droning cassettes of whoever the current Pakistani star and *femme fatale* is, I realize he may have a point.

The ANA are still arguing when dinner finally starts, and even those of us who haven't been fasting have earned scoff in the dark because the controlled explosion has blown the power lines for the whole valley (Happy Ramadan from the IEDD team), but at least my morning's first decision is vindicated.

I *did not* get blown up today.

★★★

A very clean and fresh and unbearded-looking captain runs off the back of the Chinook and, exactly as I did what seems like a long time ago but is actually only six weeks, heads off through the brown-out in completely the wrong direction.

We're all hugely excited to be meeting 'the relief', the living, breathing evidence that we're on the verge of going home, so we only quietly smirk at the naivety of the remaining seven guys who jump with celebratory cheers off the back of the next chopper. Sherlock, Sgt T and myself enjoy a last

WMIK moment securing the landing site, smoking like the grizzly vets we are and trying to suppress our delight. The new boys have arrived, and school's almost out.

As the handover begins it's clear from the new faces just how far we've come, and I realize how ridiculous all the briefing notes must sound, trying to remember how similar notes sounded to us nearly seven months ago. Before they've had a chance to meet the ANA we're crashed out to pick up a casualty from the C Company patrol and half the 2 Yorks find themselves charging out of the gate, tooled to the max and dangling off the Snatch, trying to keep up with our WMIK, which in turn tries desperately to keep up with Hazrat's Ranger vehicle charging off down the 611. The laughs that we elicit from C Company when we arrive are partly at the ANA and ourselves for our even more than usually chaotic state of attire, with the crash-out no notice, so shorts and all sorts of dress irregularities, partly at the general wonder on the faces of the new boys.

To make room for the casualty is going to be a squeeze, so I jump on the back of Hazrat's Ranger and stand over the dushka with Goldie, who's grinning like the lunatic he is, loving that the British *toran* is up on top-cover with him and more likely to die from the Afghan driving than anything lurking back down the road. I'm aware, as Sgt T shakes his head resignedly as we set off and tries in vain to keep up, that this is very much the last 'patrol', and I'm glad that it's as irregular as it is; last-minute, largely unplanned and with me in the Ranger probably not exactly by the book, but slicker and more efficient than it would have been otherwise and with me where I've always believed we were supposed to be to do this job, right there with the Afghans. Speeding past C Company stacked up in the shade of the compound walls, nodding what will be final goodbyes to by-now familiar faces, no reflection on them, an excellent fighting unit, but I'm in no doubt that these are my comrades – Hazrat, Mohammed Nabi, Azim, mad mad Goldie and brilliant Qiam – and if we're going to miss anything beyond the buzz of the whole thing, it's going to be these guys.

Back in camp I can't quite comprehend my own briefing. I watch myself deliver the 'Afghan Fighting' PowerPoint presentation I've prepared, wondering if there's ever been such a dubious boardroom, and I'm gratified again by the genuinely awed stares which greet some of the points and, even though I'm not trying to lay it on thick, Sgt T sits at the back, watching video clips of himself in disbelief, and it's only then, watching faces hungry and curious like mine must have been for years, that I realize it's come full circle. There's no way I can brief this to the incoming boys, no adequate way of explaining the ANA, describing the relationship which we have, must have, with them. Instead, I note with amusement how the video clips and memories which just make us glad to be getting out of here are the very ones which make the Yorks glad to have arrived. But they're also memories I'd always wanted to have, and I seem to lose them in the official retelling and correctly staff-written notes. After all the waiting and imagining the stories I have are everything we could ever have imagined and more, and I'm aware how unfamiliar this is. Only the Afghans, now alert across the whole camp to the RiP and reluctantly moody like children losing their nanny, have seen this all before. To cheer them up, Sherlock agrees to 'tap dance' one last time on the roof, not as funny as when he suddenly started jigging away with an entertainer's spontaneous genius to lighten the mood in the middle of the long defensive battle, but the ANA roar with approval and nonetheless join in.

Most of the ANA move to resigned silence, but a few

maintain the bolshy stance and insist they'll either prevent us from going or refuse to fight without us and sneak on to our chopper home. I understand how difficult it must be for them to have brand new mentors every six months. To have to wait again for us to catch up and get the novelty and excitement out of our systems and I'm saddened myself at the realization that we are just a cog in the machine, but at our last supper when the boys finally join me down in the Afghan compound there's an amazing sense of melancholy we're off and I believe their protests that they will miss us and that we have been a good mentoring team. I'm even more touched when, having come back up the hill for final packing touches, the S4 sergeant races up to present me with a brand new ANA uniform as a leaving present, something they have so little of at the best of times that I can't escape the generosity of the

Pensive, waiting for the chopper home – Patrol Base Inkerman, September 2007.

gift and, however much I can't wait to get out of Inkerman and out of Afghanistan, my insistence to him that I want to come back is immediately genuine.

And then, finally, through a cloud of dust and lost hot metal minutes wedged uncomfortably and noisily and dreamily in the back of the Chinook, we touch down in Shorabak and we're back inside the wire.

29.ix.2007 — They sicken of the calm who know the storm
i'm trying really hard to conjure up the feelings of relief and elation which should accompany the choking brown-out as the Chinook finally hammers down into the sand and shitty moon-dust behind Patrol Base Inkerman and we run on to thumbs-up and smiles from the door-gunners who've obviously been briefed that we're getting out of here for good. but thundering low over the desert dropping chaff like confetti and swinging hard behind the mountains in helicopter hide-and-seek with the rocket positions in the green zone i can't feel anything other than a sort of dull emptiness.

and on reflection it was probably for the best that we didn't have internet in Patrol Base Inkerman. didn't have anything in Inkerman except the terrified choppers that dropped in every other day to keep us going through the siege, caught between the need for food and water and ammo and the hope of a rare letter and the knowledge that with each heli-drop the shelling would kick up again. it fucks you up being stuck in defence, ducking with every thud of incoming and always closing your eyes as if that's going to make a difference when a mortar slams into your mosi-net.

300

didn't make a difference for young Gilly, blown up by a Chinese 107mm rocket as he followed me down the hill into a wall of enemy fire to try and hold the front position. 19 years old and fresh out of training, wide-eyed walking cliché who'd only been in theatre 3 weeks and had spent them scrapping hard and growing up fast and who was still stupid or brave enough to try and stammer an apology as i ran back up to him idly wondering in the adrenalin rush of it how i had landed 40m down the hill, deaf as a post but without a scratch, and he had been unlucky enough to cop the full blast and lose an eye and hand in the bargain but still have the sheer guardsman like stubborn balls to be worried only that we get a suitably gory photo of him for *Nuts* and *Zoo* and could he have a fag instead of more morphine?

didn't make a difference for LSgt Ball, the fastest runner in the company whose leg was clean blown off as the Taliban kicked up an ambush with a mine and followed up with RPGs which cut the lead afghan in two before the 'terp's head exploded with a pretty good shot from somewhere and in the chaos one of the stammering and panicking new guys is practically crying as he picks up LSgt Ball's perfectly intact foot, thirty metres down the road.

didn't make a difference for Dave Hicks, fragged on the roof during one of the by now daily hammerings the base was taking whose wide eyed expression betrayed what his insistence that he didn't need to morphine couldn't accept and who hung in with fearful, gasping breaths while we won the fight and then died in the medevac chopper. but then maybe he was just the most unlucky of another dozen guys up in Sangin in the last 2 months which have passed not in hours or days but seconds and where only grim statistics and phoney newspaper percentage calculations that we had a 1 in 36 chance of being hit in Afghanistan made us laugh with the black humour of it as we pushed out on patrols with 8 blokes while hundreds of fat cunts sat eating pizza hut in the safety of Camp Bastion wondering if they'd been factored into the numbers.

it can't be good for us in the long run, we push off into the GZ looking for revenge and the release of the fire fight in which all the worries fly down the barrel of your weapon and our only concern is to cheer like thugs the A-10s roar low overhead and we smash in and blast the black-turbaned fuckers back to the stone-age where they belong, the instant hit of the moment the shadow in your sights drops like a stone and like perverts for death we push forward past the poetic and eerily beautiful sight of bright red blood, exploded heads and twisted torsos against the brown dry poppy and lush green ganja, well-tooled up pakistanis and iranians oozing life into the muddy water of the ditches they ambushed us from with the relentless and unimaginative frequency, quickly bustled away by the smiling local villagers for the undignified funerals deserving of the murderers of teachers and rapists of little boys.

but it's all a bit different licking wounds and feeling sick on rich fresh food and burger king at kandahar airfield surrounded by the planners in neatly pressed combats and fat bellies arguing over the cost-effectiveness of the bases we've just been fighting tooth and nail to hold for the ungrateful bastards. the world is a headache inducing whirl of colour and pepsi and comfy chairs and air-con and beds and women and even the dust can't be the same as that which we were crawling through only 36 hours ago and if it's this strange in a military base which, after all, is still in southern afghan i wonder what the fuck it will be like back in london and how do the men show photos of dead afghans to adoring wives and kids and expect them to understand?

the company i deployed with 6 months ago was 36 strong when we kicked out on first op and looking around at my boys, unrecognizable with thick mops of hair and deep tans, making the most of the leniency which everyone applies to us as they give a wide berth to the combat troops letting off steam and leering hungrily at the NAAFI girls on the way home, i wonder if any of them would have deployed with 1 in 3 odds at the start of the tour. we've lost 12 blokes, 1 killed in action and 3 of the 6 officers. i'm the only platoon commander left and even though i've only lost one guy out of the 26 i've commanded it doesn't seem like any fucking consolation. we've lost far more of our crazy brave afghan soldiers killed in action and allah only knows how many injured in their ridiculous style of *inshallah* lets just charge the enemy position even though we've run out of grenades fighting. our 'official' stats reckon we've accounted for between 180 and 190 taliban and i should surely be disgusted that i'm just gutted we didn't get a double century but clearly we checked in our humanity when we checked in our personal items at the start of the tour and swapped them for heavy osprey body armour and extra ammo.

problem is we've handed the ammo and body armour back in again now and got the personal effects back and they seem to belong to a world so far away from the dust and destruction of PB Inkerman or the pure 'Nam chaos of the thick green zone that they're all barely recognizable and i guess this is why winning the peace is harder than winning the war. the incoming teams taking over from us, pale and well-fed and boggle-eyed with apprehension and anticipation ask a series of questions almost impossible to answer beyond a snort of disconcerting laughter.

'have we made any progress?' – you know what, probably not but it doesn't fucking matter because at least we're going home.

my afghan commander sees me off with a final ramadan feast and bear hug which has me choking back emotion because he's a good lad and we've fought side by side for 6 months and i feel like a tourist who's had his fill and is going back home and i assume he is just talking about the british army in general or the regiment when he looks at me and smiles that we'll be back in afghanistan fighting again soon. i assure him that i'll be tucked up safely back in london enjoying the nightmares in a comfy bed with cotton sheets and killing the memory cells with grossly over-priced booze from wanky gastro-pubs and he shakes his head and scares the fuck out of me by pointing straight at me and practically quoting dorothy parker as he reels off some old Pansher Valley wisdom – they sicken of the calm, who knew the storm.

maybe, but for now i'm soaked wet through and sick to the pit of my stomach with the sound of thunder and the flash of lightning so the storm will have to do without *Toran Padi* for a while

i'm going home.

VI

Decompression

The statistic that floats around, probably dubious but with its own momentum, is that more Falklands War veterans have killed themselves in the twenty-five years since the conflict than died in the fighting. We'd always been taught that the figures were much worse among the troops who had flown straight home, rolled victoriously from the airport and then back into happy but unknowing homes and communities, than they were among the Marines and sailors who'd seen and done similarly horrible things but who had started to process it all on the ship on the way back.

How all that added up to thirty-six hours on the lash in Cyprus we weren't really sure, but neither did we care in the amazing holiday atmosphere on Tunnel Beach, everyone as skinny as they'd ever be, shrunken cheeks exaggerated by enormous mops of hair that no one had the heart to start bothering people about yet. Given how drunken the following months were perhaps it was all for the best that the first massive night of freedom and booze was self-contained, the boys all running around naked by midnight trailing 'flaming arseholes' and already squaring up over whose war stories were best and passing out in hedges.* It took the pressure off when the coach finally pulled up back into Lille Barracks and families were reunited under the Aldershot drizzle with cringy

---

* It might have only been me who passed out in a hedge, but I was pretty comfortable thanks to Harrison, who saw me, realized that he couldn't shift me and so just brought my mattress and sheets out and rolled me on to them. Be the best.

media lurking in the background, so the best thing was to race off down the M3 as if the last seven months had never happened because the cars and the traffic and the tunes and the beds at home were all exactly the same.

Except that the last seven months *had* happened, and in quiet moments at exuberant dinner parties and the endless debauch that ensued we'd know that we were the only people round the table who'd seen and done what we'd seen and done. Tea and toast became scotch and toast as the frustrated lads got out of hospital and bedlam reigned in the mess.

No one wanted or chose to be a scotch-drinking, night-spoiling, glass-smashing, relationship-bashing cliché, it was just as unavoidable as slamming on the brakes in a car on ice and watching the wall come sliding towards you anyway.

And of course then no one really knows what to say, friends slightly stunned by your proud video montage and old teachers and godparents who sat down with their Monday-evening soup and glass of wine and watched the little boys they used to know swear and kill their way across the screens. How could we tell them that what we felt most about being home was jealous of 52 Brigade who were out there in our bases, with our Afghans, shooting our enemy? How could you rationalize the moments when you'd break into a cold sweat at the traffic lights, clench your teeth, caught between tears and laughter and not a clue why? How could you explain to the well-meaning, well-intentioned, sensitively phrased questions that you'd loved it, that everything was flat and that you were sad that there were no more e-mails to send?

You couldn't. So we drank, and mess nights and Friday nights and weeks of leave blurred into one long inevitable repeated violent pattern, where Evans and Finch had to take it in turns to lash with you for safety, and you found yourself staring down the wrong sort of men on the wrong sort of streets just because deep down you wanted a fight. Wanted to slam someone into the wall of a club and be able to say with utter calm and terrifying confidence in your eyes that he had picked the wrong fight because you were a fucking killer. The first night the Micks got back from Iraq, bitter at their overshadowed tour and mouthing off ill-advisedly on the streets of Aldershot, how could you not feel a surge of pride at the boys who'd stood up and the ruckus that had ensued and the bleating of the Hampshire Constabulary who had used up all their CS gas in one night of glorious fist-whirling mayhem.

The CSM beat the crap out of his dishwasher, which wouldn't work. Everyone had stories of irrational anger, frightened kids and confused wives. London was a land of parking tickets and light bulbs which needed changing. We were fucking supermen, *übermensch* who'd chewed up and spat out the massive Taliban summer offensive and had had it beamed into ten p.m. BBC1 living rooms for good measure. We were the point of the spear against which the forces of mad medieval darkness had hurled themselves in the open-invitation playground scrap, Infidels XI vs. Extremism All-Stars, which was taking place behind the bike sheds of the world, the fight for what we thought was civilization and the right for our future daughters to learn and wear what they wanted, and we hadn't budged an inch, and now we found ourselves back home and unadored and owing the fucking congestion charge.

When 'our' *Panorama* aired we all trooped down to London to watch a screening, awkward in suits and already filling out again, watching ourselves in loosely hanging combats. We were so far from it then it might as well have been years, not weeks, previously, but it only felt like days. The SWAGs had been invited – soldiers' wives and girlfriends sceptical at having to relive their own tour nightmares and see how close their husbands came but not going to pass up the BBC's free booze. In those last minutes as we settled down to watch I slipped my hand out of Jen's and couldn't explain to her, beautiful and confused as I abandoned her in the back row with Viva and the rest, that I could only do this sat next to the boys, watch it side by side with the guys who'd fought it side by side. LSgt Fear's wife stifled sobs as she watched her husband's thumb get shot off – I hated the distance it put between us all, but couldn't explain or fight it.

The CSM with reflective poetry in his soul had carved into the wall of the Sangin District Centre the legend 'for those who have fought for it, life will always have a flavour the sheltered cannot taste', which was about the truest thing in the whole town.

Of course we went off the rails.

Even now I still count time back from Afghanistan. Each morning brings an unavoidable mental calculation and the image of what was being done exactly a year ago. Without pretension or guile I'd catch myself months after we got back referring to having come home just weeks ago. If realizing it had been a year since we'd gone out, or a year since the first contact, had been hard, I can only imagine what it's going to feel like when it's been a year since we got back. We bounced hard from the re-entry and, with nothing better to do, we carried on drinking.

★★★

If we'd thought that we'd get closure with the medals, we were sorely disappointed. We knew that Churchill had said, 'Every medal casts a shadow' (it was a pretty safe bet, Churchill had said everything). We didn't know it was an under-statement.

308

No one joined the Army to win medals; they were extra glitter that even through Sandhurst you were only vaguely aware of and imagined would probably require extra polishing. But part of giving-in to the culture was giving-in to the mythology of gallantry – learning the improbable citation narratives of regimental history and *Telegraph* obituaries. The first step had been aching for campaign medals, plotting thirty-one-day mini-breaks to Kosovo or Northern Ireland to add a line to your mess kit chest CV, gazing enviously at the LEs who'd been out on light-blue UN tours of Cyprus and the strange rainbow ribbon of Op Granby and knowing they were medals you could *never* wear.

But once we'd been out on a real tour, a war-fighting tour with its own rosette and people performing heroics every day, suddenly we wanted more. Lying under the mosi-net, swinging in a hammock or waiting after stag for the fatigue to kick in and sleep to close as the evenings got fresh enough to wrap yourself up in a liner, we'd turned over the thoughts of who had done what on our tour, who deserved what and why. The commanders read the rules, the stark mathematical calculations involved (the higher the assessed percentage likelihood of death as a result of the action, the higher the distinction) and diligently wrote up the guys we thought deserving, all the while who could help turning a few slack thoughts over in their own heads.

In those dangerous flights of night-time fancy, peppered by the distant rattle of an incident further down the Sangin Valley (well, there was no further up from us at that stage) it wasn't those close to me I imagined impressing. Family and friends, they already knew, would understand, would have read between the lines of blueys and Facebook profiles and see in a distant shimmer in the eyes that something important had happened in the last few months. They were in the bag.

It was the thought of cocks you had met along the way being secretly disappointed on the loo as they read *Soldier* magazine, the thought of the good guys being quietly proud, of being able to drive down to Sandhurst and find out CSMs White and Coates and owe it to them. It was childish and indulgent, but it was fun.

Back at home, it was more serious.

It was about legitimacy.

It was about the sense that official recognition would somehow rehabilitate us, would end the awkward silence that descended in the room when anything about the Army came on the news, parents of friends glancing involuntarily over at you and wondering. Would end the tedious self-justification, the coded references to missions and incidents which varied depending on the audience: sanitized understatement for uncomprehending civilians, gratuitous overstatement for the war-hungry lads, apologetic middle ground for comrades in other units who hadn't quite shared the glory and somewhere elusive in the middle the relaxing truth which could only be shared with those who knew because they had been standing right there next to you.

The back-slaps of those who'd seen you on TV and the patient, obligated understanding of close friends and family was one thing; we wanted documents signed in black and white and glinting metal forged with our names to shout to the rafters that what we had done was not wrong, not bad, but glorious and heroic, and we weren't sick to feel that it had all been such fucking good fun.

But when the papers trumped the largest haul of medals for generations, the bulging Honours and Awards List a groaning litany of gallantry, what stood out were the names that weren't on it. Sat around the luxurious tables for Ladies Dinner night in the mess, dazzled by the play of candlelight on the triple-ranked array of ornamental silver which occupied every spare inch of the table, what should have been a celebration was forced jollity and strained stoicism which ebbed as the bitter, champagne-filled horns came out, and we raised endless toasts to Harold Macmillan,* got more and more drunk and more and more angry.

We understood that it was all relative. That down in Helmand people were getting thanked for the sort of stuff they were getting written up for in Iraq, and in Iraq getting a quiet nod for the sort of stuff that would have been headline news in the eighties, in the good old days when company commanders got MBEs for bringing all their boys home across the Irish Sea and that was that.

Rampaging through the mess that night in a sullen orgy of destruction, feeling sorry for Martin and Seadog, who'd at least got something though still less than they deserved, we wanted justice and revenge, wanted the bastard brigadier or the idiot committee or anyone to blame. But the commanding officer just looked sad, like a captain whose ship had hit an iceberg in tropical waters. It turned out later that the Afghans had named a mosque after him, which certainly kicked the DSOs and OBEs into touch, but it didn't make it any easier to face the guys the next morning – banging hangover regardless, I had to force myself to look up and down the line at roll call, watch guys manfully pretending to be proud hearing they'd been awarded certificates when they should have got medals and wonder where I'd let them down.

* In the First World War the young Harold Macmillan was famous across all four battalions of Grenadiers for his singular bravery and, though thrice wounded, never received so much as a Mention in Dispatches (which, given that his contemporary, Viscount Gort, picked up a VC, DSO and three bars, MC and eight MiDs, put our little tantrum in perspective).

There was a lovely anecdote about a commanding officer who was awarded a DSO – I think for something in Africa but the story changes – and got the entire battalion into the gym to explain to them that he was humbled by the medal which he didn't consider to be 'his award' but 'the whole battalion's award'. Later that week one of his lance-corporals presented himself at the door to his office to explain that he had a wedding at the weekend and was wondering if he could sign-out the 'battalion's medal'. He was, of course, told to piss off. We tried to laugh it off, but it stung.

It stung because there was no closure. Out on Salisbury Plain, back in green with muddy boots and blank ammunition, we trained the Royal Irish for their forthcoming deployment, and all we wanted was to go back out with them, as if we had unfinished business.

★★★

Sometimes the system really does know better. There was no way in our state of mind the commanding officer was going to let us charge back out into the desert. With either exceptional emotional intelligence or a desire to get us out of his hair he sent me and Slothy – his two gobbiest and potentially troublesome captains – off to train the US Marine Corps, figuring the two young officers with the greatest delusions of war grandeur would perhaps be cured by a stint with the jarheads. I guess in a way we were.

Out in 29 Palms, the sprawling Marine Corps base in the middle of the Mojave Desert, while we marvelled at the training and the resources and the expertise and cohesion of the yanks and wondered what the hell we could teach them, I sunbathed and thought about where we'd all gone. Marlow back out to Afghanistan soon, this time with the Paras, which suited him fine, but still hurting for the boys he'd lost, charging up the escalator with a certainty I could only envy. Marlow knew what was at the top for him; I felt myself getting higher and higher and still didn't. Slothy knew what was at the top as well. He'd be a general one day and a good one, but that meant the time had come to hang up his fighting boots and start some desk-fighting – his hardest battle by far.

The rest of the boys? Harrison, out, surfing Biarritz and growing hair with enough Mummy credit in the bank for decades. Fergus in his element in well-cut suits in London, lunching furiously in Whites with the old boys to pull in millions of pounds for the charity we'd set up for the injured guardsmen – a civvie in all but name. Mark, out. Tobin, out. The old guard, Sidney, Gabriel, Seb, long gone. In their place when we got back there'd be new young thrusters like Holcroft to take up the reins. The Amber 63 boys were going the same way. CSgt Yates and Sgt T had both picked up well-deserved promotions but were back with their own units, serving out their last few years and wondering what the hell the real world could offer them. Even the bright prospects had put their papers in; LCpl Price, Lloydy, Mizon in and out of trouble. They'd joined for excitement, they'd had it and now they wanted to try and find a normal life, whatever that was. Only Kuks and Will were heading back, they really did have unfinished business, and probably Sgt Gillies would still be puffing alongside. Next time they would be the grizzly medalled veterans, taking the crows under their wings and hopefully doing a better job than I did.

And yes, it was good to know that you were part of something bigger, something more important than yourself which had been before you'd joined it and would carry on without noticing you'd left, a reassuring anonymity in this wonderful beast of thousands of ordinary men doing

313

extraordinary things every single day. There was something comforting in the inevitability of it all, the certainty that, if we hung around long enough, we'd become the outdated ones tutting at the flagrant disrespect of the junior officers and boring them with stories about this one time, on the dam in Helmand . . .

Goodbye to All That

And as it had all started, for no reason and for every reason, so I dug out the formal service writing guide, dusty at the bottom of a chest untouched since Sandhurst, and penned my letter of resignation.

It would have been credible, maybe even helpful, to have left because of the inefficiencies, to point at the good guys haemorrhaging from the Army at the three- and five- and twelve-year points and the bright hopes gunning towards the generals' stars at the top and ask who was going to sort out the mass in between. To point at civvie friends no longer, at thirty, being treated like naughty schoolboys and quite probably being paid a damn sight more. Was there even the incentive to go all the way? General Richard had been the most popular head of the Army for years, a soldier's soldier who'd stuck by his boys on principle, and we loved him for it, and his reward for not toeing party-political lines had been to be passed over in favour of a pilot. It could have all been the familiar refrain of over-stretched and undervalued.

But it was none of these things.

No one would really have murmured if it had been about the money – everything else was after all. No one would have minded if it had been about the months away from home, but they wouldn't have bought it after all the times I'd been in and out of offices asking for trips. Mark had pulled off a feat even greater than his famous Iraqi withdrawal and convinced a girl at least seven times more beautiful than he deserved to marry him, so it was only natural and right and proper that he should leave to focus on family and other things. All these would have been, were and are perfectly good reasons for leaving the Army.

But I don't think they were mine, not entirely.

It wasn't even the lingering, persistent off-the-rails boozing or the inevitable self-indulgent sofa afternoons which followed. Sure, you felt good after an hour with a shrink, striding back through London, refreshed by the ego trip, with a veneer of civilization freshly glossed on, but something lurked beneath the reintegrated citizen, and the fear was that it always would.

Perhaps it was the sense that there was nowhere left to go, not right then, not right now. Like the top scoreboard at the end of some massive video-game could only be anticlimactic after you'd completed level after level after level. Like the Olympic medallists who all suffered depression because the one thing worse than silver was gold – what was there to aim for after that? Through every country and possible escalation, wanting more and more and more, until you suddenly landed back home, and what else was there? More of the same, but each time the fun slightly diminished, the frontier spirit slightly quelled and the enemy probably slightly more distant, the roadside bombs more numerous and deadly, and we knew about that sort of fighting and didn't like it. Eight years of desk jobs, monkeying at the report-writing mercy of the sort of guys I'd already spent my young and enthusiastic credit on pissing off was too big an ask for the vague promise of one day commanding a whole company of men.

And of course the joke was that, while we sat in the corner

of the mess with a knowing smile and watched the new young guys, chuckling at their cluelessness, there are guys out there who have sat chuckling at us. Every time you thought to yourself you'd got to the top, of course you hadn't. Someone, somewhere, would always be doing something cooler and more dangerous, someone would always have better war stories, and you'd always want more like a drug, so maybe the thing was to get out while you could, while you still had the solid pavement underneath your feet because you were just starting to discern that there was nothing cool about the guy in the corner with the biggest scar and the winning stories – he was just fucked up.

If you could hold your head together for long enough, you suddenly discerned the massive spinning wheel we were all on, whirring round faster and faster, wanting better and better jobs or more and more violence, and for the sated ambitions of the Reading Club guys you could only be spun faster into the lost world of blacked-out eyes and special missions, or take the plunge and sharpen your ambition and pencils into the world of super-staff work and maybe emerge blinking one day at the end of the tunnel, the very model of a modern major general. A sandy-coloured blur of Iraq and Afghanistan and the Plain and London and round and round again until the dots of red might have been tunics or they might have been casualties on ops, but you just couldn't tell with the blur.

Or you could jump off.

Take the leap, the plunge, the hold-breath jump away from the safety net and the coddled, built-in sense of importance and the party banter and the uniforms and the excitement and paddle off into the sunset, knowing you'll always gaze enviously at whatever news reports follow, will squirm behind your desk when the boys step off for Darfur or Trans-

316

Dniester or wherever will be next but jump anyway. Yossarian lives.

The Last Post

This book ends in freezing August on the Falkland Islands.

I like that it ends here.

I like that after consecutive summers of deserts and just

Junior Officers' Reading Club, South Atlantic Branch – Falkland Islands, August 2008.

when we thought we might make it to Ibiza with everyone else, the company was tasked to go and keep an eye on the Argentinians. The whole thing has a neat circularity. Two months before I'd been born the Argentinians had surrendered, there were probably still squaddies getting drunk in Stanley as the midwife handed me to my mother, and all my life, though most of it unbeknownst to me, the British Army had retained an infantry company on the Islands, 100 fighting men to support and protect the airfield complex and to deter further Argentinian aggression. I like that after fighting the three-block war in three years, idle Balkan peace-keeping to tense Iraqi counter-insurgency to bloody Afghan combat, my brief military career was going to end in pointless manoeuvres on the hallowed turf of gritty, conventional warfighting.

Six years earlier, a clueless civilian student, I'd have trudged these mountains bored and cold, possibly slightly dismissive of the men who threw themselves up heavily defended slopes for the epitome of nothing – two bald men fighting over a comb.

Four years ago, a shivering Sandhurst victim, I'd have sat in the Argentine positions exasperated, hauled myself over Onion Ranges, running on the sheer spite of my conviction that everything we were doing was out of date, that it was based on the anomaly that had happened down here and that surely it would never again come to bloody right-flanking, left-flanking or up the guts with bags of smoke.

Two years ago, bitten and keen, I'd have read the memorials and citations with a mixture of awe and fear, respect and envy. Wanting so much to have been and done these things and wondering so much whether we would do them again, could do them again, wanting and not wanting to find out.

I was wrong, and I was right.

Hundreds of people roam the Mount Pleasant Complex, the moon-base camp and airfield where the RAF outnumber the islanders and a farcical cold war somehow rumbles on. There are no trees on the island, bleak beyond austere and impressive with it. When the weather turns, the cold runs through and the corridors which link the whole complex throng with people shut in, shuffling the concrete indoor streets in quilted North Face jackets from room to gym to mess to café and back. They said before we came down that it was like an operational tour, just without the enemy. It's not.

The RAF, bless them, think it actually is an operational tour, and the last part of me that still holds on, the part that reads last year's diary just before I go to bed to see what we were doing last year, the part that I know will yearn just a little but every day to once more be charging through the crack and thump, coasting the high of each zing of a passing round, that part of me wishes it suddenly was. To watch the embarrassing carnage that would ensue if the process-driven mediocrity which seems to dominate down here was put to the test. That part of me resents the air-traffic controllers for wearing camouflage as if they ever went outside, had ever wished and prayed as those boys who started the job out here must have done, for the slightest ditch or hedge to dive into. That part of me resents the easy tolerance with which the fool who takes four hours to zero his weapon is treated. That part of me wants Argentinian battalions to drop from the sky and to be able to fuck off every whingeing bar-coded, blue-rankslided war-dodger back to look after his engine parts while the real fighting is done.

What galled us more than the sudden exposure to how old and fat the officers all looked away from the deployable brigades, how much institutional boozing went on down in 'their' operational theatre, was the extraordinary way in which we were treated. From the unthinking, rank-driven inflexibility of the upper-echelons to the catty bitch who turned to the lads and told them that all the infantry were good for was carrying their mates' coffins. Not a sensible thing to say to boys who *had* carried their mates' coffins, and now you know why the gag was that it wasn't the public who were abusing the RAF in uniform in Peterborough, but resentful soldiers and sailors.

But there's another part of me that's glad.

There's no point to raging up and down the base against those who haven't done what we've done, seen what we've seen, known what we know. There's a part of me that's glad it ends here, glad for the warmth of the ops room and the tedium of its staff, safe in the knowledge that it isn't for real and almost choking on the unimaginable frustration that a future in this world would have held. I like that it ends here in the Falkland Islands, where we can walk the iconic hills and smile a knowing smile or gulp a knowing gulp. And, just occasionally, catch a glimpse of one of the younger guys watching in a different way, listening in a different way and realize that was you three years ago, and feel, for that split second and for everything that has been and gone before, closer to the legends of this place than the fools who now police it and pass their months in a drunken stupor.

The penguins are the only things noteworthy on these ridiculous snow-bound rocks. Mesmerizing lined up on the beach but like the ripples which meet obediently, tottering along in their marked and measured lines, one after one. Maybe it's for the best, no distractions from the writing now, nor reading. The Junior Officers' Reading Club could never have imagined such luxury, the well-stocked library, the gorgeous Thailand photo of Jen on my desk, next to the phone, a landline back to the UK and happy-making chats every night, tasty sofas and comfy brownies on which to gorge ourselves while we idly read and work steadily through the Olympics and endless DVD box-sets in our bar.

We're not in Shaibah any more, not even in Baghdad, the

papaerbacks aren't melting any more, and we're sure as hell not in Helmand.

I know that it ends here because, for all the time on our hands, there's nothing else to write home about.

> Vix duellis nuper idoneus
> Et militavi non sine gloria★

★ 'Lately I have lived amidst battles, credibly enough / and not without glory fought' – the epigraph to Henry Reed's *Lessons of the War* poems, to which he returns in the final verses:

> Things may be the same again; and we must fight
> Not in the hope of winning but rather of keeping
> Something alive: so that when we meet our end,
> It may be said that we tackled wherever we could,
> That battle-fit we lived, and though defeated,
> Not without glory fought.

Acknowledgements

There are a number of people to whom I am greatly indebted, they fall broadly into two groups: those without whom the book would never have been written and those without whom I'd have had nothing to write a book about – for help writing and fighting my deepest thanks.

The Junior Officers' Reading Club had an unusual genesis. The backbone of the book is a series of e-mails I sent to friends between starting Sandhurst in January 2004 and the end of our Afghanistan tour in autumn 2007. What started as a light-hearted way of staying in touch became an important therapeutic outlet, and for their various replies which sustained me wherever I was and for their encouragement for my increasingly fraught missives I owe these friends a huge debt of gratitude. A number will recognize themselves in the book, many more were cut when I realized that I wasn't supposed to be writing a 300-page in-joke for all my friends. Thanks to all of you; if you missed out I'll try and get you in the next one.

My e-mails would have remained bouncing around in cyberspace, however, had it not been for the kindness of the editors of the *Literary Review*, and in particular the encouragement and continued support of the wonderful Philip Womack, in humouring a bored soldier and printing my whimsical reflections on literary life (or lack of it) in Iraq and Afghanistan. The two pieces I wrote for the *Literary Review* not only persuaded me that it was worth writing for a wider audience but also gave me something for my Taid to be proud of. (I don't think the *Guards Magazine* counted!)

It was my further good fortune that these articles caught the eye of Jim Gill, who should have known far better than to ask an English graduate if he thought he had a book in him. It was Jim's vision and confidence that turned a vague and boozy brainstorming lunch into an exciting idea, and his tireless work while I was gallivanting (at the tax-payers' expense) in the Californian desert and the French Alps which turned that idea into a potential book. It must be unnerving for any agent to take on a retiring soldier: forever in and out of the country, prone to sending middle-of-the-night hysterical e-mails as if calling for air support and requiring frequent calming-down sessions usually involving beer and quoting war films. Jim steered me through the course of writing a book; I wouldn't and couldn't have done it without him.

But I am most indebted to Helen Conford, my brilliant editor at Penguin Press. Helen has given me more time and attention than I'm sure any writer should require, and her guidance and skilful editing rendered an awkward compendium of mess anecdotes and swear words into something better than I could ever have imagined. Her patience and unflappability have been amazing, and her ability to see at once the minute detail and the whole would be the envy of every general. From a position, I think it would be fair to say, of relatively little 'military' knowledge she has led a person of extremely little 'writing' knowledge with great understanding, for which she has my heartfelt and enduring thanks.

I extend my gratitude to everyone at Penguin who has endured strange Palace dress codes, dangerous cocktails in silver tankards, windy video-conferences from the Falklands and who graciously failed to bat an eyelid when an incongruous camouflaged figure in combat boots stomped through the office for various meetings. It is a source of astonishment and admiration and the result of a lot of other people's hard work that the messy e-mails I sent off at various last possible moments before deadlines have become an actual book. For that, in particular, I must thank Thi Dinh for all her amazing publicity work while simultaneously fending off dubiously helpful friends, and also Fiona Buckland, Nicola Hill, Nikki Lee, Gina Luck and Natalie Ramm; Paula Edwards at DGMC for her official advice; and David Watson for his meticulous attention.

Thanks too to Jeremy Quarrie, Bertie Dannatt and Andrew Tiernan for a balanced military perspective and a whole lot more.

As we say in the Army, shit only rolls one way – I am at the bottom of the hill, and any mistakes are entirely mine.

It has been an overwhelming privilege and honour to serve in the British Army, and my particular fortune to have spent my time in its finest regiment, the Grenadier Guards. It is really to all the Grenadiers and all the men that I have trained, served, marched and fought with that this book is dedicated, but perhaps especially to 10 Platoon and the Inkerman Company (2005–6), to the Nijmegen Company veterans of the endless 350th birthday marches and to the Queen's Company (2007–8). Even over as brief a time in the Army as mine I have worked with or for, been rescued by or from, and laughed and cried with more people than I have the space or the memory to list. I apologize to anyone I have omitted; the following, for better or for worse, deserve particular mention.

Charlie Bowmont, Charlie Church, Oscar Holloway, Jonty Moore, Nick Tobin, Jim Doig, Andy Batty, Claydon-Swales, C-T and all the men of XV Platoon (even the U-man), without whom I'd never have got through Sandhurst in the first place, and in memory of James Donaldson.

'Chalky' White, Roger Coates, Gus Hindmarsh, 'Uncle' Kev Vacher and the omnipotent presences of Neil England and Vince Gaunt, the inspirational men who actually taught us the stuff worth knowing at Sandhurst and then terrified us into remembering it.

Si Hillard, Gussie, Evo and Sarge, who kept the Blue-Red-Blue together; JB, Lewey, Nishal, Mad-Man Mannock and all the boys who made Brecon bearable and Bully, the finest jungle buddy and list-compiler in all of Africa.

Seb 'Gaiters' Wade, Marcus 'Box' Elliot-Square, Martin David MC and Alex 'Monty' Cartwright, who have endured a clueless ensign, a rampant know-it-all subaltern, a captain who thought he was an Afghan and a 2I/C who was writing a book instead of clearing the in-tray. I doubt there are four finer (or more tolerant) company commanders in the British Army, and to get to one day be them would be the only reason for staying in.

Harrison, Marlow, Fergus, Mark, Bysshe, Sugden, Tobin, Barty, Seadog and the rest – the original JORC and the guys who made a suffocating tent in the middle of the desert fun to live in.

Stumpy Keely, Daz Chant, Paddy Farrell, Wayne Scully, Danny Andrews, Chris Gillham, Glen Snazle, Simon Edgell and Rick Hampson (not forgetting thrashings at the hands of the likes of Butcher, Smith, Bates, Munroe, Robbinson, etc.). On my first day at Sandhurst I accidentally confused a company sergeant major with a major and got the classic response: *Don't fucking salute me, sir, I work for a living!* One and all outstanding warrant officers with whom (should that be for whom?) it's been a treat to work.

Phil Childs, Matt Betts, Pete Yates, Dickie Davis, Jon Thornborrow, Clint Gillies have all been exceptional Platoon Blokes, made my life easy at various stages over the last five years and have always had my back. Likewise Nick Rowe, Big-George Roper, Andy Austin, Roughers, Robbo, Benny, Wisedog, Pezza and Sir Edward Redgate have all been noted section commanders and partners in crime.

Col David and Col Carew for being benign, understanding and tolerant commanding officers, thank you both.

The officers' mess has been a wonderful home: Slothy, Sidney, Gabs, Foxy, Henry, Rupert S, Will, Kuks, Worthers, Neil, Jim, Piers, Ben, Paddy R, Greavesie, G-L, Eddie P, Rupert K-E, Fozzy, Chow, Tom, John, Alex, James, Chips, Joe, Bernie, Skid, Dave,

Saxby, L–P, Hartley, Harper, Holtby, Thorold, Andrew, Guy et al., a wonderful if occasionally dysfunctional family.

To Olly Holcroft and the next generation I pass the baton.

From that strange and foreign body of 'civilians' I somewhat apprehensively find myself joining thanks must also go to the following.

Charlie Bartlett, Louise Rogers, Quintin Fraser and Charlotte Bird for a perfectly timed stay in France so that we can pretend one day I wrote this somewhere suitably beautiful and pretentious and not in assorted overpriced coffee shops around central London.

Olivia Breese and Laura Roberts for unfailing support and ideas; Ned Williams and James Boylan for (questionable) help with the tricky issue of titles.

Viva, Katie, Alex and Jo – the Nuns – and Charlie and Francesca, for looking after Jen while I was off playing soldiers and then putting up with a smelly boy crashing around their nunnery in the middle of the night making coffee to try and hit deadlines when I got back.

Dr Maggie Mills for just about keeping me from smashing up the new refrigerator.

My mother and father, to whom I owe everything and apologize for all the smoking and swearing.

And to Jenny Dean, my amazing girlfriend, who has supported me above and beyond, without whose advice this would be a lesser book and without whom I'd be a lesser person.

Glossary of Military Terms

A-10: the A-10 Thunderbolt II, a US Air Force close air support (i.e. primarily engages targets on the ground rather than other planes) aircraft, a.k.a. the Tankbuster or Hog (its guns make a noise like a warthog)

AGS-17: Soviet automatic grenade launcher (*Automat Granatmyot Stankovyi*: automatic grenade launcher, mounted)

AK47: Soviet semi-automatic rifle (*Avtomat Kalashnikova obraztsa 1947*: Kalashnikov's automatic rifle 1947)

APOD: air point of disembarkation, the airport that is the main troop entry point into the country

Banner: UK operations in Northern Ireland (1969–2007)

BMP: Soviet amphibious tracked vehicle (*Boyevaya Mashina Pekhoty*: fighting vehicle of infantry)

BSU: Baghdad Support Unit, British HQ in the Green Zone.

BTR: Soviet amphibious wheeled vehicle (*Bronyetransportyor*: armoured transporter)

C17: Boeing C17 Globemaster, US and UK giant military transport aircraft

CIMIC: civilian–military cooperation

Corporate: UK operations in the South Atlantic (1982)

CP: checkpoint

CWS: common weapon sight, a primitive night-vision device

D-Fac: dining facility, US slang for a mess or cookhouse

Dragunov: Soviet semi-automatic sniper rifle (7.62mm) designed by Evgeny Dragunov

DTDF: divisional temporary detention facility: the British prisoner of war camp in Southern Iraq which didn't contain 'prisoners' because we weren't fighting a 'war'

81s: 81mm mortars

F15: F15 Strike Eagle, US fighter plane specializing in long-range interdiction of ground targets

.50 cal: technically the ammunition used in the .50 (12.7x99mm) Browning heavy machine-gun, but used as frequently to describe the gun itself

FLYPRO: flying programme, daily and weekly schedule of helicopter traffic

FOB: forward operating base

FUP: forming-up point, the final administration and preparation area just before the Line of Departure crossing which would be the no-turning-back moment of the start of an assault

GMG: grenade machine-gun, a modern UK equivalent of the AGS-17

GPMG: general-purpose machine-gun, the venerable 'general'

Granby: UK operations in the Persian Gulf (1990–91)

Herrick: current UK operations in Afghanistan

Hesco: steel cage boxes filled with rubble and hardcore to form defensive fortifications

Humvee: HMMWV high mobility multi-purpose wheeled vehicle, US troop carrier

i-com: radio scanner

IED: improvised explosive device

I-Law: interim light anti-armour weapon, UK version of the widely used AT-4 anti-tank rocket

IRT: Incident Response Team in Helmand specifically the Chinook-borne medical crew probably engaged in more daily heroics than anyone else in theatre

ISAF: International Security Assistance Force, NATO mission to Afghanistan

JDCC: Joint District Command Centre

KAF: Kandahar airfield

KBR: Kellog Brown Root, US contracting firm

LAV: light armoured vehicle

LE: late entry officer, the most senior and often best soldiers, commissioned at the end of their twenty-two years in the ranks

loggy: logistician, an officer or soldier of the Royal Logistic Corps.

LUCIE: light-intensifying night-vision binoculars

Mastiff: armoured six-wheel patrol vehicle

MRE: meal ready to eat, US version of our ORPs

NAAFI: Navy, Army, Air Force Institute cafeteria and shop

9-liner: standard format to call for medical assistance

NVG: night-vision goggles

1-bit ammo: ammunition mix which is one tracer round for every one ball round

ORP: operational ration pack or 'Rat Pack', 24-hour supply of boil-in-bag meals, etc.

Palk: the last major operation of 12 Brigade's tour, September 2007

PCD: platoon commanders division, fourteen-week course for Infantry second-lieutenants

Pinzgauer: 4x4 and 6x6 military utility vehicle

PKM: Soviet medium machine-gun (*Pulemyot Kalashnikova Modernizirovanniy*: Kalashnikov's machine-gun, modernized)

PRR: personal role radio, platoon-level communication

PSYOPS: psychological operations, propaganda, etc.

RiP: relief in place

RPG: rocket-propelled grenade (*Ruchnoy Protivotankoviy Granatomyot*: hand-held anti-tank grenade launcher)

Sangar: defensive position

SF: special forces

SITREP: situation report, basic radio call detailing the time, your current location, your current activity and your future intentions – usefully remembered as 'when, where, what, what, what'

SO2: staff officer level 2, a major

SPG-9: Soviet 73mm recoilless gun (SPG-9 *kopye*: self-propelled gun, 'the spear')

SUV: sports utility vehicle

T2: T fortriage system: T1 immediate medical attention, T2 high priority, T3 walking wounded (T4 is a euphemism for dead).

T72: Soviet main battle tank

teeth arm: quasi-official Army shorthand for 'Combat Arms' (Infantry, Cavalry and Army Air Corps) as distinguished from 'Combat Support Arms' (Artillery, Engineers, Signallers, Intelligence Corps) and 'Combat Service Support' (Royal Logistic Corps, Adjutant General's Corps, Royal Army Medical Corps, etc.)

Telic: current UK operations in Iraq

tracer: rounds modified with a small charge on the base, ignited on firing so that the bullet is visible, especially in the dark, usually loaded one in four (4-bit) or every other round (1-bit)

UGL: underslung grenade launcher, a grenade launcher fitted to a standard rifle

UNSCR 1456: the resolution passed on 20 January 2003 by a meeting of the UN Security Council which specified (among other things) the rules governing the handling of detainees in Iraq

VCP: vehicle checkpoint

Vector: variation of the Pinzgauer utility vehicle

WMIK: a weapons mounted installation kit: a stripped-down and up-gunned Land Rover